The Sacraments
An Interdisciplinary and Interactive Study

Joseph Martos

A Michael Glazier Book

LITURGICAL PRESS
Collegeville, Minnesota

www.litpress.org

A Michael Glazier Book published by Liturgical Press

Cover design by Ann Blattner

Excerpts from documents of the Second Vatican Council are from *Vatican Council II: The Basic Sixteen Documents*, by Austin Flannery, OP. © 1996 (Costello Publishing Company, Inc.). Used with permission.

Excerpt from *Psychology and Religion: An Introduction to Contemporary Views* by George Stephens Spinks. Copyright © 1965 by George Stephens Spinks. Reprinted by permission of Beacon Press, Boston.

Excerpt from *The Religious Situation* by Donald R. Cutler. Copyright © 1968 by Beacon Press. Reprinted by permission of Beacon Press, Boston.

An earlier version of this book, *The Catholic Sacraments*, was published by Michael Glazier in 1983.

© 2009 by Order of Saint Benedict, Collegeville, Minnesota. All rights reserved. No part of this book may be reproduced in any form, by print, microfilm, microfiche, mechanical recording, photocopying, translation, or by any other means, known or yet unknown, for any purpose except brief quotations in reviews, without the previous written permission of Liturgical Press, Saint John's Abbey, PO Box 7500, Collegeville, Minnesota 56321-7500. Printed in the United States of America.

Library of Congress Cataloging-in-Publication Data

Martos, Joseph, 1943–
    The Sacraments : an interdisciplinary and interactive study / Joseph Martos. — [New ed.].
        p. cm.
    "A Michael Glazier book."
    Rev. ed. of: The Catholic Sacraments, 1983.
    Includes index.
    ISBN 978-0-8146-5369-2 (pbk.)
    1. Sacraments—Catholic Church.   I. Martos, Joseph, 1943– Catholic Sacraments.
II. Title.

BX2200.M357 2009
264'.0208—dc22   2009019619

Contents

Preface

In the mid-1970s, I was a young professor of philosophy and theology teaching at a small Catholic college in Iowa. Since I had been a parish religious education director with responsibility for sacrament preparation programs, my department head asked me to teach a course on the sacraments. I wanted to use a historical approach, but I discovered that no one had collected all of the historical research on the sacraments that was readily available in an array of scholarly works. First I taught the course without a textbook, and when the students complained about that, I wrote *Doors to the Sacred: A Historical Introduction to Sacraments in the Catholic Church*, published in 1981. Rather than a straightforward history, it was an exercise in what Bernard Lonergan calls dialectic, showing how sacramental practice and sacramental theology moved forward by interacting with each other while being influenced by a succession of social and cultural environments.

Shortly after that book's appearance, I was asked by Monika Hellwig to write an introductory volume for a set of books on the sacraments being published by Michael Glazier. My approach to writing *Doors to the Sacred* had been interdisciplinary, but most of what I understood about psychology, sociology, and spirituality had remained in the background while the book itself focused on history and theology. In writing *The Catholic Sacraments*, I summarized the historical and theological developments detailed in the earlier work and added chapters on the psychology of religion and the sociology of religion, showing how those disciplines shed light on Catholic religious rituals. Part II of the latter work sketched out some implications of the sacraments for spirituality.

To a large extent, those chapters have been incorporated into the present work because the ideas in them remain valid. During the last few decades, however, a new discipline has emerged to shed more light on the human aspects of sacraments, and so the current volume includes a chapter on ritual studies that was not in the original. During the same period, both Catholic and Protestant theologians have been drawing out the ethical implications of liturgy and worship, and their work inspired an additional chapter on personal morality and social justice. Perhaps there's something about the number seven; that's how many chapters you will now find here.

In the introduction, I make some strong claims about the significance of this book. I did not make those claims when I wrote the first edition because I believed that readers would see for themselves the revolutionary implications of this interdisciplinary approach to sacraments. Now decades older and somewhat wiser, I have decided to tell you up front what you are in for.

Joseph Martos
The Feast of All Saints, 2008

Introduction

If you read this book, and especially if you engage in the interactive study to which it invites you, your understanding of sacraments will be changed forever.

Most Catholics think of sacraments as invisible realities that are administered and received through seven special church rituals—baptism, confirmation, Eucharist, reconciliation, anointing of the sick, marriage, and ordination. Although there was a time when that view of sacraments worked quite well, it has become dysfunctional. Trying to be a minister in today's church while holding the traditional view of sacraments is like trying to guide people around a city that you lived in many years ago. You keep running into problems because what you remember from the past does not match the current reality.

While reading this book, you may experience what people felt when they first read *The Revolutions of the Celestial Spheres* by Nicholas Copernicus. People in the sixteenth century felt sure that the earth stood still while the sun, moon, and planets revolved around it. Copernicus told them that the sun, not the earth, was the center of our planetary system, and that the earth was flying through space at 67,000 miles per hour while rotating on its axis doing 25,000 miles per hour at the equator. This is not what their senses told them, and they found it hard to accept a picture of reality that was so different from what they were accustomed to seeing and thinking.

To prove his point, Copernicus filled his book with observations, measurements, and calculations, and he invited his readers to make the same observations, take the same measurements, and do the same calculations—to verify for themselves, in other words, the claims that his revolutionary work was making. And even though many people did not believe him at first, his understanding of the solar system eventually became the basis of modern astronomy. It is my hope that this book will perform a similar service for sacramental and liturgical theology.

1

So that you can prove to yourself what you find in this book, it is written in nontechnical language, and its web site offers mental exercises that will help you to see that the Catholic sacramental system is something very different from what you thought it was when you picked up this book. Not everyone will need to do all the exercises and respond to all the questions before they get the book's main point, but the more you take the book's ideas and check them out against your own experiences, the more comfortable you will be with seeing sacraments for what they are—and aren't.

Like Copernicus' rearrangement of the heavens, this is largely a rearrangement of things with which Catholics are already familiar, primarily sacramental rituals, liturgical symbols, and spiritual realities. It was not the heavenly bodies but their arrangement in relation to one another that made Copernicus' work revolutionary and, for some ecclesiastical authorities, heretical.

If you are acquainted with traditional sacramental theology (the scholastic theology that reigned supreme from the Council of Trent to the Second Vatican Council, and that is still found in the church's Code of Canon Law), you will find that the approach taken in this book accepts the reality of what were known in Latin as *sacramentum tantum* and *res tantum*, that is, the sacramental ritual and the grace with which it is associated. There is no room in this approach, however, for *sacramentum et res*, a third entity that in effect mediates between visible ritual and invisible grace in scholastic theology. From the perspective of this book, *sacramentum et res* is an explanatory concept, a hypothetical entity, that medieval theologians invented in order to explain the effectiveness of sacramental rituals in terms of Aristotelian philosophy. Since theology in the twenty-first century does not rely on Aristotelian philosophy, it does not need explanatory concepts such as *sacramentum et res*.

If you are not acquainted with traditional sacramental theology, you are probably familiar with a sacrament being spoken of as something that is received—as in the phrase, "receiving the sacrament of penance." Clearly, the sacrament being talked about here could not be the ritual, so it must be something else. In fact, it is what scholastic theology called *sacramentum et res*. This "sacramental reality," as it was termed in English, is what is understood to be "administered" and "received" whenever the ritual is properly performed. So you have been influenced by traditional sacramental theology even though you did not know it. Moreover, you and other Catholics did not realize that the sacramental reality is not real; it is only a concept—an idea introduced in the Middle Ages to explain how sacraments work.

Nonetheless, *sacramentum et res* is still a central concept in official Catholic thinking about sacraments, not only in canon law and in the 1994 catechism, but also in ecclesiastical pronouncements about sacraments, and even in most of what Catholic theologians write about sacraments regardless of whether they are conservative or liberal. It is an idea that Catholics simply take for granted, and to which they refer whenever they speak about administering or receiving a sacrament, even though they never use the Latin term and even though they do not know where the idea came from. But if *sacramentum et res* has no value for thinking about sacraments today, then many of Catholicism's claims about its sacraments do not refer to the real world as it is today. Catholics know from experience that baptism does not make a person Christian for life, that confirmation has little or no noticeable effect, that Christ is not physically present in the consecrated bread and wine, that confession and anointing of the sick are nice but hardly necessary, that marriage is not indissoluble, and that priesthood is not necessarily permanent. For the Catholic Church to be credible in the twenty-first century, it must let go of this medieval concept.

Catholic Christianity did well for over a thousand years without the concept of *sacramentum et res*, which was introduced into European schools of theology around the twelfth century. The concept resolved a number of theological questions about how church rituals produced their effects, but since the sacraments no longer actually have many of those effects (as noted in the preceding paragraph), there is little point in retaining it. Indeed, the concept has never been important in the Orthodox tradition, which in some respects is older than Roman tradition, and it never found its way into Protestant theology either. Yet both Orthodoxy and Protestantism have flourished as religious traditions, which suggests that our own Catholic tradition can also do well without this theological concept, especially if it has become dysfunctional.

A fashionable word today is deconstructionism, by which is meant mentally taking apart what we take for granted (about art, society, science, relationships, etc.) and showing that it is often based on questionable assumptions that lead to misleading and even harmful conclusions. Unfortunately, most writings by self-styled deconstructionists are intellectually torturous and linguistically illogical, perhaps because they attempt to undo the ordinary logic with which most of us naïvely interact with the world around us. One contemporary Catholic theologian, Louis-Marie Chauvet, has attempted to apply this mode of postmodern analysis to the sacraments in order to show how their effectiveness can be understood without resorting to medieval metaphysics and concepts such as *sacramentum et res*.

Reading Chauvet's works is challenging, and although he does reconstruct sacramental theology using linguistics rather than metaphysics, his work often suffers from the same convoluted thinking that characterizes many postmodern writings. On the one hand, Chauvet has perceived the importance of rethinking the Catholic sacramental system, but on the other hand, the way he does it is accessible only to academics.

The book that you are about to read is also a work of reconstruction, but it is written in a way that ought to be accessible to most people currently engaged in ministry, as well as to most students of theology. I hope that it will enable you to get a better grasp on what happens and what does not happen in sacramental rituals, and if you are in a liturgical ministry, understanding sacraments from the inside out may help you to design and implement religious rituals that are more spiritually effective.

This is not a book of sacramental theology, although it is in part a book about sacramental theology. In fact, seven different sacramental theologies are summarized in chapter 5, and one of the things you will be asked to do is to determine whether or not they make sense to you. In chapters 6 and 7, you will find some of my own ideas related to sacraments, morality, and spirituality, and you will not be asked to accept them at face value but to consider them and judge whether or not they have some merit. If you are interested in sacramental theology—that is, in an understanding of sacraments that makes sense in light of the scriptures, the Christian tradition, your acquired knowledge, your experience, and your observations—you will have to develop one for yourself. Hopefully this book—or rather, what you learn from interacting with this book—will help you to do that.

Invitation

As you read this book, you will notice the symbol □ at many places in the margins. Each of them is an invitation to engage the topic at hand and personalize your study of the sacraments. At www.TheSacraments.org you will find questions designed to help you examine what is being said at that point in light of your own ideas and experiences. Feel free to answer the questions in your head, on paper, in a word processor, or on the web site itself. If you choose to work on the web site, you may also be able to see what other readers have written in response to the questions. The web site also contains other material that I hope you will find helpful.

In addition, I have set up a special e-mail account so you can send me your thoughts. You may disagree with me, ask me questions, or even agree with me. If I am unable to reply within a week, I will quickly let you know how long it may take to get back to you. Please send all correspondence to: TheSacraments@Gmail.com. I look forward to hearing from you.

Joseph Martos

CHAPTER 1

Psychology and the Sacraments

Sacraments are not for the unconscious, the asleep, or the dead. They are for the awake and aware, the living and growing. Sacraments are signs, and they function as symbols: they resonate in the thoughts and feelings of those who perceive them. Sacraments are actions, and they function as rituals: they repeat gestures and words that are meaningful to those who perceive them. Sacraments do more than affect thoughts and feelings, but they affect the minds of participants in ways that need to be understood psychologically as well as theologically.

1. Psychological Dimensions of the Sacraments

In the early 1960s two books appeared in English that had a dramatic impact on Catholic sacramental theology: Edward Schillebeeckx's *Christ, the Sacrament of the Encounter with God* and Bernard Cooke's *Christian Sacraments and Christian Personality*. They reminded us of the broadly psychological dimensions of our sacramental celebrations that traditional theology had tended to neglect or obscure. Schillebeeckx pointed out that in each sacrament we come in contact with the saving presence and power of Christ, and that on our part this should be an existentially personal encounter. Cooke showed how in responding to the grace that is offered in each of the sacraments our personality becomes more Christlike.[1] After that, Catholic authors, most notably Aidan Kavanagh and Joseph Powers, paid further attention to the experiential dimensions of the sacraments. In

---

1. Edward Schillebeeckx, *Christ, the Sacrament of the Encounter with God* (New York: Sheed and Ward, 1963); Bernard Cooke, *Christian Sacraments and Christian Personality* (New York: Holt, Rinehart and Winston, 1965).

1967 Kavanagh observed, "Ritual is the hinge on which personal interiorization of religious tradition swings, the experiential source from which a sense of religious identity, dedication, renewed freedom and effectiveness proceeds."[2] And in 1973 in *Spirit and Sacrament* Powers explored the experiences that are pointed to through the linguistic symbols, "God," "Spirit," "Christ," and "church," and further in the context of the sacraments, "grace," "salvation," "rebirth," and "forgiveness."[3] In the years since, it has become increasingly taken for granted that participating in and reflecting on the sacraments should have psychological ramifications.

Of course, this understanding has never been entirely absent from Catholic theology. St. Paul was undoubtedly reflecting on his own religious experience when he formulated many of his teachings,[4] and similarly the fathers of the church and the early scholastics often used symbolic language to express what they felt was otherwise ineffable. The same has been true of the great Christian mystics, St. Teresa of Avila, St. John of the Cross, and others. But in the Middle Ages Catholic theology developed a technical language that was objective and metaphysical, with the result that the subjective and experiential dimensions of doctrine were often relegated to the realms of personal piety. To some extent the liturgical renewal, which began with the Benedictines during the nineteeth century and continued well past Vatican II, reintroduced Catholics to the psychological dimension of liturgical spirituality. This dimension was recognized in such books as *The Inner Life of Worship* and in many of the writings of Thomas Merton.[5] As summarized in the words of Jacques and Raissa Maritain:

> The worship rendered to God by the church is necessarily an exterior worship, but it is a worship in spirit and in truth, in which what matters above all is the interior movement of souls and the divine grace operating in them.[6]

---

2. Aidan Kavanagh, "How Rite Develops: Some Laws Intrinsic to Liturgical Evolution," *Worship* 41 (1967): 342. See also Kavanagh's many articles on liturgy and sacraments in *Worship* and other journals during this period.

3. Joseph Powers, *Spirit and Sacrament* (New York: Seabury Press, 1973). See also his *Eucharistic Theology* (New York: Herder and Herder, 1967).

4. This shows through most clearly in such passages as Rom 5–8; 1 Cor 2–4; 7–14; 2 Cor 4–6; 10–12; and Gal 2–4.

5. Charles M. Magsam, *The Inner Life of Worship* (St. Meinrad, IN: Grail Publications, 1958). See, for example, Thomas Merton's *The Living Bread* (New York: Farrar, Straus and Cudahy, 1956).

6. Jacques and Raissa Maritain, *Liturgy and Contemplation* (New York: P. J. Kenedy and Sons, 1960), 14f.

Even before the Second Vatican Council, reputable theologians such as Henri de Lubac, Piet Fransen, and Karl Rahner acknowledged that the supernatural reality of grace was something that entered the realm of human consciousness, and after the council the experience of grace received further attention from Catholic authors.[7] Moreover, religious conversion is an area of religious experience in which the psychological aspects have long been recognized (think, for example, of St. Augustine's *Confessions*). And finally, some of the sacraments have normally been expected to have psychological implications for those who participated in them: the Eucharist, as the sacrament of Christ's presence and God's love, and penance, as the sacrament of human contrition and divine compassion. (It is perhaps noteworthy that of the seven, these two are ordinarily the only two frequently repeatable sacraments.)

2. The Sacred Dimension

Those engaged in the scientific study of religion acknowledge that the sacred is a genuine dimension of human consciousness. Although not all people can point to times in their lives when they have felt what they might call the presence of God or the power of grace, there are many who can. In tribal and ancient societies psychological encounters with the sacred were considered normal and what was experienced in those moments was regarded as real. The same was true to a greater or lesser extent in traditional Christian society. In today's secular society there is a tendency to dismiss such experiences as "merely psychological," but people who do so apparently do not recognize that *all* human experiences (including the experience of colors, sounds, smells, tastes, and touches) are at root psychological.[8] Thus in the psychology of religion, the sociology of religion, and the history of religion,

---

7. This is not to suggest, of course, that everything referred to in the traditional theology of grace is available to our experience. On this subject, see Piet Fransen, "Towards a Psychology of Divine Grace," in *Intelligent Theology*, vol. 3 (Chicago: Franciscan Herald Press, 1969), 7–45; Karl Rahner, "Concerning the Relationship between Nature and Grace," in *Theological Investigations*, vol. 1 (Baltimore, MD: Helicon Press, 1961), esp. 298, 300; also his "Reflections on the Experience of Grace," *Theological Investigations*, vol. 3 (Baltimore, MD: Helicon Press, 1967), 86–90; William W. Meissner, *Foundations for a Psychology of Grace* (Glen Rock, NJ: Paulist Press, 1966).

8. On this point, the history of modern philosophy from Descartes and Locke onward bears adequate testimony. For a brief and clear exposition of this matter, see Garrett Barden and Philip McShane, *Towards Self-Meaning* (New York: Herder and Herder, 1974), 42–47. On the reason why the complete subjectivity of our experience does not imply the complete subjectivity of human knowledge, see Bernard Lonergan, *Insight: A Study of Human Understanding* (New York: Philosophical Library, 1957), chap. 13.

the experience of the sacred, the divine, or the transcendent is regarded as an authentically human experience. "It is as if there were in human consciousness a sense of reality, a feeling of objective presence, a perception of what may be called 'something there.'"[9]

That "something there" was extensively described in 1917 by Rudolf Otto in his now classic study, *The Idea of the Holy*.[10] In its most intensive moments the object of that experience appears to be "wholly other," a *mysterium tremendum et fascinans*, a mystery that is at the same time both frightening and fascinating, a "numinous reality" charged with power and radiating energy, to which we respond with feelings of reverence and awe. In less intensive moments it is experienced as no less real but still indescribable, familiar yet strange, sublime and deserving of respect. Experiences of this sort are so characteristic of religious life that religion itself has sometimes been defined in relation to them.[11]

When we encounter the holy in our own lives (and Christians tend to designate these moments as experiences of God or experiences of grace) we enter, as it were, another dimension of reality. It is called in contemporary religious studies the world or realm of the sacred, in contrast to the ordinary, profane, everyday world that we normally inhabit.[12] It is a world in which we have an altered sense of space and time: the space that we inhabit is somehow sanctified, and the time or period in which it occurs is likewise made holy. At some times, it is not unlike the experience of being in love, and of being in the presence of one's beloved. At other times, it is more like the experience of what Protestants call "conviction," an awareness of their sinfulness and guilt in the presence of the One who is all pure and

---

*This symbol in the margin indicates an interactive question that can be found at http://www.TheSacraments.org.

---

9. William James, *The Varieties of Religious Experience* (New York: Modern Library, 1932), 58; italics removed.

10. Rudolf Otto, *The Idea of the Holy* (New York: Oxford University Press, 1950). For a more contemporary account of this and other religious experiences, see William F. Kraft, *The Search for the Holy* (Philadelphia, PA: Westminster Press, 1971).

11. For example, "'Religion,' it might be said, is the term that designates the attitude peculiar to a consciousness which has been altered by the experience of the numinosum" (G. Stephens Spinks, *Psychology and Religion: An Introduction to Contemporary Views* [Boston, MA: Beacon Press, 1967], 6).

12. Note that "world" here is understood psychologically (or more accurately, phenomenologically), in the sense that each of us may be said to live at the center of our own world, or that the world of the scientist is different from the world of the artist.

all good. There is a wide variety of such religious experiences.[13] And yet they all seem to take place in what Mircea Eliade calls sacred space and sacred time.[14]

Very often the occasions for these religious experiences (Eliade calls them "hierophanies" or manifestations of the sacred) are particular objects and gestures, places and occasions that have come to be regarded as special and sacred in themselves.[15]

For early humans and for people who live in tribal cultures even today, these are very often things associated with nature, such as certain plants and stones, particular mountains and rivers, the winter solstice and springtime. For Catholics and other Christians they tend rather to be such things as relics and statues, churches and shrines, scriptures and hymns, liturgies and sacraments, Christmas and Easter times. In the technical language of religious studies, objects, rites, places, and occasions of this sort are perceived by believers as possessing "mana," a numinous power or supernatural aura that penetrates them and radiates from them.[16] Persons too can be imbued with mana, but following the suggestion of the pioneering sociologist Max Weber, such personal mana is usually referred to in religious studies as "charisma." In the history of religions Moses, Jesus, Buddha, Mohammed, and other great religious leaders have all been seen by their followers as having sacred powers or qualities. In the history of Judaism and Christianity, the kings and prophets of Israel, the martyrs and saints of the church, as well as individuals such as Augustine and Chrysostom, Luther and Calvin, Martin Luther King and Mother Teresa of Calcutta have been perceived as charismatic persons. Finally, persons can come to be regarded as having

13. See Gordon Allport, *The Individual and His Religion: A Psychological Interpretation* (New York: Macmillan, 1950), 29; also James, *The Varieties of Religious Experience*, 42–49.

14. See Mircea Eliade, *The Sacred and the Profane: The Nature of Religion* (New York: Harcourt, Brace and World, 1959), 20–65, 68–95. For a more scholarly treatment, see his *Patterns in Comparative Religion* (New York: Sheed and Ward, 1958), 367–408. For a discussion of these phenomena more related to contemporary religious experience, see John E. Smith, *Experience and God* (New York: Oxford University Press, 1968), 57–62.

15. See Eliade, *Patterns*, 2–4, 8–13, 23–30. See also Bernard Lonergan, *Method in Theology* (New York: Herder and Herder, 1972), 108f.

16. "Mana" is originally a Melanesian word, but it has been adopted by anthropologists and others to refer to what is called *wakan, orenda, maga* (an ancient Persian word with the same root as our "magic"), and so on in various tribal cultures. The reality to which these words point seems to be a fairly universal phenomenon in all religions both ancient and modern. For a good summary treatment of mana, see Barbara Hargrove, *The Sociology of*

charismata worthy of respect in virtue of their office or function in a religious society, for example, priests and bishops, nuns and religious superiors, evangelists and healers.[17]

In traditional Christianity, the religious experience that is pointed to in contemporary religious studies by such words as "hierophany," "mana," and "charisma" is the experience of mystery. Intellectually, mystery can be conceived of as something that is only partially understood and never completely understandable; on the level of experience, however, mystery is often perceived to be present when what we are aware of is sacred or precious, important or serious, meaningful or significant, numinous or holy, even if it is not thought of as supernatural or divine.[18] In this sense the experience of the disciples on Pentecost, of St. Paul on the road to Damascus, of St. Peter when he had his dream, and of countless other saints and mystics can all be classified as hierophanies. But so too can the even more frequent experiences in which ordinary Christians sense the presence of God or the power of grace. "In this perspective," says Jean Mouroux, "religious experience can be defined as the act—or group of acts—through which [people become aware of themselves] in relation to God." Thus, "one may say that God is not given in experience but grasped in it."[19]

Similarly, people who saw the power of God in Jesus' miracles, or who sensed the dynamism of the Holy Spirit in the apostles' laying on of hands, or who felt a spiritual regeneration through the ritual of adult baptism, or who were aware of a divine presence in the Eucharistic host—in the language of secular religious studies they can be said to have experienced mana, while in the language of Christianity they can be said to have experienced mystery or some aspect of the divine mystery. In fact, for most Christians the encounter with mystery is "a mediated experience. The presence and grasp of God that it involves are both realized through the mediation of a sign, or series of signs."[20] Finally, for Christians the primary person imbued with charisma and radiating divine power is the figure of Jesus.

Religion: Classical and Contemporary Approaches (Arlington Heights, IL: AHM Publishing Corporation, 1979), 16–18.

17. Note that in sociology "charisma" is a religiously neutral term, so popular figures in secular society can be referred to as charismatic individuals: persons like Napoleon, Churchill, Kennedy, Princess Diana, and Oprah Winfrey, and even scoundrels such as Hitler and Stalin. See Thomas F. O'Dea, *The Sociology of Religion* (Englewood Cliffs, NJ: Prentice-Hall, 1966), 22–24; also Max Weber, *On Charisma and Institution Building* (Chicago: University of Chicago Press, 1968).

18. On this point, see Jean Mouroux, *The Christian Experience: An Introduction to a Theology* (New York: Sheed and Ward, 1954), 17–20.

Those who walked with him in Palestine, who bore testimony to his resurrection, and who acknowledged him as the Christ sensed in his person the spirit of God. For them and for all Christians afterward, *the* mystery of Christianity is the mystery of Christ, believed certainly, but primarily experienced as the mystery of God.

In contemporary Christianity, however, both in liberal Protestantism and increasingly in Catholicism, there seems to be a loss of the sense of mystery, an absence of the traditional types of religious experience such as those just described. Although there are notable exceptions to this trend, Christians in general seem to have a harder time seeing God at work in their everyday lives than, say, their parents and grandparents did. Catholics in particular seem to find it more difficult to sense the mysterious power of the sacraments or even to experience the presence of Christ in the Eucharist.[21] And there are those, both Protestant and Catholic, who find it more comfortable to relate to Jesus as a good man, perhaps even as a prophet or a great man, than to encounter him as God's incarnate Word.

There appear to be a number of reasons for this decline in the experience of the sacred, the psychological sense of mystery. One that is often pointed to is the gradual secularization of society. As the secrets of nature become known to science, as the world becomes more filled with the products of technology, as people's affairs become less regulated by religious institutions and more regulated by secular institutions, God seems to become less and less relevant to their daily lives. Along this line one can also point to contemporary religious studies, to the "demythologizing" of the scriptures that seems to rob them of their literal truth, to the "sociologizing" of the church that makes it look like just one more institution among many, and even the "psychologizing" of religious experience that seems to make it just another human, but all too human, experience. Another factor seems to be that traditional religious language and symbols (like the doctrine of original sin, the symbol of the Sacred Heart, or even the pastoral imagery of the New Testament parables) no longer connect with people's experience of themselves and their world. Along with this, traditional Christian spirituality often seemed to demand self-abasement and slavish dependence on God and the clergy, but these are attitudes that today appear strange if not perverse to people

19. Ibid., 15, 21.

20. Ibid., 21.

21. On some of the reasons for this development in relation to the sacrament of penance, see Monika Hellwig's introduction to her book, *Sign of Reconciliation and Conversion: The Sacrament of Penance for Our Times* (Wilmington, DE: Michael Glazier, 1982).

seeking self-fulfillment and personal and social liberation.[22] One can point to other factors as well, including (for Catholics especially) a loss of a sense of personal community, a disenchantment with church authority, a weakening of institutional identity in the wake of the changes wrought by Vatican II, and even the rejection of the belief that the sacraments are magically □   effective.[23]

Anthropologist Mary Douglas, however, has argued that there is another key factor at work in the diminishing experience of the sacred. In her book *Natural Symbols: Explorations in Cosmology* she demonstrates that socially static and hierarchically organized societies are more prone to express their religious ideas in ritual and to respond to the symbolism of such ritual. The reasons for this are apparently psychological in as much as in static, stratified societies people tend to accept things the way they are in both the natural and supernatural orders. These rituals are plausible, and people can see through the symbols to the realities that they symbolize without much difficulty. Moreover, these rituals are acknowledged to be efficacious, for people in such societies easily believe in the mysterious effects that the rites are supposed to have, such as appeasing the gods through sacrifice or having a demon dispelled through exorcism.[24] As Catholic society goes through its present period of turmoil, therefore, the traditional sacraments (which are symbolic rituals) become less capable of conveying a common understanding of God, or even of mediating a common experience of the sacred. In other words, fixed and standardized religious rituals work well only in stable and stratified societies. And so to the extent that the culture of European and American Catholicism is changing and destratifying, standard rituals such as the sacraments are less effective symbols than they used to be. Put succinctly, "when the social group grips its members in tight communal bonds, □   religion is ritualistic; when this grip is relaxed, ritualism declines."[25]

22. See Harvey Cox, *The Secular City: Secularization and Urbanization in Theological Perspective* (New York: Macmillan, 1965); Gregory Baum, "Religious Experience and Doctrinal Statements," in *New Directions in Religious Experience*, ed. George Devine (New York: Alba House, 1971), esp. 5 and 9f.

23. The rejection of magic in Catholic rituals may be premature. Not long ago it was abhorrent to think that certain biblical stories might be myths; today that view is commonly accepted, due in part to a greater appreciation and understanding of myth as a valid form of human communication. A parallel rethinking and rehabilitation of the nature and function of magic in earlier cultures may shed great light on medieval religion and sacramental theology. See the discussion of magic in chap. 3, sec. 4d of this work.

24. See Mary Douglas, *Natural Symbols: Explorations in Cosmology* (New York: Random House Vintage Books, 1973), esp. chaps. 1–4.

25. Ibid., 32. Note that Douglas' analysis suggests why elaborate religious ritual remained very effective in Eastern Europe and Russia until the downfall of communism, after which

This does not mean, however, that experiences of the sacred or encounters with mystery are entirely absent from people's lives today. It implies only that when such experiences occur, they often do not occur in traditional religious contexts like standardized church rituals. For religious people, such experiences tend to occur more frequently in periods of private prayer, in the individual reading of the scriptures, or in the context of small religious groups. For nonreligious people they occur in analogous moments of meditation, in reading literature and poetry, in viewing films and plays, and in interpersonal encounters. Psychologist Abraham Maslow refers to such moments as "peak experiences":

> In moments of such experience, one is gathered up into a vision of the universe as a coherent unity to which one feels intimately related. One is delivered from egoistic concerns into a clearer perception of others as well as one's own uniqueness. . . . This experience is self-validating; it needs no external justification. Values are sacred; emotions of awe and surrender predominate; dichotomies are transcended; fear and confusion are left behind. One feels more receptive in one's cognition, more able to love and to respond to others and to life as a whole.[26]

Maslow also admits the occurrence of "plateau experiences," which are heightened, if not peak, moments of existential awareness. These are less rare and they are more liable to be repeated in situations such as religious and civil, and even personal, ritual. When they happen, and especially when they repeat themselves, such heightened moments of awareness tend to be touched off by the occurrence of a situation or the appearance of a signal that seems to function as a symbol for them. Indeed, most sacramental experiences appear to fit the description of plateau experiences rather than peak experiences, for they gather together in a moment of heightened awareness a rerealization of values, beliefs, and feelings that have already been experienced and affirmed as sacred. ☐

---

it began to decline. Ritual is also highly effective in structured groups such as military units, monastic orders, and rigidly conservative groups. If highly ritualistic religion and belief in its magical efficacy is natural and normal in rigidly stratified societies, it is likely that medieval Christianity contained more magical elements than Catholics are usually willing to consider.

26. Ann and Barry Ulanov, *Religion and the Unconscious* (Philadelphia, PA: Westminster Press, 1975), 52f. See also Abraham H. Maslow, *Religions, Values, and Peak-Experiences* (New York: Viking Press, 1970); and Charles R. Meyer, *The Touch of God: A Theological Analysis of Religious Experience* (New York: Alba House, 1972).

3. The Symbolic Dimension

In contemporary philosophy, it was largely through the work of Ernst Cassirer and Susanne Langer that we began to understand the value and importance of symbols.[27] Until recently Catholics thought of their sacraments primarily as signs, perhaps because medieval theology did not work out the ramifications of the difference between signs and symbols. Saints Augustine and Thomas Aquinas both defined sacrament as "a sign of something sacred," and similarly the Baltimore Catechism said, "A sacrament is an outward sign instituted by Christ to give grace."[28] But Catholic theology also understood that the sacraments were a special kind of sign: they were "effective signs." Today we realize that part of their effectiveness, at least, is due to their being symbols.

There are a number of ways of differentiating signs from symbols.[29] For our purposes, perhaps the best way is to do it psychologically, that is, in terms of how they affect us and how we respond to them. We can say that signs tend to affect us simply and we tend to respond to them simply, but symbols tend to affect us complexly and we tend to respond to them complexly. Perhaps in terms of the meaning that they have for us, we can say that signs come across to us as having a basic denotation (or meaning) and not much connotation (or associated meaning), whereas symbols may even have many denotations and they are rich in connotations.[30] Some illustrations may make this clearer. Ordinarily, words are simply signs for us. They are signs of what the words mean, or of what they stand for. Like the words in this sentence that you are reading: they have meaning for you, and the meaning registers. Simple input, simple response. Or the signs on doors that say "Entrance" and "Exit"; you know what they mean, and you use the correct door. Or the road signs in Europe, which do not use words

---

27. See Ernst Cassirer, *The Philosophy of Symbolic Forms*, 3 vols. (New Haven, CT: Yale University Press, 1953, 1955, 1957), esp. vol. 2, *Mythical Thought*; also Susanne Langer, *Philosophy in a New Key: A Study in the Symbolism of Reason, Rite, and Art*, 3rd ed. (Cambridge, MA: Harvard University Press, 1957).

28. Augustine, *Letters*, no. 138, I; Thomas Aquinas, *Summa Theologiae* III, q. 60, a. 2; *A Catechism of Christian Doctrine* (Paterson, NJ: St. Anthony Guild Press, 1941), q. 304.

29. See, for example, Langer, *Philosophy in a New Key*, 57–59; Thomas Fawcett, *The Symbolic Language of Religion* (Minneapolis: Augsburg, 1971), chaps. 1 and 2; George S. Worgul Jr., *From Magic to Metaphor: A Validation of Christian Sacraments* (New York: Paulist Press, 1980), chap. 3.

30. The English language does not always use the words "sign" and "symbol" according to these psychological criteria. For example, what we ordinarily call mathematical symbols would here be classified as signs, and what are ordinarily called signs of affection would here be called symbols.

but indicate "Stop" and "No parking" and so on. These are all conventional signs invented and produced by human beings. But there are also natural signs. Smoke is a sign of fire. Laughter in a room means that people are having a good time. Trees turning green is a sign of spring.   □

Things that usually function as signs, however, can sometimes function as symbols. Words like "God," "freedom," "sex," and so on can evoke subtle emotions even by themselves, and when used in the context of a religious sermon or a political speech they can resonate deep in our feelings. We react to sentences like "I love you" and "You're a pig" not because of what they blandly denote but because of what they powerfully connote to us. Our country's flag and national anthem are not just cloth and music, but they remind us in our depths of memories and beliefs, ideals and values, hopes and fears that we share in common with so many others. Again, words, emblems, music, and the like are conventional symbols, but there are also natural symbols. The greening of springtime can symbolize for us the end of winter confinement, invigorating freshness, the promise of summer's warmth, and hope for new beginnings. And it is hard to be kissed (especially unexpectedly) without feeling and thinking of a number of things simultaneously.   □

Interestingly, almost anything can be viewed as a sign or symbol of something else, if it is taken that way. Books can be just books, or they can be taken as a sign of learning. Fire can be just fire, or it can be taken as a symbol of warmth and life, or conversely, of destruction and death. Because of this, signs and symbols are said to point to what they signify; they refer to something besides themselves. But whereas things taken as signs usually have a single or simple referent (like the label on a box to what is inside it), things taken as symbols have a multiple or complex referent (they can mean many things simultaneously). Because signs or symbols do not stand simply for themselves, they sometimes have to be interpreted or deciphered or translated for those who do not know what they mean or refer to.   □

In the current literature on religious symbolism, the ability of symbols to have multiple or complex meanings is designated by a variety of terms: multivalence, multivocality, coalescence of meaning, richness of expression, condensation, polysemy, and surplus of meaning.[31] All these terms, however, refer to the same basic fact, namely, that when some object or image or natural phenomenon is apprehended symbolically, it conveys many things simultaneously. As Mircea Eliade insists, it is a drastic mistake to reduce a symbolic image to just one of its meanings:

---

31. See Victor Turner, *Forest of Symbols: Aspects of Ndembu Ritual* (Ithaca, NY: Cornell University Press, 1967), 50–52; Fawcett, *Symbolic Language*, 28f.; Langer, *Philosophy in a New Key*, 94–97.

It is therefore the image as such, the whole bundle of meanings that is *true*, not any *one* of its meanings, nor one alone of its many frames of reference. To translate an image into a concrete terminology by restricting it to any one of its frames of reference is to do worse than mutilate it—it is to annihilate, to annul it as an instrument of cognition.[32]

One of the ways that symbols get their ability to communicate many things to us at the same time is through the psychological association of overt or surface meanings with covert or subliminal meanings and feelings. At least some of the meanings of any symbol are hidden or depth meanings when the symbol is doing its work. Modern-day advertisers know this much about the psychology of symbolism very well, which is why they often associate the products they are selling (the overt message) with symbols of sex, power, wealth, motherhood, patriotism, or anything else that will make us feel positively about them (the covert message). Psychologically sophisticated advertising thus carries a double message, although in this case the connection between the overt and covert messages is often contrived and usually manipulative in intent.[33] In the ordinary use of symbols, the association between the levels of meaning is more spontaneous and natural, and the intent is communicative: to say in symbol what cannot be said otherwise.

Anthropologist Victor Turner has documented how these two levels of meaning relate to one another in the religious rituals of tribal and other cultures.[34] Borrowing Turner's analytical ideas (but not his technical terminology),[35] we can say that when a symbol resonates in our minds and hearts, it is often because meanings and feelings at the depth level of the symbol get psychologically associated with meanings and images at the surface level of the symbol. Thus at the surface level, for example, a picture of Our Lady of Lourdes refers to Mary, the mother of Jesus, and her appearance to St.

---

32. Mircea Eliade, *Images and Symbols: Studies in Religious Symbolism* (New York: Sheed and Ward, 1961), 15. See also his *Patterns*, chap. 13.

33. The classic work on this subject is Vance Packard, *The Hidden Persuaders* (New York: David McKay, 1957).

34. For a good summary of Turner's ideas, as well as references to his other works, see appendix A of Victor and Edith Turner, *Image and Pilgrimage in Christian Culture: Anthropological Perspectives* (New York: Columbia University Press, 1978), 243–55. Turner's work has already been applied by Catholic scholars to the sacraments. See, for example, Michael G. Lawler, "Christian Rituals: An Essay in Sacramental Symbolisms," *Horizons* 7 (1980): 7–35; also Worgul, *From Magic to Metaphor*, 98–104.

35. His terminology is quite precise, though not very descriptive. Turner analyzes symbols by grouping them around what he terms the orectic (or sensory) pole and the ideological (or normative) pole. They may be thought of as the surface and depth levels of meaning, or the specific and generic referents, of a symbol.

Bernadette. But at the depth level (for those who are open to it) the symbol evokes meanings and feelings associated with motherhood, virginity, divinity, and compassion (since she was the virgin mother of God who deigned to appear to a peasant). Or to take another example, oil had a set of culturally accepted meanings in the Middle East around the time of Christ: oil was used as a salve and medicine, and so it meant health and healing; it was used to moisten dry skin and hair, and so it meant leisure and luxury; it was used to anoint priests and kings, and so it meant divine presence and power. Thus when anointing became part of the Christian initiation ritual (and it was in part because of this rich complex of cultural meanings that it came to be used in the ritual), although new meanings were attached to it, the use of oil brought with it a whole host of generic meanings that reinforced those specifically Christian meanings and aroused ideas and ideals, feelings, and desires that had been traditionally associated with oil.[36]

The fact that Marian devotion has declined in recent decades, however, and the fact that the use of oil in our sacraments no longer calls forth the depth meanings that it had in the ancient world illustrate that neither the intellectual nor the psychological effectiveness of symbols is automatic. Just as personal symbols may not mean to others what they mean to us, so ecclesial symbols of the Christian experience of the sacred may not mean to one generation or culture what they mean to others. Nor is the situation unique to Catholicism. Protestant theologian Paul Tillich has observed about symbols, "They grow when the situation is ripe for them, and they die when the situation changes."[37] Normally when a symbol stops being significant to people, they stop using it. After Vatican II, many in religious orders stopped wearing their traditional habit because it no longer expressed what they wanted to say about themselves, and ordinary Catholics stopped buying traditional statues and pictures because such art no longer spoke to them. This fact is more adequately demonstrated in the history of religious symbolism, and even in the way that the symbols and rituals of a religion other than our own can seem odd and foreign to us. "Symbols are effective only so long as they are relevant to life," and so, "when a symbol loses its meaning it may continue as a historical sign but as a symbol it is dead."[38]

---

36. Ralph Keifer applies this analysis to the Paschal Vigil in chapter 6 of *Blessed and Broken* (Wilmington, DE: Michael Glazier, 1982). Keifer refers to the orectic meanings as the human element or the primal layer in the symbolic experience.

37. Paul Tillich, *Dynamics of Faith* (New York: Harper and Row, 1958), 43.

38. Spinks, *Psychology and Religion*, 98; italics removed.

At the same time, however, there are some fundamental *types* of religious symbols that seem to never die. Mircea Eliade has abundantly demonstrated that although individual symbols may come and go, there are some general symbolic types that keep recurring in the history of religion: sky symbolisms of transcendence and infinity, sun and fire symbolisms of light and life, moon and seasonal symbolisms of cyclical renewal, rock and stone symbolisms of stability and endurance, tree and plant symbolisms of life and growth, water symbolisms of potentiality and ambiguity.[39] To these fundamental nature symbols we must add physical human realities such as masculinity and femininity, genital sexuality, blood and menstrual flow, plus common human gestures such as laughter and tears, embracing and distancing, food sharing and abstinence, postures of authority and submission, and so forth.[40] Eliade calls these general and basic types of symbols "archetypes" or fundamental symbolic images, as does psychologist Carl Jung, who found such recurring symbolism not only in the dreams of his patients but also in many of the world's religions:

> The fact is that certain ideas exist almost everywhere and at all times and they spontaneously create themselves quite apart from migration and tradition. They are not made by the individual but rather they happen— they even force themselves on the individual's consciousness.[41]

This sort of archetypal symbolism is found not only in religious objects, images, and gestures; it is also found in religious stories or myths. Although the words "myth" and "mythic" once had exclusively pejorative connotations (and the words are still used this way in ordinary speech), contemporary religious studies understand myth to be a fundamental form of symbolic narrative, an expression of symbols in story form. In this sense of the term, creation accounts in the Old Testament and the infancy narratives in the New Testament, for example, are today accepted as mythic in character, for they attempt to say in the concrete imagery of story what their authors understood about the human situation and about the person of Jesus.[42] Moreover, just as

---

39. For many of these, see Eliade, *Patterns*, cited above.

40. For many of these, see Victor Turner, *Dramas, Fields and Metaphors: Symbolic Action in Human Society* (Ithaca, NY: Cornell University Press, 1974).

41. Carl Jung, *Psychology and Religion* (New Haven, CT: Yale University Press, 1932), 4. For more on archetypes, see Robin Robertson, *C. G. Jung and the Archetypes of the Collective Unconscious* (New York: Peter Lang, 1987).

42. On myth in general, see Ernst Cassirer, *An Essay on Man: An Introduction to the Philosophy of Human Culture* (New Haven, CT: Yale University Press, 1944), chap. 7; Mircea Eliade, *Myth and Reality* (New York: Harper and Row, 1963), chap. 1; Fawcett, *Symbolic*

one finds repeated patterns of archetypal symbols in the world's religions, so also one finds repeated archetypal patterns and images in religious myths. There are stories about the creation of the world and about the origins of everything that is important to human beings; there are stories about gods and goddesses, heroes and heroines, and how they interact with one another; there are stories that show how to do things (like hunting and farming), how to make things (such as homes and boats), and how to behave in various situations (as in times of danger or in times of celebration).[43]

It is important to emphasize that ancient myths were not imaginative stories devised to cover up human ignorance or to fill in the gaps between the few things that people knew about themselves and their world. Rather, they were symbolic expressions of what people actually *did* understand about life, its meaning, and how it is to be lived. Behind every myth there stands an insight that some individual or society in the past has had into the nature of reality, into the meaning of life, and into the value of thinking and behaving in certain ways. The myths of different religions sometimes vary greatly in what they say (the content of the insight) and in how they say it (the symbolic language or story used to express it), and so we can distinguish between the Judeo-Christian myths and those of other religions. But at the level of archetypal patterns the form and function of myths in all religions seem to be similar; they offer paradigms or models of the way things are, or of the way things ought to be, or of the way things should be done. In Eliade's words, "The foremost function of myth is to reveal explanatory models for all human rites and all significant human actions—diet or marriage, work or education, art or wisdom."[44]

It is on this basis, then, that some tribal peoples distinguish truth from falsity in their symbolic stories. A story that describes the correct way to do things, that portrays the right way to live, or that displays the proper values and attitudes is "true." Conversely, a story that departs from these norms is "false" to a greater or lesser degree. From this perspective, tales that say that hunters are brave and that children respect their parents are "true," whereas tales that suggest the opposite are "false." From this same

Language, chap. 6. On myth in the Old and New Testaments, see for example, John L. McKenzie, *Myths and Realities: Studies in Biblical Theology* (Milwaukee, WI: Bruce Publishing Company, 1963), chaps. 8 and 9; James P. Mackey, *Jesus, the Man and the Myth* (New York: Paulist Press, 1979).

43. See Eliade, *Patterns*, chap. 12. From a somewhat different perspective, see Joseph Campbell, *Myths to Live By* (New York: Viking Press, 1972); and *The Hero with a Thousand Faces* (Cleveland, OH: World Publishing Company, 1956).

44. Eliade, *Myth and Reality*, 8; see also *Patterns*, 410, 419, 425–27, 430.

perspective, though at a slightly higher level of generalization, both of the creation stories in the book of Genesis are "true" because they correctly describe human beings' relation to God and nature, even though in the first account man and woman are created last, and in the second account man is created first among the inhabitants of earth and woman is created last.

What has just been said of myth, which is symbolic narrative, can also be said of ritual, which is symbolic action. Although it is generally conceded that ritual developed before myth, and that myths are to some extent a spelling out in words what rituals depict in actions,[45] it is sometimes easier for us today to understand the meaning of a ritual by relating it to the myth that is its verbal expression. Perhaps at an earlier stage of human evolution all that was needed was the repetition of the "true" action for individuals to feel and enter into its "truth," but in all known religions (including Christianity) the significance of rituals is narrated in myths and the significance of myths is acted out in rituals. In fact, it is often through ritual that religious people enter into the symbolic world of the myth and experience its deep significance for their lives. What Eliade describes in the context of tribal religions is analogously true of all religions, including our own:

> "Living" a myth, then, implies a genuinely "religious" experience, since it differs from the ordinary experience of everyday life. The "religiousness" of this experience is due to the fact that one re-enacts fabulous, exalting, significant events, once again witnessing the creative deeds of the Supernaturals; one ceases to exist in the everyday world and enters a transfigured, auroral world impregnated with the Supernaturals' presence. What is involved is not a commemoration of mythical events but a reiteration of them.[46]

It is primarily through symbols, therefore, that people express what they have experienced in the world of the sacred and communicate that experience to others. Sometimes particular symbols are so tied to particular individuals and societies that what "says" the sacred for them does not say anything to others. There are, however, archetypal symbols that seem to be able to mediate experiences of the sacred in many different cultures, partly because while their surface meaning is peculiar to each religion their depth

---

45. See Louis Bouyer, *Rite and Man: Natural Sacredness and Christian Liturgy* (Notre Dame, IN: University of Notre Dame Press, 1963), chaps. 4 and 5, and esp. p. 73; also Adolf E. Jensen, *Myth and Cult among Primitive Peoples* (Chicago: University of Chicago Press, 1963), esp. 39–45.

46. Eliade, *Myth and Reality*, 19.

meaning is common to human beings no matter where and when they live. ☐

In some way, all symbols "image" the reality that they call to mind or make psychologically present to us. Such images can be natural objects or simple diagrams that appear to be filled with mana. More frequently the images are complex: either the complex stories narrated in myths, or the complex activities performed in rituals. Sometimes the same encounter with the sacred is expressed in both myth and ritual, and so the same mystery is revealed through both. Moreover, both myth and ritual are judged to be true or false according to whether or not they represent the right way to live, the way that is disclosed in the world of the sacred. ☐

4. The Ritual Dimension

Some years ago, Erik Erikson developed a theory about the psychological importance of ritual and the sequential development of the various elements that are found in adult rituals.[47] Although this theory is not as well known as his theory of the eight stages of human development,[48] it is of particular interest for understanding the role of ritual in psychological development and the contribution that each stage makes to the experience of ritual in adulthood.

Envision, if you will, the interactions between mother and infant. He cries, and she comes to him. She cares for his needs, overcoming the nameless feeling of aloneness that threatens to engulf him. He responds with trust that expresses itself in a calm relaxation. She smiles; he gradually recognizes the source of his comfort and learns to smile back. "The encounter of the maternal person and small infant, an encounter which is one of mutual trustworthiness and mutual recognition is the first experience of what in later reoccurrences in love and admiration can only be called a sense of 'hallowed presence,' the need for which remains basic in [human beings]."[49] It is in infancy that we first need to find a sacred "other," and it is through responding to our mother's affection that we both develop the capacity to perceive other people as able to be trusted and loved, and we

---

47. See Erik H. Erikson, "The Development of Ritualization," in *The Religious Situation, 1968*, ed. Donald R. Cutler (Boston, MA: Beacon Press, 1968), 711–33. This theory is at the core of his *Toys and Reasons: Stages in the Ritualization of Experience* (New York: W. W. Norton, 1977). His ideas have also been applied to the sacraments by George Worgul in *From Magic to Metaphor*, 52–62.

48. For a clear summary, see Erik H. Erikson, *Childhood and Society*, 2nd ed. (New York: W. W. Norton, 1963), chap. 7.

49. Erik H. Erikson, *Identity: Youth and Crisis* (New York: W. W. Norton, 1968), 105.

develop the ability to sense the sacred presence of God in religious worship.
For the first important element in religious ritual is a sense of the sacred.

The second stage of ritualization in human development may be called the "judicial" stage because during it we learn to judge between right and wrong at a very basic level. During early childhood we are repeatedly told what is "good" and "bad," and we learn to distinguish the two partly by learning and repeating socially approved behavior and by ritualistically avoiding actions that are not acceptable to our parents and others. In other words, in early childhood we learn how to behave in public and we accept that doing things with people means conforming to certain rules. Through such ritualization, then, we both develop the capacity to interact with others in ways that our society accepts as normal, and we develop the ability to sense what is appropriate and inappropriate behavior in religious worship. For the second important element in religious ritual is the sense that this is the proper thing to do.

The third stage of everyday ritualization may be called the "dramatic" stage because at this point in our lives we first develop the ability to see sequences of events as little dramas with a beginning, middle, and end. Preschool children play with dolls and doll houses, building-block villages and their inhabitants, cars and trucks, and in doing so they also create miniature plays in which people and objects interact with each other in appropriate patterns. Children at this age also play at roles, pretending to be mommy and daddy, cowboy and cowgirl, nurse and fireman, modeling their dramatic actions on what they perceive as adult roles and interactions. Through these little rituals, therefore, we both develop the ability to cooperate with other persons through more prolonged periods of social interaction, and we develop the capacity to perceive human rituals as dramatic wholes, whether those rituals be ballets or sporting events, operas or plays, Bible services or eucharistic liturgies. For the third main element in religious ritual is its form as drama, having a period of preparation, a moment of climax, and a period of coming to completion.

The fourth stage of ritualization in our ordinary experience may be called the "formal" stage because through it we come to appreciate the perfection of performance in the things that we do by ourselves or with others. During our years at school, for example, "play is transformed into work, game into cooperation, and the freedom of the imagination into the duty to perform with full attention to all the minute details which are necessary to complete a task and do it 'right.' "[50] The human need to develop

---

50. Erikson, "The Development of Ritualization," 726f.

through ritualization at this age is met by the gradual mastery of school subjects and musical instruments, by participating in team sports and practicing until it's perfect, by joining youth organizations and earning awards for the acquisition of new skills. Through such ritual devotion to formal tasks we develop the ability to attend to and delight in the fine details of activity, and we develop the capacity to focus on, perform, and appreciate the external and internal intricacies of ritual worship. For the fourth main element in religious ritual is its character of being formal or stylized behavior. ☐

If the formal aspect of ritual is insisted upon but the ceremony (whether it be secular or religious) does not arouse a sense of the sacred, is not perceived as the right thing to do, or loses its dramatic integrity, it can appear as empty formalism. This is especially true for adolescents, for whom the fifth stage of ritualization brings a demand for solidarity of conviction. At this stage of self-identification and social commitment the rituals learned in childhood need to be accepted as one's own and integrated into one's identity as a member of the social group from which they were learned. It is through the performance of rituals during adolescence, therefore, that we add our own assent and approval to what we have become in the preceding stages of our development. In this way we become able to perform civil ceremonies and religious rituals with conviction, that is, we recognize them as symbolizing what we believe and value, and we identify with what the symbols stand for. For the fifth principal element in religious ritual is the sense that this symbolic action is both "mine" and "ours," plus the affirmation that what it signifies is real and worthwhile. ☐

It is important to remember that according to this theory of sequential development, while each stage builds on the accomplishments of the preceding stages, the accomplishments of those stages are retained in the more developed ritualization of the later stages.

> [Human] epigenetic development in separate and protracted childhood stages assures that each of the major elements which constitute human institutions [whether they be everyday rituals or specifically ceremonial rituals] is rooted in a distinct childhood stage, but, once evolved, must be progressively reintegrated on each higher level.[51]

Nevertheless, Erikson believes that by adolescence all of the psychologically important elements of ritual have been developed in each person. But what then of adulthood? Doesn't this stage of human growth contribute

51. Ibid., 725.

something to the development of ritual? Erikson believes not, and instead he suggests that "a dominant function of ritual in the life of the adult" meets a "need to be periodically reinforced in his role of ritualizer" for the younger generation.[52] In Erikson's overall theory of human development, the primary task of the adult years is generativity, which encompasses both biological creativity and social accomplishment, and he envisages adult participation in ritual as a means of accomplishing this generative task of passing on one's personal and cultural achievements to others.

This does not imply, however, that developmental psychology can offer nothing more to our understanding of religious ritual. For one thing, if it is true that the accomplishments of each lower stage of personal development are retained as one grows through the later stages, then liturgy and worship can both reaffirm those accomplishments and reinforce them in addition to encouraging them in those who have not yet succeeded in doing so. Erikson himself suggests this when he says that religion is "the institution which throughout human history has striven to verify basic trust," which is the foundation for all further human development.[53] Certainly baptism and Eucharist, for example, can be seen as both affirming and enabling the development of trusting relationships among members of the church and between individuals and God. Confirmation may be viewed as a celebration of autonomy and initiative in Christian living (Erikson's stages two and three) as well as an encouragement toward greater activity within and identification with the church (stages four and five). Penance can be at least one means of effecting reconciliation between persons and between individuals and God, and so bring about a greater measure of intimacy (stage six) in human living. Both marriage and ordination are celebrations of generativity in human living (stage seven). And the anointing of the sick can help those in later years to perceive the fundamental integrity of their lives within a Christian perspective (stage eight).[54]

For another thing, Erikson's developmental theories are not the only ones in psychology, and there are others that trace other dimensions of human development or that explore other areas of human experience and living.[55] So although Erikson offers us a model for the development of ritu-

---

52. Ibid., 729, 730; italics removed.

53. Erikson, *Identity*, 106.

54. On this latter point, see James L. Empereur, *Prophetic Anointing: God's Call to the Sick, the Elderly, and the Dying* (Wilmington, DE: Michael Glazier, 1982), 159–81.

55. See Jean Piaget, *Genetic Epistemology* (New York: Columbia University Press, 1970); and *The Child and Reality: Problems of Genetic Psychology* (New York: Viking Press, 1973); Lawrence Kohlberg, *The Philosophy of Moral Development: Moral Stages and the Idea of*

alization, his work certainly does not fully explore the psychological richness of sacramental rituals.[56] Here we shall have to be content with reviewing some of the other psychological aspects of religious ritual in general.

In the preceding section on symbolism we looked primarily at symbols as *expressions* of religious experience, although we also saw how through association with basic human emotions and ideas symbols can also make a deep *impression* on people. This is just another way of saying that symbols can be causes of hierophanies, and it turns out that in the history of religions most symbols that give rise to hierophanies occur in the context of rituals. How then do rituals make the impression that they make on people? How do they occasion hierophanies that occur in sacred space and time? □

This is a complex matter that is slowly becoming better understood, with a major insight coming from anthropologist Victor Turner, who discovered that most religious rituals take place in a situation of "liminality" or in-between-ness. This is most clear in the case of so-called rites of passage or rituals that bring about a transition from one state in life to another (for example, puberty rites in tribal religion, ordination to the priesthood in Catholicism, and marriage ceremonies in either), but it is also found to a greater or lesser degree in all religious worship and sacramental ceremony, and it is even found outside the context of religion. Liminality may be described as a condition of being outside a social group, of being on the fringe of a certain social structure, or of being in-between and in transition from one social group or structure to another. Psychologically it is a condition of feeling neither here nor there in the standard social order. To some extent adolescents have this feeling naturally, for they are in psychological and social transition from childhood to adulthood. Artists, intellectuals, and social critics are also often liminal individuals both in regard to their social standing and in regard to their own psychological attitude. It is important to recognize, however, that we all go through liminal periods in our lives (not only adolescence but also courtship, illness, graduation, career change, relocation, etc.) during which our normal ways of behaving and looking at life come a little unglued. Psychologically, part of our old perception of reality is disintegrating or is in suspension, and we are open to a new integration, a new vision of reality. □

Justice (San Francisco: Harper and Row, 1981); James Fowler, *Stages of Faith: The Psychology of Human Development and the Quest for Meaning* (San Francisco: Harper and Row, 1981).

56. For further direct applications of developmental psychology to sacramental instruction, consult the director's guidelines and/or scope and sequence charts for the religious education programs of the major Catholic catechetical publishers.

What happens in religious rituals, then, is something akin to this phenomenon. It is not something that is automatic, but if we seriously intend to enter into the ritual with our minds and hearts, we leave our ordinary patterns of thinking and feeling behind us. This transition is helped by the entrance procession and preliminary prayers at the beginning of the eucharistic liturgy, and by analogous periods of preparation as we enter into other types of worship. To talk about it in terms that we have already met, we enter the world of the sacred, but here we notice that this world for most of us is a liminal world in the sense of being marginal, because for most of us it exists on the edges of our practical life. It is also liminal in the sense of being in-between, because we come into it out of our profane world of everyday concerns and a little later we return from it to that same profane world. While we are in that liminal realm of experience, however, the ordinary pragmatic ways of thinking and feeling are temporarily suspended, and we find ourselves open to those ideas and values that are presented to us through the symbols of the sacramental liturgy (including the linguistic symbols of the prayers, readings, and homily).[57]

That religious experience is characterized by liminality comes as no surprise once we recognize that Moses and the prophets, Jesus and the apostles, and indeed most charismatic religious leaders were liminal figures vis-à-vis the established social structures of their day. Moreover, their followers were often either social outcasts (like Mary Magdalene) or willing to question the established view of things (like Joseph of Arimathea). But as Turner points out, people who share the same liminal experience often develop a psychic bond between them that he calls "communitas," that Catholic writers tend to call community or spiritual unity, and that Protestant writers sometimes call fellowship or oneness. As an experience, however, communitas is not unique to religion, for the experience of togetherness is also found in families, among the poor and oppressed, among gang members and goths, and among victims of natural disasters, to mention but a few instances. It is an experience of commonality and togetherness that disregards the differences that social structures impose on people. "The bonds of communitas are anti-structural in the sense that they are undifferentiated, equalitarian, direct, extant, nonrational, existential, I-Thou . . . relationships."[58]

57. When people complain that the Mass or sacraments don't mean anything to them, part of the reason is often that they are psychologically unable (for whatever reason) to fully participate in the ritual by entering into this liminal realm of religious experience.
58. Turner, *Dramas*, 274. On the relation between liminality and communitas, see also *Ritual Process: Structure and Anti-Structure* (Chicago: Aldine, 1969), 95–97.

Muslim pilgrims to Mecca often remark afterward that the required wearing of plain white robes that hide any differences of social status or national origin adds immensely to their experience of Islamic unity and deepens their comprehension of the meaning of that brotherhood. To some extent all religious rituals do this, for during them we no longer play our accustomed social roles but instead become together "this parish" or "the church" or "the people of God." And the fact that we sit and stand together, that we see and hear the same things, and that we sing together and pray in unison—all these symbolically suggest at a depth level that despite our differences we are all united in a common reality.   □

For all that symbolism, however, the experience of spiritual community is not automatic. As was noted in the section on symbolism, although symbols can express experiences of the sacred, they can in turn be recognized as such only by people who can find in the symbol a representation of what they themselves hold sacred. If they do not see through the symbol to something that is real for them at a depth level—or to say it the other way around, if the symbol does not signify something that they have experienced as true and valuable—then the symbol fails to be effective for them. Applied to the experience of oneness in worship, this means that people can find the unity that all the sacraments (but especially the Eucharist) symbolize only if they have already found it in activities other than worship. As Turner says succinctly, "Communitas in ritual can only be evoked easily when there are many occasions outside the ritual on which communitas has been achieved."[59]   □

This should not be taken as implying that rituals can have no effect at all on people who have not fully experienced what they symbolize, however. To the extent that they employ archetypal symbols that connect with fundamental needs such as trust, intimacy, generativity, or the others that Erikson speaks of, and to the extent that they image basic human values such as fidelity, hope, altruism, and so on, to that extent they can draw those who are willing to let go of their profane concerns into the realm of the sacred and into the realization that what it discloses is true. Moreover, the fact that rituals are repeated over and over again makes it possible for people to be constantly reminded of what they ought to be experiencing and believing and valuing even when in fact they are not living what their rituals symbolize, and so rituals can to some extent over the course of time engender and shape the very depth realities that they signify.[60]   □

59. Turner, *Dramas*, 56.
60. See Worgul, *From Magic to Metaphor*, 88f.

Rituals are therefore symbolic actions that represent in word and gesture realities that people have already experienced, or may be led to experience. With regard to our everyday experience, it is in fact this latter aspect of ritual that is the more important, for, as Erikson has shown, it is through ritualization that we come to experience ourselves as trusting, autonomous, and creative persons, and it is through ritualization that we come to know ourselves as members of a social group with definite beliefs and practices. In short, it is through ritualization that in many ways we come to be what we are, both individually and socially.

With regard to religious experience, however, it is the former aspect of ritual that is the more important, for it is in these special rituals, set apart from the rituals of everyday life, that we express and find expressed the beliefs and practices, values and ideals of our everyday rituals. As Turner has shown, these rituals often entail experiences of liminality not only because they sometimes occur at transition points in our lives but also because they are in fact special and thus set apart from our ordinary routines. In such rituals we find symbolized many of the deepest realities that we experience every day, in a bond of communitas with others who share that same experience and acknowledge those same realities. But such rituals also give us the opportunity to perceive ideas and ideals that we have perhaps lost sight of and are not fully enacting in our lives. In religious rituals such as the sacraments, then, we see what we are and what we want to become, and we are given the chance to say yes to it in our heart of hearts.

Additional Reading

NOTE: Here and in subsequent chapters, when works cited in the text were later revised, the reading lists make reference to the later editions.

Psychology of Religion

Loewenthal, Kate M. *The Psychology of Religion: A Short Introduction.* Oxford, England: Oneworld Publications, 2000.

Scobie, Geoffrey E. W. *Psychology of Religion.* New York: John Wiley and Sons, 1975.

Spilka, Bernard, Ralph W. Hood Jr., Bruce Hunsberger, and Richard Gorsuch. *The Psychology of Religion: An Empirical Approach.* 3rd ed. New York: Guilford Press, 2003.

Spinks, George Stephens. *Psychology and Religion: An Introduction to Contemporary Views*. Boston: Beacon Press, 1965.

Thouless, Robert H. *An Introduction to the Psychology of Religion*. 3rd ed. London: Cambridge University Press, 1971.

Religious and Spiritual Experience

Appleby, R. Scott. *The Ambivalence of the Sacred: Religion, Violence, and Reconciliation*. Lanham, MD: Rowman and Littlefield, 2000.

Atkins, Peter. *Memory and Liturgy: The Place of Memory in the Composition and Practice of Liturgy*. Aldershot, England: Ashgate, 2004.

Chamberlain, Theodore, and Christopher A. Hall. *Realized Religion: Research on the Relationship between Religion and Health*. Philadelphia: Templeton Foundation Press, 2000.

d'Aquili, Eugene, and Andrew B. Newberg. *The Mystical Mind: Probing the Biology of Religious Experience*. Minneapolis: Fortress Press, 1999.

Dunn, James D. G. *Jesus and the Spirit: A Study of the Religious and Charismatic Experience of Jesus and the First Christians as Reflected in the New Testament*. Grand Rapids, MI: William B. Eerdmans, 1997.

Gaudoin-Parker, Michael, ed. *The Real Presence through the Ages: Jesus Adored in the Sacrament of the Altar*. New York: Alba House, 1993.

Godin, André. *The Psychological Dynamics of Religious Experience*. Birmingham, AL: Religious Education Press, 1985.

Groeschel, Benedict J., and James Monti. *In the Presence of Our Lord: The History, Theology, and Psychology of Eucharistic Devotion*. Huntington, IN: Our Sunday Visitor, 1997.

Hogue, David A. *Remembering the Future, Imagining the Past: Story, Ritual, and the Human Brain*. Cleveland, OH: Pilgrim Press, 2003.

Hood, Ralph W., ed. *Handbook of Religious Experience*. Birmingham, AL: Religious Education Press, 1995.

Jackson, Edgar N. *The Role of Faith in the Process of Healing*. Minneapolis: Winston Press, 1981.

James, William. *The Varieties of Religious Experience*. New York: Modern Library, 1932.

Johnson, Luke Timothy. *Religious Experience in Earliest Christianity: A Missing Dimension in New Testament Studies*. Minneapolis: Augsburg Fortress, 1998.

Lane, Dermot A. *The Experience of God: An Invitation to Do Theology*. New York: Paulist Press, 1981.

Lynch, Martin, and Sally Lynch. *Healed for Holiness: The Role of Inner Healing in the Christian Life*. Ann Arbor, MI: Servant Books, 1988.

Maslow, Abraham H. *Religions, Values, and Peak-Experiences*. Columbus: Ohio State University Press, 1964.

Pearson, David. *No Wonder They Call It the Real Presence: Lives Changed by Christ in Eucharistic Adoration*. Ann Arbor, MI: Charis Books, 2002.

Proudfoot, Wayne. *Religious Experience*. Berkeley: University of California Press, 1985.

Riley, Bruce T. *The Psychology of Religious Experience in Its Personal and Institutional Dimensions*. New York: Peter Lang, 1988.

Sanford, John A. *Healing Body and Soul: The Meaning of Illness in the New Testament and in Psychotherapy*. Louisville, KY: Westminster John Knox, 1992.

Sokolowski, Robert. *Eucharistic Presence: A Study in the Theology of Disclosure*. Washington, DC: Catholic University of America Press, 1994.

Stapleton, Ruth Carter. *The Experience of Inner Healing*. Waco, TX: Word Books, 1977.

Twiss, Sumner B., Walter H. Conser and Mac Linscott Ricketts, eds. *Experience of the Sacred: Readings in the Phenomenology of Religion*. Providence, RI: Brown University Press, 1992.

Wach, Joachim. *Types of Religious Experience: Christian and Non-Christian*. Chicago: University of Chicago Press, 1951.

Symbol, Myth, and Ritual

Beane, Wendell C., and William G. Doty, eds. *Myths, Rites, Symbols: A Mircea Eliade Reader*. New York: Harper and Row, 1975.

Campbell, Joseph, and Bill Moyers. *The Power of Myth*. Edited by Betty Sue Flowers. New York: Doubleday, 1988.

Cassirer, Ernst. *An Essay on Man: An Introduction to the Philosophy of Human Culture*. New Haven, CT: Yale University Press, 1944.

Doty, William G. *Mythography: The Study of Myths and Rituals*. University: University of Alabama Press, 1986.

Dupré, Louis. *Symbols of the Sacred*. Grand Rapids, MI: William B. Eerdmans, 2000.

Empereur, James L. *Worship: Exploring the Sacred*. Washington, DC: Pastoral Press, 1987.

Erikson, Erik H. *Toys and Reasons: Stages in the Ritualization of Experience*. New York: W. W. Norton, 1977.

Fawcett, Thomas. *The Symbolic Language of Religion*. Minneapolis: Augsburg, 1971.

Gallagher, Michael Paul. *Clashing Symbols: An Introduction to Faith and Culture*. New York: Paulist Press, 1998.

Grainger, Roger. *The Language of the Rite*. London: Darton, Longman and Todd, 1974.

Mitchell, Nathan D. *Liturgy and the Social Sciences*. Collegeville, MN: Liturgical Press, 1999.

Power, David N. *Unsearchable Riches: The Symbolic Nature of Religion*. New York: Pueblo Books, 1984.

Rees, Elizabeth. *Christian Symbols, Ancient Roots*. London: Jessica Kingsley, 1992.

Rowell, Geoffrey, and Christine Hall, eds. *The Gestures of God: Explorations in Sacramentality*. London: Continuum, 2004.

Smart, Ninian. *The Religious Experience*. 4th ed. New York: Macmillan, 1991.

Turner, Victor, and Edith Turner. *Image and Pilgrimage in Christian Culture: Anthropological Perspectives*. New York: Columbia University Press, 1978.

Womack, Mari. *Symbols and Meaning: A Concise Introduction*. Lanham, MD: Rowman and Littlefield, 2005.

CHAPTER 2

Sociology and the Sacraments

Sacraments are not just for individuals. In fact there is not one of them that can be performed alone.[1] Sacraments are group actions, and under normal conditions they involve a number of persons in dramatic interaction with one another. The participants do or say things to each other and their ritual action simultaneously speaks to those others who observe it. Sacraments are also group actions in the sense that they are stylized behaviors developed by religious communities that both signify something important about the group and make it to be what it is.

1. Social Dimensions of the Sacraments

For a long time the communal and ecclesial aspects of the sacraments were so taken for granted that they were largely overlooked by theology even though they were never entirely forgotten. Medieval theology paid close attention to the minister and subject of each sacrament, and discussions about sacramental effects were pretty much confined to talking about those produced on individual souls.[2] Early modern sacramental piety likewise focused on the importance of the sacraments for individual growth toward God and ultimate salvation in heaven.[3] It was mainly in canon law that the

1. Even the "private Mass" of medieval and modern times, said by a priest without congregation present, was offered in the name of the church and usually on behalf of someone else besides the celebrant.

2. For a summary of the traditional theology of each of the sacraments, see the articles in the *New Catholic Encyclopedia* (New York: McGraw-Hill, 1966) under "Sacraments, Theology of" and under the names of the individual sacraments. For an older treatment, see the 1917 *Catholic Encyclopedia* online at http://www.newadvent.org/cathen/index.html and type "sacraments" in the search box in the upper right corner of the home page.

3. See, for example, A.-M. Roguet, *Christ Acts through the Sacraments* (Collegeville, MN: Liturgical Press, 1954).

sacraments were viewed as vital for the institutional life of the church, and so their proper performance was duly regulated and their ecclesiastical consequences were thought out in some detail.[4]

Starting in the nineteenth century, however, the liturgical movement tried to deepen the Catholic understanding of the sacraments by examining their historical development.[5] One of its first discoveries was that during the patristic period, congregations did not passively watch but actively participated in the Mass. Later it learned how the whole community had once been involved in adult baptism and public penance, sacraments that in the Middle Ages had become private clerical performances. But the real interests of the movement were not antiquarian but practical, and so cautiously at first it proposed such radical innovations (for that time) as allowing people to use missals and encouraging them to sing Gregorian chant. This gradual reintroduction of lay participation in Catholic worship eventually led to an increasing awareness that all of the sacraments did have a communal dimension that ought to be better reflected in the rites themselves. By this time, Vatican II was only a step away.[6]

In the middle of the twentieth century the liturgical movement gained added impetus from the scriptural movement in the church.[7] When Pope Pius XII in his encyclical *Divino Afflante Spiritu* instructed Catholic scholars to begin using modern methods of scientific research to develop a better understanding of the Bible, they were able to show how in many ways the New Testament was a product of the early Christian community and not just the work of individual writers. Many gospel passages, for example, show evidence of having been used in community worship before being written down and collected. And the same is true of what we now recognize as early hymns in the letters of St. Paul. A better understanding of the Old Testament too revealed how Jewish worship was intrinsically communal, and it suggested that if the church is truly the new Israel then the Catholic liturgy should not be an opportunity for private prayer but an occasion in which the people of God assemble for common prayer.

4. Before Vatican II the sacraments were often treated within moral theology, and moral theology was in large measure governed by canon law. For an example of this, see Dominicus Prümmer, *Handbook of Moral Theology* (New York: P. J. Kenedy and Sons, 1957), part 2.

5. See the essays collected in *The Liturgical Movement* (New York: Hawthorn Books, 1964); and *Liturgy in Development* (Westminster, MD: Newman Press, 1966).

6. Significantly, the first document promulgated by the bishops at the council was the Constitution on the Sacred Liturgy (December 4, 1963), and it emphasized "active participation" in Catholic worship.

7. For a good introduction to the renewal of Catholic scripture studies, see Raymond E. Brown, *New Testament Essays* (Milwaukee, WI: Bruce Publishing Company, 1965), chap. 1.

These advances in liturgical and scriptural scholarship in turn led systematic theologians to rethink the meaning and function of the Mass and the sacraments in the Catholic life of worship. After the introduction of the notion of the church as sacrament by Otto Semmelroth and others in the 1950s,[8] a number of theologians strove to find a social aspect in each of the seven sacraments and to integrate it within the traditional framework of sacramental theology.[9] Eventually, however, Catholic thinkers began to abandon scholastic philosophy in favor of more contemporary intellectual frameworks, and once they did this, the social dimension of the sacraments began to be appreciated even more.[10] Today in academic, pastoral, and catechetical treatments of the sacraments, their intrinsically social nature is both recognized and emphasized.[11]

2. The Functional Dimension

Until relatively recently in the history of the human race, the social worlds that people grew up in were dominated by a very few social institutions, namely, their family, their religion, and their government.[12] These social institutions are still around, but they are not the only important ones any more. Today there are peer groups, social and political organizations, educational institutions, and mass media all vying for our attention and our allegiance. Moreover, they are perceived as different from each other and the traditional three, partly because they do not all say or stand for the same things. Traditionally (which here means for thousands, even hundreds of thousands of years) family, religion, and government all stood for the same basic beliefs and values. Together they supported one another, the social

---

8. Otto Semmelroth, *Church and Sacrament* (Notre Dame, IN: Fides Publishers, 1965) was originally published in German in 1953. Likewise, Edward Schillebeeckx, whose seminal works were not translated into English until the following decade, was being published in Europe during this period.

9. See, for example, Bernard Leeming, *Principles of Sacramental Theology* (Westminster, MD: Newman Press, 1956), chap. 11; Karl Rahner, *The Church and the Sacraments* (New York: Herder and Herder, 1963), part 2.

10. See George McCauley, *Sacraments for Secular Man* (New York: Herder and Herder, 1969); Bernard Häring, *The Sacraments and Your Everyday Life* (Liguori, MO: Liguori Publications, 1976).

11. See George S. Worgul Jr., *From Magic to Metaphor: A Validation of Christian Sacraments* (New York: Paulist Press, 1980), esp. chap. 5; William Bausch, *A New Look at the Sacraments*, 2nd ed. (Notre Dame, IN: Fides/Claretian, 1983); Tad Guzie, *The Book of Sacramental Basics* (New York: Paulist Press, 1981).

12. In hunting-gathering societies, these three are even often united into one: the tribe or clan.

structure in which they were enmeshed, and the individuals who grew up within that social structure.[13] □ *

Today the situation is much different. For instance, the role that religion plays in introducing individuals to social realities is much smaller than it used to be. Nevertheless it is still important. For one thing, although religion is not a part of education and government as it once was, it is still an element in family life, and the first world that children grow up in is the home. For another thing, the subjects taught in school are supposed to be "value free" (or at least "value neutral"), government is no longer perceived as the guardian of national virtues, and the values proposed through the mass media are conflicting at best. Therefore, although we cannot even say that religion is important in everyone's life, helping them to develop a sense of what is true and valuable, we can say that when religion is important to people it does perform some significant social functions.[14] □

Early anthropologists and sociologists sometimes defined religion in terms of its psychological or cognitive aspects: the experience of the sacred or the acceptance of beliefs about transcendent realities.[15] Others preferred to focus on the structural elements in religion such as myth, ritual, and hierarchical leadership.[16] Since the 1950s, however, sociologists who follow Talcott Parsons' theory of structural functionalism have focused on the various functions that religion performs for individuals and societies.[17] Such functions include providing a meaning of life, legitimizing the existing

---

*This symbol in the margin indicates an interactive question that can be found at http://www.TheSacraments.org.

13. See Peter Berger and Thomas Luckmann, *The Social Construction of Reality: A Treatise in the Sociology of Knowledge* (New York: Doubleday, 1966); also Gerhard Lenski, *The Religious Factor: A Sociological Study of Religion's Impact on Politics, Economics, and Family Life* (New York: Doubleday, 1961). For a more general perspective, see Peter Berger, *Invitation to Sociology: A Humanistic Perspective* (New York: Doubleday, 1963).

14. See Elizabeth K. Nottingham, *Religion: A Sociological View* (New York: Random House, 1971), 44f.

15. For example, in his *Sociology of Religion* (Chicago: University of Chicago Press, 1944), Joachim Wach approvingly quotes Rudolf Otto's definition that "religion is the experience of the Holy" (13).

16. For example, Émile Durkheim in 1912 defined religion as "a unified system of beliefs and practices relative to sacred things, that is to say, things set apart and forbidden—beliefs and practices which unite into one single moral community called a Church" (*The Elementary Forms of the Religious Life* [New York: The Free Press, 1965], 62).

17. According to J. Milton Yinger, religion "can be defined as a system of beliefs and practices by means of which a group of people struggles with these ultimate problems of human life" such as death, suffering, and existence itself (*The Scientific Study of Religion*

social structure, maintaining a code of morality, and explaining the ultimate nature of reality.

Thomas O'Dea has grouped the functions of religion under six main headings.[18] First, religion "provides *support, consolation* and *reconciliation*" to people when they are faced with uncertainty, confronted with disappointment, and alienated from each other or from society as a whole. Second, "religion offers a *transcendental relationship* through cult and the ceremonies of worship" to a divine being and even to other human beings, giving people a greater sense of security and stability amid the flux and changes of life. Third, "religion *sacralizes the norms and values* of established societies" by placing them within a divinely revealed moral code, but it also provides ways that individuals who violate those sacred norms can overcome their own guilt and be forgiven by others. Fourth, religion also has *"the prophetic* function" of holding forth ideals "in terms of which institutionalized norms may be critically examined and found seriously wanting." Fifth, "religion performs important *identity* functions," helping people to situate themselves in the cosmos and in society, giving them a sense of who they are and what they are supposed to be. Sixth, "religion is related to the growth and maturation of the individual," guiding his or her passage through the various stages of human development and various changes in social position. According to the functionalist view, therefore, the primary functions of religion are integrative, since it aids the integration of the individual within society and also the self-integration of the individual in terms of self-knowledge, self-identity, and self-acceptance. But religion also has an innovative function, since besides maintaining the established order it can also criticize and transform social institutions and individual habits.

One of the principal ways that religion performs these various functions is through the use of symbols. The primary symbols in any religion are archetypal paradigms that reveal the hidden meaning of life and clarify the mysterious nature of the universe. In Mircea Eliade's words, "The symbol reveals certain aspects of reality—the deepest aspects—which defy any

[New York: Macmillan, 1970], 7). For an overview of Parsons' structural functionalism, see Jonathan H. Turner, *The Structure of Sociological Theory* (Homewood, IL: Dorsey Press, 1974), chap. 3. For an extensive application of structural functionalism to religion, see Louis Schneider, *Sociological Approach to Religion* (New York: John Wiley and Sons, 1970), chaps. 3–5. And for a summary history of sociological attempts to define religion, see P. H. Vrijhof, "What Is the Sociology of Religion?" in *Readings in the Sociology of Religion*, ed. Joan Brothers (New York: Pergamon Press, 1967), 38–50.

18. See Thomas F. O'Dea, *The Sociology of Religion* (Englewood Cliffs, NJ: Prentice-Hall, 1966), 13–16. All of the following quotations are from those pages.

other means of knowledge."[19] For Christians the primary symbol is the life, death, and resurrection of Jesus Christ, which is the ultimate revelation of the mystery of God and the definitive exemplar of how we are to live out the mystery in our own attitudes and actions. The same is true to a greater or lesser extent of the rest of revelation in both scripture and tradition. "Christian truth is symbolic," says sociologist and theologian Gregory Baum, because it "reveals the hidden structure of human life and by doing so significantly transforms the self understanding of those who receive it."[20] The human imagination is not fixed; people are not born with a set of a priori ideas about reality or thought forms through which they interpret their experience. The wide diversity of cultures and religions past and present bears adequate testimony to this. Rather, "experience has a structure in which the symbols governing the imagination have a creative part," and so people's response to the world is in large measure "determined by the symbols operative in their imagination." In other words, the function of these symbols is to "define the vision of life out of which people operate and thus orient their actions in a certain direction."[21]

☐

As we have already noted in the previous chapter, symbols are not only expressions of religious beliefs and attitudes but also a means through which people learn about them and reaffirm them. Thus for Christians, "if symbols reveal the divine presence in the universe, then their assimilation in the imagination will make people follow the divine will and lead them on the way of salvation."[22] But this internalization of the symbolic truths of faith happens primarily in and through the church, by active participation in the believing community. There Christians "share life with people enjoying the same vision. There they are surrounded by the signs of faith. There they listen to the scriptures, join in the liturgy and study Christian teaching."[23] In and through the church they learn to live the Christian myth, if you will, by assimilating into their imagination the fundamental structures of reality that are disclosed in the scriptures and the person of Jesus, and by incorporating into their lives the pattern of attitudes and actions that is congruent with that reality.

☐

19. Mircea Eliade, *Images and Symbols: Studies in Religious Symbolism* (New York: Sheed and Ward, 1961), 12. Likewise Paul Tillich: The symbol "opens up levels of reality which are otherwise closed for us" (*Dynamics of Faith* [New York: Harper and Row, 1958], 42).

20. Gregory Baum, *Religion and Alienation: A Theological Reading of Sociology* (New York: Paulist Press, 1975), 241.

21. Ibid., 242.

22. Ibid., 243f.

23. Ibid., 246.

Archetypal symbols are found not only in the language of myth, however, but also in the gestures and objects used in ritual. Functionally speaking, rituals are "repetitive activities that provide a sense of participation in the mythic framework" of any given religion.[24] Most religious rituals are cultic actions, stylized activities set apart from the routine of everyday living, in which the religious group conceives and enacts its sacred meanings and values. It conceives them in myth and it enacts them in ritual; thus myth and ritual are correlative and inseparable. To say it another way, ritual supplies "ways in which the individual or group may participate in the myth through re-enactment in one form or another."[25]

The roots of religious ritual are to be found in everyday rituals such as those discussed in the previous chapter. Many activities that are patterned by religious ritual in primal cultures later become secular routines as technology develops: hunting, farming, tool making, house building, and so on. Initially, such technological breakthroughs are sacred in the sense that they are awesomely important for the survival and well-being of the group. Their importance is illustrated in mythic stories, and knowledge of them is communicated from one generation to the next through periodically repeated rituals: hunting dances, fertility rites, house-building ceremonies, and the like.[26] In a geographically limited tribal society, the rituals dramatize, as far as anyone in that society can see, "how human beings do this," and the myths narrate "how people came to know this" or explain "how this fits into the overall pattern of human living." In a very real sense, therefore, early humans and tribal peoples learned how to be human by acquiring and then living the patterns of behavior that are preserved and handed down through ritual. Early human rituals encompass not only the technological routines mentioned here but also virtually all cultural activities (sharing food, coping with illness, making agreements, waging war, etc.) and social relationships (parents and children, in-laws and outcasts, rulers and subjects, etc.). And although in the course of time many of these rituals become so commonplace that they are no longer religious, their sacredness is still preserved in the attitudes that regard them as "the right way to do things,"

24. Barbara Hargrove, *The Sociology of Religion: Classical and Contemporary Approaches* (Arlington Heights, IL: AHM Publishing Corporation, 1979), 11.

25. Ibid., 10. See also, Aidan Kavanagh, "The Role of Ritual in Personal Development," in *The Roots of Ritual*, ed. James D. Shaughnessy (Grand Rapids, MI: William B. Eerdmans, 1973), 148f.

26. See Wach, *Sociology of Religion*, 41. The classic treatment of this phenomenon is found in Bronislaw Malinowski's 1925 essay, *Magic, Science, and Religion, and Other Essays* (New York: Doubleday Anchor Books, 1954), esp. chap. 2.

the unquestioned rules of custom and etiquette, or "the tradition of which we are proud."

As the sacred rituals needed for survival and civilized living become profane routines, therefore, specifically religious rituals tend to be reserved for those dimensions of life that are still imbued with mystery (for example, birth, growth, sex, sickness, death), those aspects of reality that are still not fully comprehended (for example, the cycles of the seasons, the weather, natural catastrophes, the experience of the supernatural), and those elements of culture that are regarded as ultimately important (for example, authority, family relationships, national origins, memorable persons, and events of the past). These rituals dramatize ideas and values that the group holds in common and that hold the group itself together: "Ritual is perhaps the strongest nonbiological bond that unites people into a functioning social unit."[27] Participation in religious rituals can raise consciousness to a state of heightened awareness of ideas and values, which not only reinforces those attitudes but also deepens the commitment of people to those others who share them.[28]

In summary, then, religion—and specifically religious myth and ritual—performs a number of important social functions. In an increasingly secularized society many of these functions can get taken over by nonreligious ideologies and purely cultural rituals, either for a large minority or even for a majority of individuals. But for religious persons (and we are speaking here not about mere churchgoers but about persons who are deeply committed to what their religious symbols represent) many if not most of these functions are performed by many if not most of their religious activities (which is not to say that such people do not have secular commitments as well). For Catholics this means that consciously and deliberately participating in the eucharistic liturgy and other sacraments does much more than fulfill external religious obligations. Through these rituals (although these are not the only ways it happens) we both express our inner commitment to the Christian way of life and we interiorize the ideas and values, beliefs, and attitudes that are congruent with the Christian revelation. Expressed theologically rather than sociologically, we put on the mind of Christ, become one with our Lord, and build up his body, which is the church.

---

27. Hargrove, *The Sociology of Religion*, 79.
28. See O'Dea, *The Sociology of Religion*, 39–41. For a summary of the classical analyses of ritual, see S. P. Nagendra, *The Concept of Ritual in Modern Sociological Theory* (New Delhi: Academic Journals of India, 1971).

3. The Effective Dimension

Closely allied to the functional dimension of religion is the effective dimension of religious ritual, which is just another way of saying that rituals can and do affect people. They effect alterations in their attitudes and changes in their lives. Traditional theology spoke of sacraments as effective signs, but it analyzed their effectiveness using metaphysical concepts such as instrumental causality. Today we no longer think in terms of metaphysical causality, but we can still recognize the phenomenon of sacramental effectiveness. And now we can speak of it in other terms as well.[29] Using the techniques of linguistic analysis we can examine the types and levels of sacramental language. Anthropology and comparative religion can give us insights into the impact of myth and ritual on religious peoples everywhere. Depth psychology can shed light on the nature of religious experience and the effects of religious symbolism. And we can use sociological concepts for understanding the social dynamics of religion and ritual.[30]

Yet speaking about the sacraments in psychological and sociological terms can sometimes be disconcerting and even seem disrespectful. One reason for this is that throughout our history as a church we have focused on the sacraments' theological effects: by baptism we are freed from sin and incorporated into Christ, by confirmation we are spiritually strengthened by the Holy Spirit, in the Eucharist we become united to Christ, through penance our sins are forgiven, and so on. These may be called the intended effects of the sacraments, for they reflect what presiders and other participants have in mind when engaging in sacramental ceremonies, and they reflect the meaning of the words and gestures found in the rites themselves. When we think about our experience of sacramental ceremonies, however, and especially when we ponder the multiple effects that they have had on us or others, we begin to realize that there are other unintended but no less

---

29. The shift from metaphysical to sociological categories of thought among religious thinkers is simply a matter of history and culture; it does not imply that the philosophical approach is any less true than approaches based on the other social sciences. For contemporary attempts to understand the sacraments using various philosophical categories, see chapter 5 of this work.

30. For an attempt to examine traditional Catholic claims about the sacraments using concepts from the social sciences, see B. R. Brinkman, "On Sacramental Man," a series of articles in *The Heythrop Journal*: "I, Language Patterning" 13 (1972): 371–401; "II, The Way of Intimacy" 14 (1973): 5–34; "III, The Socially Operational Way" 14 (1973): 162–89; "IV, The Way of Interiorization" 14 (1973): 280–306; "V, The Way of Sacramental Operationalism" 14 (1973): 396–416. A number of Brinkman's ideas are summarized in the work by Worgul, *From Magic to Metaphor*, 79–92 passim.

real effects of these ceremonies. Among these are the effects that we have discussed in the previous section as functions of religious rituals.[31]

One reason why sacramental actions have multiple effects is, of course, that human beings are complex. We think, we feel, we act, and we interact with others both spontaneously and in culturally established patterns. And so when we participate in sacramental ceremonies we are affected by what we see, hear, and do on many different levels. Moreover, the effects can vary in both intensity and duration. And finally, the sacraments can affect us individually and personally, or they can affect us socially and alter our relationships with others, or they can do both.

Until the twentieth century, however, the principal language that theologians had at their disposal for speaking about the effects of the sacraments has been the language of theology, and Catholic theological language, at least since the Middle Ages, drew heavily from the language of scholastic philosophy. As a result, the multiple effects of the sacraments, both psychological and social, tended to get spoken of in philosophical terms such as soul, act, and habit, or in theological terms such as grace, character, and merit. But today with additional linguistic (and conceptual) tools at our disposal, derived not from medieval philosophy but from the contemporary social sciences, we can analyze sacramental rituals and their effects on us in a greater variety of ways.

We have already seen, for example, that symbolic rituals can have a number of psychological effects. They can be occasions for hierophanies or experiences of the sacred, and through their repetition they can cause the recurrence of the experiences that they symbolize. In a very real sense, then, sacraments make God's word and power present to us if we are predisposed to receiving them. Since these hierophanies appear through the symbols, as it were, the experiences take on the structure and meaning of those symbols. Thus the sacraments call to mind events and facts in the life of Christ (for example, his last supper or his healing ministry), and they can also reawaken or deepen our appreciation of Christian beliefs and values (for example, God's forgiving love or the importance of self-sacrifice). Rituals thus revitalize ideals and attitudes, but they also promote their initial occurrence in us. Because sacramental rituals can be occasions for the religious experiences that they symbolize, during the liturgy and other sacramental ceremonies we are more prone to feel at one with God and others, to have our conscience disturbed, to have our anxieties calmed, and to pray in any number of ways. Finally, some rituals represent reasons

31. See also Nottingham, *Religion*, 62–64.

for joy and celebration, and so participating in sacramental worship can also give us feelings of festivity.

Psychologically, however, it is unlikely that we would feel much festivity if we were alone in our ritual, and so it becomes apparent that many of the psychological effects of the sacraments are tied up with their social aspects. And although there are a number of ways to discuss the sociological effects of rituals,[32] we may for the purpose of convenience divide them into three categories: unification, transition, and communication.

First and foremost, then, rituals have a *unifying effect* on those who participate in them. Performing a common ritual with others (even though not all the performers have the same function in the ritual) unites people in a common action. Rituals therefore have an inherent power to say to people, "We're in this together," for that is precisely what is happening on the level of physical behavior. It renews their identity within a religious group, and it creates a sense of solidarity with the other members. In our religious experience as Catholics this occurs most frequently during the eucharistic liturgy, not only because it is the one sacramental ritual that regularly brings us together as a community, but also because its central symbol is one of communion. Moreover, being together in the same religious ritual heightens people's awareness of common beliefs and values, deepens their appreciation for them, and intensifies their commitment to common ways of thinking and behaving.[33] No matter which sacrament we participate in, we have a sense that this is what we all believe in, this is what is important, and this is the right thing to do. Finally, in the symbolic drama of ritual people see a pattern of living that is appropriate not only for the present but also for the future. And so through the sacraments we learn not only how to behave during the ceremonies but also how to relate to God, to ourselves, and to others in our lives as Christians.[34]

In a discussion such as this, however, it must also be remembered that the psychosociological effects of the sacraments basically reflect and intensify the felt social realities of the celebrating group (though they can also to some extent engender and communicate them, as we shall see later). For example, if there is no sense of unity among people in a parish before

---

32. For a rather comprehensive treatment of this, see Anthony F. C. Wallace, *Religion: An Anthropological View* (New York: Random House, 1966), chaps. 3–5.

33. On this point, see Michael G. Lawler, "Christian Rituals: An Essay in Sacramental Symbolism," *Horizons* 7 (1980): 8, 13, 32.

34. On sacraments as a means of entering into the realm of properly Christian behavior, see Stephen Happel, "The Bent World: Sacrament as Orthopraxis," *CTSA Proceedings* 35 (1980): 88–101.

they come to Sunday worship, it cannot be reflected in the Mass. And if there are not shared commitments to common values and ideals, they cannot be intensified in liturgical worship. More generally and somewhat more accurately, we can say that, to the extent that these realities are present or lacking in any given group, they will be present or lacking in their sacramental celebrations. And what holds true for the group also holds true for individuals and subgroups. For instance, sometimes individuals can be alienated from what everyone else is experiencing, or sometimes small groups at a parish Mass can be celebrating a shared life that others have no sense of. So just as the psychological effects of the sacraments are not automatic but vary with the degree of our conscious self-involvement in the ritual, so also these social effects of the sacraments are not automatic but vary according to the degree of our commitment both to what the sacraments symbolize and to those with whom we share that commitment.[35] □

The second major category of the sociological effects of ritual is *transition*. Primarily the transition here is social, that is, a change from one set of social relationships to another; but secondarily it is also psychological, that is, a change in the way people perceive themselves in relation to God, themselves, and others. In many religions there are various "rites of passage" through which individuals pass from one social status or role to another: puberty rites effecting their transition from childhood to adulthood; initiation rites making them members of special groups within the society, such as leaders, food providers, healers, or diviners; wedding rites that make them married and give them an extended family of relatives. Invariably, rituals of this sort have three basic phases to them: separation from one's previous status or group, suspension in a marginal state or liminal condition, and incorporation into one's new status or group.[36] Typically, symbolic gestures signal what is happening during each phase of the ritual: first, individuals are physically removed from their previous social environment, and/or signs of their status within it are removed or covered over; second, the candidates are taken to a place apart, and/or they undergo a testing or are given special instructions that prepare them for their new role, and/or they are ritually processed into persons with a new status; and

35. On this point in reference to the liturgy, see Joseph M. Powers, *Eucharistic Theology* (New York: Herder and Herder, 1967), 5–18, 24–26, 73–74. With regard to the sacraments in general, see Regis A. Duffy, *Real Presence: Worship, Sacrament, and Commitment* (San Francisco: Harper and Row, 1982).

36. See Wallace, *Religion*, 127–30. This analysis of transition rituals has been generally accepted since it was first introduced in 1908 by Arnold van Gennep in *The Rites of Passage* (Chicago: University of Chicago Press, 1960).

third, they are received into their new social environment, and/or they are given signs of their new status, and/or their new role is recognized and approved by the larger group.

Many of the Catholic sacraments exhibit this same triple structure. Both the ancient and the recently revised rites for the initiation of adults take it for granted, but it is most vivid in its ancient form. In early Christian initiation people were removed from their ordinary environment for a day of fasting and prayer, after which they were stripped naked (women and men separately, to be sure) as they symbolically divested themselves of their old lives. Then the candidates were immersed in water three times while three times they assented to the truths of their new faith. Finally the initiates were dried, anointed, given clean white robes, and received by the bishop and the community in their first experience of eucharistic worship.[37] Likewise, public penance during the patristic period was in many ways an elaborate reentry ritual for those who by their sinfulness had withdrawn from the Christian community, and the transition or liminal period sometimes lasted for months or even years.[38]

Marriage and holy orders are obviously transition rituals bringing about new roles in the Christian community, and even a cursory examination of their rites reveals that those who are the subjects of these sacraments pass through the three symbolic phases mentioned above.

Christianity has no puberty rites as such, but since the Middle Ages three sacraments have been used to mark the transition to adult responsibility in the church. Clearly, confirmation was and still is for many a sign of spiritual strengthening and an occasion for a more mature commitment to Christ and the church. But first confession and First Communion have likewise functioned culturally as transition rituals, marking children's entry into the ranks of those who can understand their religion and behave according to its norms.

In the not too distant days when people went to confession mainly to get readmitted to Communion, and when the confessional was a dark box symbolically well-suited to a state of liminality, penance was more visibly a rite of passage, for it was an external symbol of an internal repentance or conversion. Today, however, the confessional is just as likely to be an ordinary room, and there is often less a sense of rejoining the community as there is a sense of reaffirming one's need to be reconciled with those who

37. See Arthur McCormack, *Christian Initiation* (New York: Hawthorn Books, 1969), 43–70.

38. See Monika Hellwig, *Sign of Reconciliation and Conversion: The Sacrament of Penance for Our Time* (Wilmington, DE: Michael Glazier, 1982), chap. 2.

are in it. Yet even here there is a sense of liminality during confession and an awareness of having passed through a change of heart, if not a change in social status.

☐

Similarly, when anointing of the sick was regarded as extreme unction for the dying, it was in many respects a transition ritual. The last rites, which include confession and Communion as well as anointing, together formed a rite of passage from this life to the next, or at least they marked a change in a person's status from being ready to return to the world to being prepared to go to heaven. This passage aspect is less apparent in the new ritual for anointing, although it can still be administered to the dying, and sometimes it marks a change in a person's status from being seriously sick to being on the road to recovery. Moreover, as James Empereur points out, illness itself is a liminal state, removed from the rhythms of ordinary life, and in need of interpretation. "Anointing is the liturgy which clarifies that suffering and sickness are not symbols of sin but of grace, not of testing and purification, but of a more intimate relationship with God."[39] Communal healing services can also affect the relation between the sick and well in a parish, bringing about more caring relationships as those who attend them learn who may need their help and why they deserve to receive it.

☐

Some of the social effects of transition rituals occur quite readily, almost mechanically, while others do not. Those that occur most readily are those that are changes in social roles in the church. According to Catholic teaching, for example, a person who is baptized is immediately and irrevocably a member of the church. Likewise, someone who is ordained automatically receives a role within the ecclesiastical community, and someone who is married receives a status that can be lost only by the death of the spouse. The immediacy and permanence of these effects were historically factors in the development of the theological concept of the sacramental character, an indelible sign on the souls of individuals who were baptized or ordained, as well as in the development of the concept of the marriage bond, which was sometimes likened to a sacramental character.[40]

There is another group of social effects, however, that do not occur quite so automatically. Hopefully, those who are baptized will live up to their calling as Christians, those who are ordained will be good priests, and those who are married will be faithful spouses. The change in one's social

---

39. James L. Empereur, *Prophetic Anointing: God's Call to the Sick, the Elderly, and the Dying* (Wilmington, DE: Michael Glazier, 1982), 154.
40. See Leeming, *Principles of Sacramental Theology*, 368.

role makes it possible to carry out that role well (only those who are ordained can possibly be holy priests, for instance) but it does not make it necessary. Again historically, this aspect of sacramental effectiveness seems to have been reflected in the way that theology spoke of the further effects of these sacraments as grace, or sacramental graces. As it was traditionally understood, sacramental grace was always offered to those who received a sacrament, but its actual effectiveness in their soul depended on their willingness to cooperate with it.

Now, lest it appear that the theological dimensions of the sacraments can be reduced to their sociological and psychological dimensions, it must be pointed out that some sacramental effects can be studied by the empirical human sciences while others cannot. Changes that a sacrament brings about in an individual's relationship with God, for instance, cannot be observed or explained by sociologists and psychologists. Such scientists can only discuss changes in social relationships and changes in individual behavior and awareness. But these changes can also be understood as having theological ramifications, and so theologians can talk about them in their own ways, ways that are not available to the secular sciences. The medieval adage was that "grace builds on nature," and here it can be taken to indicate that the realm of the properly human (that is, the order of nature) is presupposed and subsumed into the realm of grace or God's free gift (that is, the supernatural order). In a parallel fashion, systematic theology builds on the empirical human sciences, for it accepts their verified conclusions but then goes beyond them to discuss things like conversion and prayer, the church and the sacraments, in its own unique manner.

Let us go on, then, to the third major category of the sociological effects of rituals, which is *communication*. Just as everyday rituals communicate the beliefs and values, attitudes and behaviors of an older generation to a younger generation, so also religious rituals communicate specifically religious ideas and ideals, affective orientations, and patterns of living to a younger generation of believers.[41] Religious ritual can be said to symbolically articulate the shared religious experience of a community by putting into words and gestures what it understands about itself, about individuals, and about the relation of both to the transcendent. In doing so it transmits both that experience and that understanding through history, and it effects its perdurability into the future. Before the gospels were written, the first Christians continued as a church and passed on the revelation they had

---

41. On ritual as communication, see Wallace, *Religion*, 233–43; also Mary Douglas, *Natural Symbols: Explorations in Cosmology* (New York: Vintage Books, 1973), chap. 3.

received in Jesus largely through their liturgical celebrations. Similarly, the Jews survived as a people and Judaism survived as a religion through the centuries of diaspora mainly by means of home-centered rituals such as the yearly Passover celebration and the weekly Sabbath supper. And in our own century Catholics were not only legally bound to attend Sunday Mass but they were also counseled that "the family that prays together stays together." Both the law and the counsel had the effect of maintaining a religious identity and passing it on to the upcoming generation.[42]

□

But young people are not the only ones in need of what can be communicated through ritual. Human memory fails; human will falters. As Monika Hellwig reminds us, the root meaning *of anamnesis* (the ancient Greek word for what happens in liturgy) is not "remembering" but "not forgetting." We all need to be regularly reminded of who we are and what we are called to be, lest we forget. And if we are growing in our understanding and appreciation of the Christian life, we need to receive direction for that growth from our religious community. Although they cannot do it all, the rituals of the liturgy and the sacraments can provide at least some of that direction. Ritual is therefore one of the places in which adult believers allow the depth and richness of their religious tradition to be communicated to them. It is also a place where they can communicate it to themselves, so to speak, by the words that they speak and the actions that they perform. Finally, it is a place where they can publicly profess their faith to other adults by joining in ceremonial enactments of their central beliefs.[43]

□

In the words of Edward Fischer, "All ritual is communication. As communication, ritual speaks to our minds, and spirits, and intuitions by means of words, sights, sounds, and smells."[44] Fischer's point as an expert in communication arts, however, is that "communication is effective only if it fits the times. Communication is blurred when one attempts to use forms that are no longer fitting."[45] As we noted in the first chapter, symbols can die; they can become empty signs. This can happen because of individual and psychological reasons when they no longer express the conscious religious experience of those who use the symbols, but it can also happen because of cultural or social reasons when people no longer perceive what they have experienced as holy through the symbols that they are given by their tradition. The history of the Catholic sacraments themselves bears adequate

42. See Kavanagh in *The Roots of Ritual*, 148–54.
43. *See* John E. Smith, *Experience and God* (New York: Oxford University Press, 1968), 58.
44. Edward Fischer, "Ritual as Communication," in *The Roots of Ritual*, 161.
45. Ibid., 165.

testimony to this. In their external forms they have sometimes changed markedly during a transition from one cultural epoch to another: periodically the symbols were altered to fit the new social situations in which the church found itself.[46]

Some of the disparity between what sacramental symbols are meant to communicate and what they actually do communicate can, no doubt, be reduced through education. As Monika Hellwig suggests, "We have in the sacraments a whole language of gestures, signs, symbols, stories, allusions, and we have long ago forgotten the vocabulary and grammar of the language. To understand what is being expressed, we have to try to remember the language."[47] On the other hand, Edward Fischer urges that education cannot be the whole answer: "To try to formulate a ritual meaningful to all people at all times is a form of pride that anyone interested in communication cannot afford."[48] In other words, for the sacraments to be effective communicators of what they symbolize, people must not only learn the language of the symbols, but the symbols must also speak the language of the people. There must be adaptation on both sides of the liturgical equation. Of course there is always a danger that adjusting symbolic rituals to the mentality of those who participate in them can lead to a loss of their original meaning, but not adjusting them is a fairly certain way of lessening their ability to communicate that meaning. "If we try to make one ritual for everyone from eight to eighty, learned and unlearned, civilized and semi-barbaric, we are out of touch with reality."[49]

In this section we have looked at religious rituals as agents of unification, transition, and communication. Although it may be that some rituals have all three effects, not all rituals must have all of them. In the past, the emergency baptism of infants, private confession, and the individualized administration of extreme unction may have had few if any socially unifying effects. In the present, most eucharistic liturgies, penance services, and healing services are not social transition rituals even though they may effect individual transitions along the order of conversion or reconversion. And although all rituals usually communicate something, in both the past and the present the effectiveness of sacramental communication has often been less than it could be.

46. See Joseph Martos, *Doors to the Sacred: A Historical Introduction to Sacraments in the Catholic Church* (Liguori, MO: Liguori/Triumph, 2001), chaps. 6–12.

47. Monika Hellwig, *The Meaning of the Sacraments* (Dayton, OH: Pflaum/Standard, 1972), 3.

48. Fischer in *Roots of Ritual*, 165.

49. Ibid.,166.

4. The Historical Dimension

It is by no means obvious that religion has a history. We may be familiar with the changes in the Catholic Church during recent decades, and we may even know something about the history of Christianity. Few Catholics suspect, however, that the past two or three millennia may be part of a larger stretch of religious history. Instead, we tend to view African religions, the Greek and Roman gods, Judaism, Protestantism, and other religions simply as "different" from our own. We also tend to judge that they are "not the true religion," although we grant that some are closer to us (and therefore closer to the truth) than others. □

To sociologists, this is a subjective and ethnocentric view of religion. In fact, every ethnic or cultural group tends at first to judge that its ways are "right" and that the ways of others are good or bad depending on how closely they approximate the "right" ways of believing or behaving. The scientific study of religion, on the other hand, tries not to favor any one religion by judging others against its standards. Instead, it tries to objectively understand each religion on its own merits, and to understand how it is related to other religions.

When religions are thus lined up side by side, so to speak, similarities between certain ones seem to suggest religious groupings or style sets. The native religions of Africa, North and South America, and Australia seem to naturally fall into one set. Traditional Judaism, Christianity, and Islam fall easily into a strongly monotheistic group. There are still other ways of grouping religions, and when these groups are placed on a historical time line, they suggest a pattern of evolution or sequential development in the complex cultural phenomenon known generally as religion. □

Robert Bellah has proposed that there are five stages in the evolution of the world's religions,[50] but for our purposes we may group them into just three main phases or cultural styles.[51] These correspond to the three main stages in the evolution of human cultures, the first being the period of tribal culture extending from the origins of the human race to somewhere around 5000 BC, the second being the period of civilized culture extending from the invention of farming and the discovery of metal to the development of modern science, and the third being that cultural style that began

50. See Robert N. Bellah, "Religious Evolution," *American Sociological Review* 29 (1964): 358–74, collected in *Beyond Belief: Essays on Religion in a Post-Traditional World* (New York: Harper and Row, 1970), 20–50. Also using this paradigm is Barbara Hargrove in *The Sociology of Religion*, chaps. 5–7.

51. See Nottingham, *Religion*, chap. 2; also, Kenneth Boulding, *The Meaning of the Twentieth Century: The Great Transition* (New York: Harper and Row, 1964), 1–16.

about AD 1500 in Europe and that is still emerging and spreading around the globe. The three main phases of religion that correspond to these cultural epochs may be conveniently called primal, classical, and modern.[52]

a. Early Forms of Religion and Consciousness

Even when primal religion is referred to as primitive religion, it is not given that label because it is crude or simple (it may be incredibly complex) but because it is the first (*primus* in Latin) and most basic form of human religiosity. It thus dates from prehistoric times but it is also found among tribal peoples today. Certain aspects of primal religion are also considered basic to all religion, for example, the experience of the sacred, concern for understanding the mysteries of life and the cosmos, and the expression of religious meaning in myth and ritual. Its main features may be quickly summarized:

> Primitive religion is based on a near fusion of the religion and the rest of life. The individual performs certain religious acts because of the role he or she plays in the group. Primitive religion is not concerned with a clearly defined mythology or theology; instead it is an expression of values, desires and emotions. It makes little use of specialized functionaries, with the exception of the shaman, who tends to provide in his or her person a center for the emotional content of crisis occasions. It is in such crisis situations that primitive religion is expected to operate, whether they be the crises of individual life—birth, death, changes of status—or those of the group—war, the cycles of production, problems of order. Primitive religion serves to bind the society together in affirmation of common purpose, giving individuals the sense of participating in such purpose and finding identity in it.[53]

In other words, early human culture is relatively undifferentiated. Societies are the size of families, clans, or tribes at the largest, and although individuals in these groups have assignable roles, the societies themselves are fairly homogeneous. The hand-to-mouth existence of small hunting and gathering societies is no place for economic stratification and extended social ranking; the predominant social reality is what Victor Turner calls communitas. Although local control is largely authoritarian, the main social controls are embodied not in individuals but in customs and traditions to

---

52. Bellah's name for the five stages are primitive, archaic, historic, early modern, and modern. He admits, however, that the fourth is something like a transitional stage. I would contend that the same is true of the second stage.

53. Hargrove, *The Sociology of Religion*, 80. Because of the word's pejorative connotations, anthropologists today no longer refer to tribal peoples or their culture as primitive.

which even the tribal leaders must submit. So on the one hand there is little room for individualism and innovation, but on the other hand there is great social stability, which allows for the passing on of accumulated wisdom from one generation to the next across tens of thousands of years.

Similarly, early human consciousness is relatively undifferentiated. There is no distinction between objective and subjective truth: what is so, is so and what is not so, is not so. But "truth" here is primarily practical: it is the truth of how to be a good child or husband or wife, of how to hunt or fish, of how to build a canoe or a house, of how to integrate oneself into the cycle of seasons and the stages of life. The emphasis is therefore on orthopraxis (right action) rather than on orthodoxy (right belief), and to a great extent all mythic embodiments of a practical truth (even seemingly contradictory stories) are equally true. Because these practical truths are also sacred truths, the natural is not distinguished from the supernatural, and the holy is experienced as something within the world. Moreover, *my* world is the same as *our* world, and *our* world is the same as *the* world, for when widely scattered tribal groups are separated from each other by distance and language there is little awareness that other people can think and behave differently. Primal consciousness is thus a holistic awareness of oneself as fitting within the pattern of existence that is portrayed in the lifestyle and myths of one's society.

Finally, primal religion is likewise holistic, covering all areas of individual and social life. Its myths portray paradigms of human action and paragons of human virtue, and its rituals give people a way of entering into these and acting them out. "In the ritual the participants become identified with the mythical beings they represent. The mythical beings are not addressed or propitiated or beseeched. The distance between [human] and mythical being, which was at best slight, disappears altogether in the moment of ritual when every when becomes now. There are no priests and no congregation, no mediating representative roles and no spectators. All present are involved in the ritual action itself and have become one with the myth."[54]

b. Religion and Consciousness in the Classical World

Such was the universal state of human culture and religion for untold millennia. Then, beginning around seven thousand years ago, a few basic

54. Bellah, *Beyond Belief*, 28. For more on primal or primitive religious ritual, see Wallace, *Religion*, 216–33.

discoveries and inventions initiated a gradual transformation of some societies primarily in the Middle and Far East. The discovery that seeds could be collected and planted, that animals could be raised for slaughter or domesticated for labor, made it both possible and desirable for large numbers of people to live relatively close to one another. Agriculture thus encouraged the rise of towns and then cities, and with cities began the style of social organization known as civilization (*civis* in Latin means city). The invention of writing to keep track of produce and business transactions later led to the rise of literature, including religious scriptures. The discovery that ores could be smelted into metals led to improvements in tools for farming and weapons for war.

Whenever it occurs, the rise of civilization brings with it a division of labor (into rulers, farmers, artisans, merchants, scribes, soldiers) and a stratification of society (into citizens and slaves, literate and illiterate, wealthy and poor). Spontaneous communitas is gone and in its place come social distinctions that alienate individuals and groups from one another. This differentiation of society is also found in religion. Religious institutions (temple, church, religious ritual) begin to be separated from other social institutions (government, family, civic ritual); religious functionaries (priests, scholars, administrators) begin to emerge as a separate class (sacred caste, clergy); and in many instances religion too is divided between the way of perfection open only to a few (saints and prophets, monks and nuns) and the way of salvation available to the many.

It can even be said that the hallmark of classical religion, both non-Christian and Christian, is the desire for salvation. Classical religion introduces the practice of sacrifice, which despite its many forms (vegetable, animal, human) is also an attempt to establish, maintain, or restore a good relationship with the divine. The aim of all sacrifice is therefore unity: either unity with a divinity in spiritual communion (and most sacrifices had ritual meals connected with them) or unity with the divine will (doing what should be done during the religious ritual and in the rest of life). But sacrifice is not the only way that salvation may be sought in classical religions; at one time or another, in one place or another, people have tried to achieve salvation through actions (obeying commandments, performing rituals), knowledge (mystical intuition, rational reflection), and devotion (dedication, fervor).[55]

---

55. See J. Milton Yinger, *Religion, Society and the Individual: An Introduction to the Sociology of Religion* (New York; Macmillan, 1957), 88. On various aspects and types of salvation, see 85–90.

Moreover, of these three elements (action, knowledge, and devotion), it is the cognitive that is emphasized during religion's classical phase. Belief is distinguished from practice, and faith is contrasted with works, but priority is regularly given to ideas rather than deeds. Classical religions therefore tend to insist on orthodoxy rather than orthopraxis, allowing diversity in practice whenever it can be reconciled with uniformity in doctrine. Compared with the indifference that comes of ignorance about others during its early phase, religion in its classical phase recognizes differences and is generally intolerant of them. Only one religion can be the true religion and so other beliefs must be either heretical (if the differences are minor) or simply erroneous (if the differences are major). Most classical religions have therefore been expansionist in one way or another (for example, the Greek pantheon displaced the Egyptian gods after the conquest by Alexander the Great; Buddhism and Confucianism have been spread by disciples; Christianity and Islam have supported both holy wars and missionary efforts), and they have provided both for the conversion of others to the true faith and for the reconciliation of those who wander from the fold. □

Clearly, then, classical religious consciousness includes strong elements of differentiation. Typically the divine is strongly distinguished from the human, the supernatural from the natural, and religion is largely conceived as an attempt to overcome human estrangement from God or the gods. Even the picturing of the divinity as one or many, and the depicting of his (or her or their) attributes, mirror to some extent the vertical and lateral distinctions that are found in society.[56] Cultic worship, or praying to the gods "up there," is a classical religious practice, and even the word *religio*, coined in ancient Rome, meant to bind back or reunite. This reunion with the divine, furthermore, is often to be accomplished by a rejection of this world and its values, either physically (asceticism, monasticism) or psychically (meditation, contemplation). Sometimes this is also accompanied by a prophetic judgment that the present social order does not meet divinely revealed standards. In other words, classical religious consciousness is able to perceive a discrepancy between the way things are and the way things ought to be, and the distinction between the sacred and the profane makes it possible for religious leaders to criticize the sinfulness of secular society.[57] □

Almost all the world's "great" religions—Hinduism, Buddhism, Confucianism, Judaism, Christianity, Islam—began during the classical phase

---

56. See Guy E. Swanson, *The Birth of the Gods: The Origin of Primitive Beliefs* (Ann Arbor: University of Michigan Press, 1960), esp. 55–81. Also Bellah, *Beyond Belief*, 35f.
57. Bellah, *Beyond Belief*, 36.

of religion. With the exception of Hinduism (which evolved slowly out of the tribal religions of India) all of them are traceable to unique individuals—Buddha, Confucius, Moses, Jesus, Mohammed—whose religious experience and insight made a break with the past and provided a foundation for a new religious tradition. They were charismatic persons in Max Weber's sense of the term, and so the religions that they initiated are to a greater or lesser extent institutionalizations of their charismatic personality. Their words are enshrined in religious scriptures, their actions become models for religious practices, their leadership is passed on first to disciples and then to religious authorities. This "routinization of charisma" makes it possible for later generations of believers to follow in their founder's footsteps; but it is also possible for noncharismatic concerns and behavior to slip into the tradition and get routinized in religious institutions that bear little resemblance to

☐   the founder's ideas or ideals.[58]

c. Modern Consciousness and Religion

It was partly in reaction to what they perceived as departures from Christ's gospel that the sixteenth-century reformers (especially Martin Luther and John Calvin) protested against the institutions of medieval Christianity. But the religious perception of the Protestants was also sharpened by the cultural shift that was beginning during the Renaissance. The invention of the printing press made books more affordable, and books made it possible to read about the world from many points of view and to develop one's own perspective on matters. European explorers found civilizations in Asia and the Americas, calling into question the classical assumption that the human race could be neatly divided into the civilized and uncivilized world. Astronomers and other scientists demonstrated that the earth was neither flat nor the center of the universe, making it possible to doubt many of the traditional conceptions of reality. Emerging nationalism was also weakening the medieval ideal of a single Christian society and at the same time it was strengthening the notion that political pluralism was desirable.[59] In other words, the Renaissance marked the beginning of the end of classical culture

---

58. See Max Weber, *On Charisma and Institution Building* (Chicago: University of Chicago Press, 1968), 48–65, 253–83. For a summary treatment, see O'Dea, *The Sociology of Religion*, 37f.

59. For a sense of how the modern world has been restructuring human perception, read Marshall McLuhan, *The Gutenberg Galaxy: The Making of Typographic Man* (Toronto: University of Toronto Press, 1962); and *Understanding Media: The Extensions of Man* (New York: McGraw-Hill, 1964).

and the beginning of the modern epoch. And the Protestant Reformation that occurred during the Renaissance was therefore both a religious protest against the routinization of corruption in the church and a modern protest against medieval ways of institutionalizing the Christian message in hierarchy, dogma, and sacrament. □

At its beginning and even through the twentieth century, Protestantism bore many resemblances to traditional Catholicism (for example, insistence on dogma, intolerance of diversity, emphasis on salvation). But early Protestantism also displayed certain elements of religion that were to become distinctive marks of the third phase of religious evolution.

> The defining characteristic of modern religion is the collapse of hierarchical structuring of both this and the other world. The dualism of the historic religions remains as a feature of early modern religion but takes on a new significance in the context of more direct confrontation between the two worlds. Under the new circumstances salvation is not to be found in any kind of withdrawal from the world but in the midst of worldly activities. . . . What the Reformation did was in principle, with the usual reservations and mortgages to the past, break through the whole mediated system of salvation and declare salvation potentially available to [anyone] no matter what [one's] state or calling might be.[60] □

It is hard for Catholics today to appreciate the radical break with the past that Protestantism initiated, since most of us share many of the same cultural religious assumptions that the Reformation was based on. Conservative Catholics sometimes complain that the church is becoming more Protestant, but from a sociological perspective it is more correct to say that Catholicism since Vatican II has been allowing itself to enter into the cultural transformation that is slowly changing the shape of human society all over the globe. Electric communication and rapid transportation pull people out of their regional isolation and force them to respect the reality of pluralism. The extended family that stayed down on the farm is being replaced by the nuclear family that moves to where the jobs are, and the stability of marriage is being overtaken by the statistical regularity of divorce. The old colonial empires have been broken up, while corporations are decentralizing and companies are diversifying. National boundaries are blurred by international trade agreements and intercontinental political treaties, as well as by multinational corporations and regional cartels. As social mobility increases, society becomes less stratified by distinct classes. As education

---

60. Bellah, *Beyond Belief*, 36.

increases, people are less willing to accept any authority as absolute. As
the rate of change increases, change itself gets taken for granted, not only
in society at large but also in religious institutions.[61]

Modern consciousness reflects this revolution in modern culture. At
least in technologically advanced countries that are experiencing the full
effects of these changes, and in those segments of society where the change
is actually occurring, people live not in one world but in many: home, business, civic, church, school, friends, recreation, and so on. As a result, consciousness becomes highly differentiated, with the greatest differentiation
generally occurring in the most educated: not only is the realm of the sacred
distinguished from the profane realm, but common sense practicality is
distinguished from scholarly research, scientific theorizing is distinguished
from technological application, and artistic creativity is distinguished from
philosophical reflection. People get used to looking at things from different
angles, and they recognize that others bring to any situation their own
perspective or unique cluster of perspectives. Consequently, they have a
greater respect for differences and a greater tolerance of pluralism. Although
they may select a career or join an interest group or push for a certain cause,
they are also aware (or at least they suspect) that their position represents
values that they themselves have chosen and that they are responsible for
actualizing.

At the same time that modern consciousness becomes so highly differentiated, however, it also becomes highly integrative. There is a growing
sense that specialization is not the last word either in human knowledge or
in personal development. There is an awareness that somehow everything
is connected with everything else, and that things must be seen in relation
to other things and to some sort of whole. World economists and international diplomats speak of interdependence among nations. Ecologists insist
that businessmen and politicians reckon with the impact of their decisions
on the natural environment, while sociologists do the same with respect to
the human environment. Educators discover the value implications of their
"value-free" disciplines, and physicians are confronted with the ethical
implications of their medical practices. In religion too, the awareness of
diversity leads not only to a respect for religious differences but also to an
ecumenical desire for religious unity, or at least to a desire to discover a
commonality that underlies diverse religious traditions.

61. For a wide-ranging assessment of the global restructuring of society, see Alvin Toffler,
The Third Wave (New York: William Morrow, 1980).

Thus modern religious consciousness is at once both differentiated and integrative. It acknowledges and respects religious diversity but it also supposes that similarities in religious ideals and values are ultimately more important than differences in doctrine or ritual. It recognizes that religious doctrines are distinct from religious experiences, and yet at the same time it insists that doctrines should be relevant to people's lives. In this sense modern religious consciousness calls for a reunification of theory and practice in a theology that has practical implications. Such consciousness also recognizes a need for holiness but, to borrow Josef Goldbrunner's phrase, it assumes that "holiness is wholeness" and not a separate sphere of development.[62] And it is more concerned with individual authenticity based on personal conversion and commitment than it is with intellectual adherence to beliefs that may or may not correspond to the way one behaves.   □

In many ways the central feature of modern religion is "the collapse of the dualism that was so crucial to all the historic religions."[63] Not long ago it was important to distinguish sharply between the natural and the supernatural, the human and the divine, truth and error, clergy and laity, Christians and non-Christians, and so on. Today, however, it seems more appropriate to speak of grace within the world, the divine incarnate in the human, the perspectival nature of knowledge, the ministry of the laity, and even unchurched Christians. Nevertheless, this rejection of classical religious dualism "is not to be interpreted as a return to primitive monism: it is not that a single world has replaced a double one but that an infinitely multiplex one has replaced the simple duplex structure."[64] On the one hand this means that modern consciousness accepts the different perspectives from which religion can be viewed (psychology, sociology, history, philosophy, political science, etc.), and it is not afraid that the unity or uniqueness of religion will thereby be lost. On the other hand this means that modern religion accepts diversity both within the totality of world religions and within the confines of a single religious tradition. Modern Catholics freely admit, for example, that there have been vast differences in their sacramental practices over the course of twenty centuries, and they are beginning to acknowledge the admissibility of simultaneous diversity in the sacramental practices in the variety of Catholic cultures around the world.   □

At the same time, however, the modern acceptance of pluralism poses a unique problem with respect to religious symbolism. In the words of

---

62. See Josef Goldbrunner, *Holiness Is Wholeness and Other Essays* (Notre Dame, IN: University of Notre Dame Press, 1964).

63. Bellah, *Beyond Belief*, 40.

64. Ibid.

Mary Douglas, "One of the gravest problems of our day is the lack of commitment to common symbols."[65] As Douglas in her own way shows, one of the greatest unifying factors of traditional Christianity was the presence of "condensed symbols," both creedal statements and ritual practices that everyone acknowledged as essential to their faith and representative of their commitment.[66] But today, in Christianity as a whole there appear to be few if any symbolic statements or actions that "say a lot" to all Christians the world over. Elizabeth Nottingham expresses this even more emphatically:

> In fact, no single universally accepted system of religious symbolism exists. Insofar as the various religious organizations are able to commend their officially sanctioned symbol systems to their membership, a plurality of symbol systems may be said to coexist simultaneously. Furthermore, many individuals, even organizational members, feel at liberty to interpret freely—or even repudiate—traditional symbol systems handed down by hierarchical or other religious authority.[67]

But the source of this inability to accept a single symbol system is not an individual or even a cultural rejection of symbolism as such. Rather, it is the other way around. The modern desire for integration leads to a rejection of symbols that are felt to be empty or powerless, even if they were traditionally rich and potent symbols, and to an insistence on symbols that authentically express and communicate religious experience and understanding. Furthermore, there is "a growing awareness among the religiously affiliated and nonaffiliated alike that symbols *are* symbols and that [people] in the last analysis [are] responsible for the choice of [their] symbolism."[68] In other words, the modern differentiation between the symbolic and the real at the same time reveals the responsibility that people have for making their symbolic statements—and sacraments are symbolic statements—truly representative of religious realities.[69]

One conclusion that can be drawn from this brief overview of religious evolution is that if Catholicism today is to be practiced and lived in tribal, agricultural, and industrial societies (for Catholicism finds itself among peoples with each of these predominant cultural patterns), then the style of

---

65. Douglas, *Natural Symbols*, 19.
66. Ibid., chap. 3.
67. Nottingham, *Religion*, 41.
68. Ibid., 42; see also Bellah, *Beyond Belief*, 42.
69. On the need for authenticity in sacramental action, see Regis Duffy, *Real Presence*; also Kenan B. Osborne, *Community, Eucharist, and Spirituality* (Liguori, MO: Liguori Publications, 2007), 1–19.

its sacraments may be expected to vary greatly once the church appreciates the sociological implications of its long allegiance to the classical style of religion (and to the correspondingly traditional style of theology). At the same time, however, an awareness of how religion and religious symbolism function in any type of culture should make it easier to develop authentic sacramental forms for each of them. ☐

A second conclusion is that if religion is currently undergoing a transition as momentous as the change from tribal to sedentary society, then the cultural style of sacraments in technologically advanced societies cannot be expected to remain as it was during the classical period of Christianity. This does not imply, however, that modern religion or sacramental practice in the future will be totally different from what they were in the past. As Erik Erikson and other developmental psychologists insist, wherever true development takes place, the accomplishments of earlier stages are retained and subsumed within later stages of growth. Modern religion, therefore, if it is truly modern and truly religious, will contain primal elements such as the experience of the sacred and its articulation in myth and ritual, but it will also contain classical elements such as concern for conceptual clarity and the ability to prophetically contrast transcendent ideals with actual realities. Likewise, modern Catholic ritual will not reject the seven traditional sacraments but rather it will retain many of the elements in them and subsume these within a new sacramental style. ☐

Additional Reading

Sociology of Religion

Baum, Gregory. *Religion and Alienation: A Theological Reading of Sociology*. New York: Paulist Press, 1975.

Berger, Peter. *The Sacred Canopy: Elements of a Sociological Theory of Religion*. New York: Doubleday, 1967.

Hamilton, Malcolm. *The Sociology of Religion: Theoretical and Comparative Perspectives*. 2nd ed. New York: Routledge, 2001.

Hargrove, Barbara. *The Sociology of Religion: Classical and Contemporary Approaches*. 2nd ed. Arlington Heights, IL: Harlan Davidson, 1989.

Nottingham, Elizabeth K. *Religion: A Sociological View*. New York: Random House, 1971.

O'Dea, Thomas F. *The Sociology of Religion*. Englewood Cliffs, NJ: Prentice-Hall, 1966.

Roberts, Keith, and David Yamane. *Religion in Sociological Perspective.* 5th ed. Los Angeles: Sage Publications, 2012.

Schneider, Louis. *Sociological Approach to Religion.* New York: John Wiley and Sons, 1970.

Ritual, Society, and Religion

Alexander, Bobby C. *Victor Turner Revisited: Ritual and Social Change.* Atlanta, GA: Scholars Press, 1991.

Chupungco, Anscar. *Liturgical Inculturation: Sacramentals, Religiosity, and Catechesis.* Collegeville, MN: Liturgical Press, 1992.

Driver, Tom. *Liberating Rites: Understanding the Transformative Power of Ritual.* Boulder, CO: Westview Press, 1998.

Finn, Thomas M. *From Death to Rebirth: Ritual and Conversion in Antiquity.* Mahwah, NJ: Paulist Press, 1997.

Flanagan, Kieran. *Sociology and Liturgy: Re-Presentations of the Holy.* New York: St. Martin's Press, 1991.

Graham, Harvey, ed. *Ritual and Religious Belief: A Reader.* New York: Routledge, 2005.

Holm, Jean, and John Bowker, eds. *Rites of Passage.* London: Pinter, 1994.

Meeks, Wayne A. *The First Urban Christians: The Social World of the Apostle Paul.* New Haven, CT: Yale University Press, 1983.

Mitchell, Leonel L. *The Meaning of Ritual.* Harrisburg, PA: Morehouse, 1988.

Pottebaum, Gerard A. *The Rites of People: Exploring the Ritual Character of Human Experience.* Washington, DC: Pastoral Press, 1992.

Rappaport, Roy A. *Ritual and Religion in the Making of Humanity.* New York: Cambridge University Press, 1999.

Shaughnessy, James, ed., *The Roots of Ritual.* Grand Rapids, MI: William B. Eerdmans, 1973.

Stark, Rodney. *The Rise of Christianity: A Sociologist Reconsiders History.* Princeton, NJ: Princeton University Press, 1996.

Stringer, Martin D. *A Sociological History of Christian Worship.* Cambridge, England: Cambridge University Press, 2005.

Tovey, Phillip. *Inculturation of Christian Worship: Exploring the Eucharist.* Aldershot, England: Ashgate, 2003.

van Gennep, Arnold. *The Rites of Passage.* Chicago: University of Chicago Press, 1960.

White, Susan J. *Foundations of Christian Worship.* Louisville, KY: Westminster John Knox, 2006.

CHAPTER 3

Ritual Studies and the Sacraments

T he sacraments have not always been thought of as rituals. For centuries, they were regarded primarily as metaphysical realities, and Catholics today still speak of administering and receiving sacraments. But whatever else the Catholic sacraments are, it is clear that they are rituals—religious rituals, church rituals. Even nonbelievers would agree to this. The difference (and the difficulty) comes in explaining the rituals, their meaning, and their effectiveness.

As the two preceding chapters have made clear, both the psychology of religion and the sociology of religion have been interested in religious rituals and their effects for over a century.[1] At the same time, cultural anthropology has been investigating the customs and beliefs of hunting-gathering, nomadic, and agricultural peoples around the world, gathering data on everything from courtship to family life to funeral practices. In the 1960s, anthropologists began turning their attention on contemporary society and discovered that the dynamics that operated in primal and classical cultures are also found in modern culture. In time, sociological and anthropological research into the nature and function of ritual gave rise to a new subdiscipline known as ritual studies.

1. The Emergence of Ritual Studies

Look at any historical survey of ritual studies,[2] and you will come across the names of researchers who were contributing to the study of religion,

---

1. William James, *The Varieties of Religious Experience* (1902) and Arnold van Gennep, *The Rites of Passage* (1908) are two of the oldest classics in the study of religion by the social or human sciences.

2. For example, Catherine Bell, *Ritual: Perspectives and Dimensions* (New York: Oxford University Press, 1997).

myth, and ritual in the early- and mid-twentieth century: James George Frazer (*Totemism and Exogamy*, 1910), Jane Ellen Harrison (*Themis: A Study of the Origins of the Greek Religion*, 1912), Émile Durkheim (*The Elementary Forms of the Religious Life*, 1912), Theodor H. Gaster (*Thespis: Ritual, Myth and Drama in the Ancient Near East*, 1950), E. E. Evans-Pritchard (*Essays in Social Anthropology*, 1962), Max Gluckman (*Essays on the Ritual of Social Relations*, 1962), Claude Levi-Strauss (*Structural Anthropology*, 1967), and Clifford Geertz (*The Interpretation of Cultures*, 1973), to name a few of the more well known. You will also find the names of some whose ideas have already been discussed in this book, such as Rudolf Otto (*The Idea of the Holy*, 1917), Mircea Eliade (*The Sacred and the Profane: The Nature of Religion*, 1959), Mary Douglas (*Natural Symbols: Explorations in Cosmology*, 1973), and Victor Turner (*Ritual Process: Structure and Anti-Structure*, 1969). For the most part, these investigators were looking at ritual as a component of larger social phenomena in which they were interested, such as religion or culture. By the 1970s, however, some researchers were beginning to consider the possibility of studying ritual itself as a phenomenon that occurs in a variety of social contexts. Instead of looking at ritual as part of something bigger, they began focusing on ritual regardless of where it occurs.

One of the first to do this was Ronald Grimes, who recalls that in the early 1980s it was hard to get his first book published "because no one knew what ritual studies was."[3] Since then, the field has grown, but it is still in the early stages of development. One difficulty is that ritual-like activity occurs in an extremely broad array of human situations: individual and social, private and public, secular and religious, civic and military, pragmatic and artistic. A second difficulty is that ritual is performed, not explained; it is demonstrated, not described; it is acted out, not spelled out. We simply do not have the words to totally translate rituals into language, so the language of the field needs to be created by those who are doing the describing and explaining. Even when a ritual is explained, it usually presents the general purpose or meaning of the ritual, not a precise articulation of its movements. A third difficulty is field study, going out and observing rituals and perhaps participating in them, then describing them on paper or recording them on video, and finally producing something in words or pictures that, in effect, reproduces at least the salient features of the ritual to someone who was not there. Are there rules or principles that hold true for all rituals?

---

3. Ronald L. Grimes, *Beginnings in Ritual Studies*, rev. ed. (Columbia: University of South Carolina Press, 1995), xi.

How does participation in a ritual change as the ritualizing group gets larger or smaller? How do rituals change over time, and what is lost and gained with the changes?[4]

There are no university departments devoted exclusively to ritual studies, so scholars who are interested in studying ritual are often found in other departments such as anthropology, religion, or even liturgy. The notion that there might be an academic discipline or subdiscipline for the study of ritual emerged for the first time at the 1977 meeting of the American Academy of Religion, an umbrella organization for academics who study any aspect of any religion past or present. Even so, ritual studies was and remains an interdisciplinary or multidisciplinary field, and articles about ritual are apt to appear in drama, literature, and even advertising journals, as well as in sociology and theology journals.

Although still a nascent field of inquiry, ritual studies has reached some basic conclusions about its object of interest. Ritual is perceived as an intentional performance that contains gestures and utterances that are symbolic. It is dramatic in the sense that it entails acting out ideas and values. It is frequently related to story and myth, and it presupposes an ideology or worldview. It can be used to legitimize the status quo and to socialize newcomers while very often it expresses power and control of some over others. But it is also a means by which power is transferred and individuals are transformed, and in that sense it embodies and objectifies relationships.[5] Nevertheless, because there is no central authority in ritual studies, researchers and theorists do not always use the same words to describe the same phenomena, nor do they draw on the same theorists in their explanations, so there is an unavoidable heterogeneity to the field.

Grimes perceives a continuing need for theory construction in ritual studies, and even though Catherine Bell has surveyed the field more than once to document how much has already been accomplished,[6] the proliferation of perspectives and explanations suggests that ritual theory is far from a unified discipline. Very possibly, researchers will coalesce into schools of thought analogous to those in psychology and sociology, each with certain strengths for interpreting different types of behavior. Such schools

4. An early attempt to bring some order to the diversity of ritual can be seen in Grimes' chapter "Mapping the Field of Ritual," written for the 1982 edition of *Beginnings in Ritual Studies*, in which he discusses ritual space, ritual objects, ritual time, ritual sound and language, ritual identity, and ritual action. Today those aspects of ritual are taken for granted in ritual studies and in liturgical studies as well.

5. Many of these ideas are discussed in Bell, *Ritual: Perspectives and Dimensions*.

6. See also her earlier work, *Ritual Theory, Ritual Practice* (New York: Oxford University Press, 1992).

of thought with differing approaches might then be viewed as complementary rather than competing interpretations of the great variety of rituals. In the meantime, however, much of the actual work in religious studies is devoted to observing, describing, and explaining ritual events with the conceptual tools that are currently available.

As both the field work and the theoretical work proceed, however, some fundamentals have begun to emerge, and these can be instructive for understanding sacraments and liturgies.

2. Types of Rituals

Perhaps the most obvious thing that can be said about rituals is that they are not all the same. Secular rituals differ from religious rituals, for example, and the rituals of one religion differ from those of another. Nevertheless, although there have been and still are countless rituals in human history and cultures, the general types of rituals are rather limited. Even so, scholars do not agree on the number of categories into which rituals should be divided, with some as low as two and others as high as twelve.[7]

□ *

In *Ritual: Perspectives and Dimensions*, Catherine Bell proposes that the majority of what people call rituals[8] can be fit into six major categories or genres: calendrical or commemorative rites, transition rituals or rites of passage, rites of exchange and communion, rites of purification and healing, rites of feasting and fasting, and political or governmental rites.[9]

a. Calendrical or Commemorative Rites

As their name suggests, calendrical rites are rituals that occur annually or with some regularity, such as new year celebrations, seasonal festivals, and annual commemorations of important events. These rituals do not make

---

　*This symbol in the margin indicates an interactive question that can be found at http://www.TheSacraments.org.

---

7. Bell, *Ritual: Perspectives and Dimensions*, 93.

8. In her list, Bell excludes conventional gestures such as shaking hands, ritualistic crowd behavior at sporting events, and other sorts of patterned behavior that might be called rituals in an extended meaning of the term but that are not considered rituals in the usual sense of the term.

9. See Bell, *Ritual: Perspectives and Dimensions*, 93–94. Note that the names given here for these six categories and the order in which they are listed are slightly different from Bell's.

anything happen but they are reminders of what has happened or is happening, they mark the passage of time, and they intensify awareness of beliefs and values.[10]

Perhaps the most obvious calendrical rituals in human culture are those that mark the beginning of a new year. In most agricultural societies, this is a spring festival that coincides with the planting of the first seeds after the passing of winter; the Jewish Rosh Hashanah and the Chinese New Year are both celebrated in the spring. In Western society today, the beginning of the year is celebrated about a week after the winter solstice (roughly between December 20 and 23), when slightly longer days begin to shorten the long nights of winter. In contrast, the Islamic New Year migrates through the seasons because their twelve-month lunar calendar is about eleven days shorter than the solar year.

All secular holidays are calendrical: Independence Day, Memorial Day, and Labor Day in the United States have their counterparts in other countries, as do remembrances of important national figures such as George Washington or Martin Luther King Jr. The Christian church calendar celebrates events in the life of Christ such as Christmas and Easter, and it commemorates saints such as St. Francis and St. Catherine. In cultures that are both religious and secular, religious feasts can also be national holidays, such as St. Patrick's Day in Ireland and for Irish Americans, and Our Lady of Guadalupe in Mexico and for Mexican Americans. When once-religious cultures turn secular, religious feasts can get transformed into secular ones, as has happened with St. Valentine's Day and All Hallow's Eve (Halloween) in the United States.

Looking at a much shorter time frame, the seven-day week is a sacred cycle that probably has its origin as a quarter part of the twenty-eight-day lunar month. Jewish tradition marks the last day of the week, the Sabbath, as the holiest, but Christians chose the first day of the week, Sunday, as the "Day of the Lord" commemorating Christ's resurrection from the dead. Observant Jews do not do certain types of physical work on the Sabbath, Catholics used to avoid "servile work" on Sunday, and Protestants used to close all stores on that day. Although these strict observances are, for the most part, a thing of the past, the five-day work week is still considered normal and weekly attendance at a church or synagogue is strongly encouraged. ☐

Of the seven Catholic sacraments, the only one that fits the pattern of a calendrical ritual is Eucharist. At the beginning, Christians gathered for a full meal that they called the Lord's Supper once a week, and even when

10. See ibid., 102–8.

this evolved into a symbolic meal surrounded by elaborate ritual during the patristic period,[11] it was still primarily a weekly celebration. Not until the Middle Ages did the Mass (as it came to be called) become a daily ritual, at least for priests, monks, and nuns. For most Catholics today, participation in the eucharistic liturgy is a weekly event, and even Protestants who do not regularly hold Communion services still attend church on Sundays to be spiritually nourished and to renew their commitment to God and their church community.

b. Transition Rituals or Rites of Passage

Rites of passage both celebrate and facilitate significant turning points in people's lives. Sometimes called life-cycle rituals, many of them occur when people leave a stage of life with one social standing and set of relationships and enter into another stage with a different standing and set of relationships, for example, the movement from childhood to adulthood or the movement from being single to being married.[12]

As mentioned earlier,[13] six of the seven Catholic sacraments have the structure of transition rituals and exhibit to a greater or lesser extent the three characteristic stages of separation, transformation, and reintegration. Before examining those sacraments in this light, however, let us first look at rites of passage in other cultures and other religions.

In many traditional cultures, especially in rural areas, childbirth is a dangerous process that frequently results in the death of the mother or child or both. For this reason, birth rituals often surround late pregnancy, the birthing process, and the initial postpartum period. Although tribal peoples may have had no concept of germs and infection, midwives understood that certain procedures led to better results than others, and these practices were often buttressed with stories, incantations, and taboos that enabled most women to have safe births most of the time. Mothers were often secluded after birth, and thus they were allowed a period of rest and healing before returning to their normal work routines. The entrance of newborns into the family was celebrated with rituals that often entailed the giving of a name by which the child would be known.

---

11. On the patristic period, see chap. 4, sec. 3 below, and my *Doors to the Sacred: A Historical Introduction to Sacraments in the Catholic Church* (Liguori, MO: Liguori/Triumph, 2001), chap. 8, sec. 2.

12. See Bell, *Ritual: Perspectives and Dimensions*, 94–102.

13. See chap. 2, sec. 3 above.

Adolescence as it exists in modern society did not occur in primal and ancient cultures. The complexity of industrial society and the need for prolonged education in the postindustrial world created a liminal period between childhood and adulthood that lasts for years and sometimes for decades. In simpler cultures, however, the transition from childhood to adulthood was effected by puberty rites that turned boys into men and girls into women in a short length of time. Pubescent boys were taken by men and taught the manly secrets of hunting, tool making, and sexual seduction; nubile girls were taken by women and taught the feminine secrets of their bodies and the skills needed to succeed as women and mothers. Emerging from their initiation, the newly made adults were soon able to marry, have children, and make their contributions as full members of society. The Jewish Bar Mitzvah and Bat Mitzvah (literally, "Son of the Commandment" and "Daughter of the Commandment") are modern vestiges of adult initiation, after which Jewish youngsters are allowed to perform certain religious functions reserved to adults.

Wedding ceremonies are found in virtually all human cultures, although the rules surrounding marriage and the ritual elements in the ceremonies can be as diverse as the cultures in which they are found. In traditional cultures even today, marriages are arranged by parents for their children, who sometimes do not meet their prospective spouses until the wedding day. In such societies, since people do not choose to marry, they cannot choose to unmarry, and divorce is relatively unknown. In modern society (in Western culture since the nineteenth century and more recently in Eastern cultures), people are more free to choose their life partners, and they are therefore also more free to leave marriage partnerships that prove unsatisfactory. Nonetheless, entering a marriage is usually a cause for great ceremony, but there are no widely accepted rituals for exiting a marriage.

Entrance into groups with special status in society is often accomplished through rites that are performed after a person has been proven worthy of membership. Temple priests and priestesses, guardians of sacred shrines, and other religious functionaries often belong to guilds into which they are initiated or to orders into which they are ordained. Again, here the requirements for membership, the rites of passage, and the duties of the initiates can vary enormously from society to society and from religion to religion. In modern societies, membership in military or quasi-military organizations (police, militia, etc.), and membership in service organizations (Masons, Elks, etc.) is often accompanied by rituals of induction and, later, by ritual promotions in rank. In the past, demotions or dismissals were often ceremonialized (for example, being literally stripped of one's rank), but this is less often the case today. □

An important characteristic of transition rituals is that they celebrate and facilitate real changes that are taking place in people's lives—entering into a family, moving into adult privileges and responsibilities, or joining a group with special rights, skills, and duties. In its ritual structure, and also because it can be performed only once in a person's lifetime, the sacrament of confirmation is a rite of passage, but for the most part it marks no real passage from or to anything. Whether children are confirmed before receiving their First Communion, or whether teenagers are confirmed some time during high school, it is unlikely that any of them are about to change their lives in any substantial way as a result of the ceremony. Since they are not going through any real change, therefore, there is really nothing to celebrate, and going through a formal rite of passage cannot facilitate a transition that is not actually occurring. Thus the sacrament is often perceived as being ineffective, and correctly so, since the ritual has no real effect except in the minds of the adults who are organizing the ceremony.[14]

This problem with the rite of confirmation has been around for decades, but recently a similar one has arisen with regard to marriage. Traditionally, a wedding celebrated and facilitated the transition of two young people from singlehood to married life, but today over half of the people who go through the wedding ceremony are neither single nor married. They are in an in-between state of living together, sometimes even with children. According to traditional Christian morality, they are living in sin, and some pastors, both Catholic and Protestant, have insisted that couples live apart and not have sexual relations during the months prior to the wedding in order to honor the Christian values inherent in the sacrament—in other words, to make the ceremony more honest. Whether or not this proves to be a successful policy, the fact remains that the wedding ceremony is no longer a rite of passage in the way that it once was. Looking at the words and actions of the Catholic rite,[15] there does not seem to be a great discrepancy between them and the current social situation, but the understanding that married life begins after the wedding may have to be rethought if the current trend continues.

14. The Anglican and Episcopal churches have apparently recognized this anomaly, and their revision of the sacrament encourages adolescents to be confirmed (with a bow to tradition and parental pressure) while allowing adults to participate in the sacrament any time in the future when they want to reaffirm their commitment to Christ and the church (thus encouraging ritual honesty).

15. See *The Rites of the Catholic Church*, vol. 1 (Collegeville, MN: Liturgical Press, 1990). The Rite of Marriage is found at 715ff.

The social fact that about half the marriages contracted in the United States today (including Catholic marriages) end in divorce poses a challenge to the concept of marital indissolubility, but it poses a distinctly different challenge from a ritual perspective. If rites of passage refer to and facilitate transitions in people's lives, divorce is a life transition that could possibly be helped by ritualization. True, not all people would want to ceremonialize their marital dissolution, but for many it could enable them to move more comfortably through the liminal period from being someone who was married to being someone who has been through a painful process and is now ready to resume life as a single person. Such a ceremony would not be a sacrament in the strict sense, but it could be sacramental in the broad sense of reminding people of important spiritual beliefs, hopes, and values. ☐

c. Rites of Exchange and Communion

The simplest ritual of exchange among human beings is an exchange of gifts for whatever reason, as happens when guests bring flowers or wine to a host who has prepared a dinner for them, or as regularly happens among friends and family members at Christmastime. The most common communion ritual is a meal, since the sharing of food facilitates the sharing of stories, the exchange of ideas, and other activities that bring people together emotionally. Religious rites of exchange and communion are built on the foundation of such basic human rituals.[16]

In the secular world, the foundational importance of such rituals can be seen in the spheres of business and commerce. Barter, or the exchange of one item for another, is the oldest form of trade, and trade is possible only if it is carried out according to mutually accepted social norms, that is, if it is routinized. In addition, bartering is usually facilitated by social rituals or customs such as haggling over the value of the goods and shaking hands to seal the bargain. Even complex trading has its ritual moments such as the signing of contracts, the presenting of checks, and the transferring of keys. Business and politics also acknowledge the importance of rites of communion such as the business luncheon and the golf outing for the purpose of making deals, as well as the company picnic and the awards banquet to recognize accomplishments.

From these secular examples it is clear that ritual behavior can engender trust and confidence, honesty and fidelity, friendship and loyalty, fellowship and community, which are basic human values and realities. When people

16. See Bell, *Ritual: Perspectives and Dimensions*, 108–14.

believe in the existence of spiritual beings that exist in a realm beyond the physical world, therefore, it is natural that they would use rituals of this sort to acknowledge their existence, negotiate with them, express their loyalty, and feel close to them.

Two forms of prayer among religious people (including Christians) are petition (asking favors) and thanksgiving (expressing gratitude). Whether people believe in benevolent deities or malevolent demons, they address inhabitants of the spirit world just as they address beings in the visible world, and they express themselves in gestures as well as words. Gift giving to the gods can be done in a variety of ways: pouring the gift on the ground, burying it, dropping it into a body of water, or burning it; giving the gift to a temple priest or priestess, or leaving it at a shrine or other sacred place; donating the gift for the care of the sick, for the welfare of the poor, for the building of a religious edifice, or for some other altruistic purpose. When done for the sake of petition, gift giving is done in the hope and expectation that the recipient will be pleased with the gift and grant a favor—whether it be health, happiness, prosperity, or a more specific benefit. When done for the sake of thanksgiving, gift giving is done to acknowledge the other's power and kindness, and specifically to express thanks for the favor received.

Although all Christians pray to God, Catholics and Orthodox have a tradition of praying to Mary the mother of Christ and the saints as well, so artistic representations of them (statues, paintings, stained glass windows, and icons) are often found in their churches but not usually in Protestant ones. Catholics sometimes ritualize their prayer requests by lighting a votive candle and leaving an offering of money in the church. Donations are also made at shrines to the Blessed Virgin and the saints known for healing, and when prayers are answered, the faithful leave tokens of appreciation (discarded crutches and other medical devices, symbolic images, medallions, handwritten letters, etc.) as a testimony to the effectiveness of prayer and as an inspiration to future petitioners. Protestants are more likely to ritualize their faith in God through the biblical practice of tithing: giving a percentage of their income to God in the hope and expectation that God will take care of their material needs.

To some extent, all seven of the Catholic sacraments exhibit the structure of petition and appreciation, asking God and thanking God for some spiritual benefit: in baptism, salvation and freedom from sin; in confirmation, the gift of the Holy Spirit; in reconciliation, forgiveness of sins; in anointing of the sick, healing and strengthening; in marriage, the blessings of wedded life; in ordination, the grace and power of the priesthood. In these six sacraments, no physical offering is made, but prayers are offered and thanks are given. Prayers of petition and thanksgiving can also be found in the Eucharist, but in that sacramental liturgy there is also something more. □

In the Eucharist, symbolic gifts of bread and wine are offered to God the Father, asking, "Let your Spirit come upon these gifts to make them holy, / so that they may become for us / the body and blood of our Lord, Jesus Christ."[17] Next, the gifts are consecrated or made sacred with a prayer recalling the Last Supper and reporting the words of Jesus, "this is my body" and "this is the cup of my blood."[18] During the eucharistic prayer, the liturgical action is repeatedly referred to as a sacrifice, and the consecrated gifts are also referred to as a sacrifice. How should these words be interpreted?

When most Americans hear the word "sacrifice," they think of Jewish temple sacrifices, especially the slaying of lambs in preparation for the feast of Passover, or they picture the Old Testament scene in which Abraham is about to kill his son in obedience to God's request, or they think of movies, such as *Apocalypto* with its bloody portrayal of human sacrifices atop an Aztec pyramid. In actuality, however, the central act in an ancient sacrifice ritual was a meal eaten in fellowship with the deity being venerated. The food brought to the sacrifice was consecrated or made sacred (the Latin *sacrificium* comes from *sacrum facere*, meaning to make sacred) through prayers and through being designated for this special purpose. The word *sacrificium* is therefore better translated as something made sacred, and a sacrifice is better thought of as a sacred meal or a meal taken with sacred food. In most temple sacrifices, in fact, once the food was offered to the deity (sometimes by being ritually disposed of, as described above), the rest of the food was eaten by those making the offering. In very few cases was the sacred food totally destroyed. So a more precise definition of a sacrifice might be a sacred meal shared in the presence of a deity.[19]

Ancient sacrifices are stereotypically thought of as requiring the blood of animals (primarily lambs, goats, or cattle), but in fact, grains, wine, and other foods could be brought for sacred meals. The reason why animals needed to be slaughtered on the spot was the same reason why they needed to be killed just before being cooked for any other meal: the absence of refrigeration. But because the event itself was sacred, even the required butchering was ritualized. □

17. Eucharistic Prayer II.
18. All four eucharistic prayers use identical formulas at this point.
19. For research into the understanding of sacrifice in the ancient world, see Michael McGuckian, *The Holy Sacrifice of the Mass: A Search for an Acceptable Notion of Sacrifice* (Chicago: Liturgy Training Publications, 2005).

When early Christians were accused of being atheists because they did not attend temple sacrifices, they replied in defense that they did indeed share a sacred meal in the presence of their god (language that their pagan accusers could relate to), and that they did this in homes rather than in separate buildings. Moreover, the bread and wine that were made sacred were the physical medium through which their Lord's presence was felt among them, so those sacred foods were called the body and blood of Christ.[20]

In the Middle Ages, the interpretation of the Mass as a sacrifice was the end result of centuries of theological development, and in scholastic theology the central action was understood to be a re-presentation of Christ's sacrifice on the cross, "sacrifice" being taken in the sense of the killing of a victim being offered to God. Through the cultic action of the priest, the sacred time of Jesus' crucifixion became present to the worshipers, the church's altar became the sacred space where the sacrifice was offered, and sacred meaning was bestowed on the bread and wine by pronouncing them to be the body and blood of Christ. Those who attended the Mass were said to participate in Christ's sacrifice in an unbloody manner, that is, they entered into the sacred time and space of Jesus' redemptive death and they felt his presence as they might have at the crucifixion. The words of the liturgical text heightened the experience of real presence for the priest, while the fact that the words were whispered in a foreign language (Latin) infused the action with an aura of mystery for the onlookers. Gazing on the consecrated bread (called a host, from the Latin word for a sacrificial victim) was said to be the same as looking at Christ himself, and devout Catholics were able to experience God's presence through this powerful combination of ritual and doctrine.[21]

The format and text of the revised rite (actually, there is more than one approved liturgical text) do not easily support the scholastic interpretation, which is a source of dissatisfaction for some conservative Catholics who correctly feel that something has been lost in the new Mass. The revised text does use the word "sacrifice" as noted earlier, but in many places it means a sacred meal, that is, the ritual of commemorating Christ's death and resurrection, repeating the words of Jesus over the bread and wine, and receiving the sacred food in communion with Christ and the church. In some places, it refers to that sacred food itself, and in others it can mean an offering or an act of self-giving.[22]

20. See Martos, *Doors to the Sacred*, 220–21.
21. On the Eucharist as a sacramental sacrifice, see Kevin W. Irwin, *Models of the Eucharist* (Mahwah, NJ: Paulist Press, 2005), 217–37.
22. As the Liturgy of the Eucharist begins, the priest says, "Pray, my brothers and sisters, that our sacrifice [= sacred meal, offering] / may be acceptable to God, the almighty Father,"

Thus the Mass is still a communion rite in the sense of being a ritual of communion with the divine, but the meaning of communion has shifted. In the Latin Mass, it was an experience of oneness with the crucified Christ, which could sometimes be an intense awareness of divine presence in the consecrated elements, especially in the host, and which could at other times be a profound sense of self-giving, of offering oneself to God in union with Christ for the salvation of the world. In the revised liturgy it is less easy to focus on the bread and wine because the words of the eucharistic prayer, now said in English (and other modern languages), draw attention away from the consecrated elements,[23] and also because participants are usually asked to sing a hymn during the distribution of Communion, which interferes with any attempt to experience personal intimacy with Christ at that moment. Moreover, since the Second Vatican Council, the Catholic Church has spoken about different modes of Christ's presence during the eucharistic liturgy: in the priest, in the assembly, in the proclamation of the scriptures, and in the consecrated elements.[24] Thus not only the structure of the revised rite but also the church's official teaching militate against traditional

---

to which the people reply, "May the Lord accept the sacrifice [= offering, sacred food] at your hands / for the praise and glory of his name, / for our good, and the good of all his Church."

In Eucharistic Prayer I, the priest says, "we offer to you, God of glory and majesty, / this holy and perfect sacrifice [= sacred food]: / the bread of life / and the cup of eternal salvation." There is a reference to the sacrifice of Abraham, but since Abraham was prevented from killing his son, the reference is to the sacred meal that Abraham enjoyed in the presence of God, eating meat from the ram that was miraculously provided. The priest goes on to pray, "Almighty God, / we pray that your angel may take this sacrifice [= sacred food] / to your altar in heaven."

There is no reference to sacrifice in Eucharistic Prayer II.

Eucharistic Prayer III says, "we offer you in thanksgiving this holy and living sacrifice [= sacred food]," and later, "may this sacrifice [= sacred meal, offering], / which has made our peace with you, / advance the peace and salvation of all the world."

Eucharistic Prayer IV says, "Father, we now celebrate this memorial of our redemption. / . . . we offer you his body and blood, / the acceptable sacrifice [= sacred food] / which brings salvation to the whole world. / Lord, look upon this sacrifice [= sacred meal, sacred food] which you have given to your Church; / and by your Holy Spirit, gather all who share this one bread and one cup / into the one body of Christ, a living sacrifice [= offering] of praise. / Lord, remember those for whom we offer this sacrifice [= sacred food, sacred meal]."

23. People attending a Latin Mass were able to focus all their attention on the sense of sight; people attending a Mass in English have to divide their attention between looking and hearing.

24. See the Constitution on the Sacred Liturgy (*Sacrosanctum Concilium*) available in Austin Flannery, ed., *Vatican Council II: The Basic Sixteen Documents* (Northport, NY: Costello Publishing Co., 1996). See also Irwin, *Models*, 238–61.

eucharistic spirituality in favor of a more diffused experience of divine presence during worship.

d. Rites of Purification, Healing, and Affliction

In our secular society, the means for obtaining spiritual and physical healing are usually routines rather than rituals. Home remedies generally work for common physical ailments: cleaning and dressing cuts and bruises, taking aspirin and other analgesics for minor aches and pains, treating colds and influenza with over-the-counter remedies and bed rest, and so on. For more severe pain and trauma, a visit to a doctor or hospital, or even calling for emergency medical assistance may be in order, sometimes followed by surgery or therapy. All of these could be considered routines of greater or lesser complexity. The same can be said of treatment for nonphysical or spiritual ailments such as mental, emotional, or relational problems. Talking things over with a friend or confidant can be good for working through anger, jealousy, stress, disappointment, and so on. If the symptoms are more severe or if the problems are more deep-seated, regular visits to a counselor, psychologist, psychiatrist, or other therapist may be called for. Empathetic listening, ownership of feelings, and taking responsibility for one's actions are skills that can be used routinely to mend broken relationships and maintain healthy ones.[25]

Before the invention of modern medicine in the nineteenth century and the emergence of mental health professions in the twentieth century, however, many of these routines for restoring health and balance in life were simply not available. Every culture had its own folk remedies for various sorts of physical ailments, and it also had ways to deal with moral, emotional, and relational problems in the community—ways such as seeking the advice of elders and shunning individuals who were socially disruptive. In tribal cultures, many restorative routines are embedded in rituals and supported by myths. An exotic herbal remedy might be known only to a shaman who learned the ritual for preparing and applying the medicine with appropriate incantations. What we would call mental or emotional problems might be diagnosed as spirit possession and treated with prayer, fasting, seclusion, massage, and other forms of folk therapy. Restoring damaged relationships and dealing with guilt feelings might be accomplished with the help of elders who are respected for wisdom and fairness, and who know the proper rituals for restoring harmony in the community and peace in the soul.

---

25. For Bell's treatment of this genre, see "Rites of Affliction" in *Ritual: Perspectives and Dimensions*, 115–20.

It should not be surprising, therefore, that religions with centuries-old traditions contain ritual means for dealing with physical and spiritual ailments. There is little information about Jewish folk medicine in the Hebrew scriptures, although they contain a few stories of physical healing through ritual and of spiritual healing through music.[26] Some Jewish laws of ritual purity may have originated with health concerns (e.g., not touching dead bodies, not eating certain types of animals, dealing with infectious diseases and mildew, dealing with body waste, menstruation, and childbirth), and various psalms and proverbs touch on physical and spiritual health and healing.[27] The main ritual for dealing with sin was through sacrifices that could be interpreted as exchange rituals (offering a gift in order to receive forgiveness) or as sacred meals of reconciliation and communion (since the root meaning of atonement is to be at one with, that is, at-one-ment).[28] But in a larger sense, the whole Jewish Law or Torah was concerned with maintaining proper relationships between human beings and God, between individuals, and between groups, for the Hebrew word *torah* is better understood as a guide for living than as a legal system.

In contrast, the Christian scriptures are full of references to physical and spiritual healing. According to the gospels, Jesus' ministry was marked by physical cures and pronouncements of forgiveness.[29] Acts of the Apostles records healings performed by the followers of Jesus, indicating that this practice continued in the early church. Although informal, the ritual of healing usually involved prayer, a laying on of hands, and an invocation in the name of Jesus.[30] The apostles proclaimed that repentance and baptism brought forgiveness of sins and that forgiveness of sins came through the saving work of Jesus.[31] There are no rituals of forgiveness described in the New Testament, but the Pauline letters make reference to a Jewish practice equivalent to the Amish practice of shunning: excluding people from normal contact with the community until they repent of their sinful behavior.[32] It was not until the second century that Christians developed a formal process

26. See 2 Kgs 5:1-16 and 1 Sam 16:23.

27. For laws of ritual purity, see Lev 11–15. For prayers and advice about spiritual and physical health, see Pss 6:2; 38:3; 41:4; 103:3; 107:20 147:3; Prov 3:8; 12:8; 16:24.

28. See Lev 4–6, for example.

29. References to Jesus' miracles, forgiveness of sins, and teachings on forgiveness are too numerous to list. In the four gospels there are eighty-six references to healing and thirty-seven references to forgiveness.

30. See Acts 1:1-16; 4:29-31; 5:12-16; 8:6-8; 14:8-10; 28:7-9. On the gift of healing in Corinth, see 1 Cor 12:9-31.

31. See Acts 2:38; 5:31; 10:43; 13:38.

32. See 1 Cor 5:1-13; 2 Cor 2:5-11.

of public repentance for serious sins, and it was only in the Middle Ages that the familiar ritual of private confession was approved by ecclesiastical authorities.[33] The development of church rituals for healing took even longer, for the first ecclesiastically sanctioned rites were not introduced until the ninth century in Europe.[34]

Catholics today are of course familiar with the rites of reconciliation and anointing of the sick, which have been counted among the seven sacraments since the twelfth century. There are in fact three forms of the sacrament of reconciliation for use in different pastoral circumstances, and the anointing of the sick can likewise be adapted to different situations, depending on whether it is done in a home or a hospital, and depending on whether the person being anointed is expected to recover or not.[35] The so-called last rites are performed by a priest for people who are close to death; they include hearing a person's confession, administering Holy Communion, and performing the rite of anointing. Although Catholic funeral rites are not regarded as sacramental in the strict sense, they are broadly sacramental in the sense of being symbolic rituals that convey sacred meaning. Funeral rituals in any culture or religion help to structure the grieving process, providing an outlet for bereavement and facilitating the transition to living without the departed.[36] So from one perspective they are rites of passage and from another they are rites that bring healing at a time of loss.

Another Catholic sacrament that falls into both categories is baptism. While primarily a rite of entrance into the church, it has long been associated with the forgiveness of sin. In the early church, people who were baptized into the church understood that the sins of their past life were forgiven and that in following Christ they were expected to lead a new life free from serious sin. In medieval Christianity, Catholic theology taught that baptism washed away original sin (a consequence of the sin of Adam and Eve as recorded in the book of Genesis), and this doctrine is still found in the Rite of Baptism for Children.[37] The Rite of Christian Initiation of Adults is actually a series of rites to mark various stages in the catechumenal process prior to full initiation into the Catholic Church. Some of the shorter rites are prayers of blessing and exorcism (asking for God's protection), rites called scrutinies (encouraging self-examination and repentance), the

---

33. See Martos, *Doors to the Sacred*, 280–95.

34. See ibid., 332–34.

35. See *The Rites of the Catholic Church*, vol. 1, 519–63 and 814–30.

36. In some religions, funeral rituals are also understood to facilitate the soul's journey from this world to the next.

37. See *The Rites of the Catholic Church*, vol. 1, 376–93.

Ephphetha rite (praying that catechumens listen to God's word in their lives), the baptismal promises (to reject Satan and follow Christ), and other prayers celebrating the decision to embrace a new life in the church.[38]   □

e. Rites of Feasting and Fasting

Large religious festivals in which great amounts of food are consumed have almost completely disappeared from religious life in North America, although their secular counterparts remain. One reason for this may be that in a society in which the scarcity of food is not a pervasive issue, special celebrations of thanks for food do not seem to be necessary. True, Americans and Canadians usually eat a lot of food on Thanksgiving Day every fall, but this celebration of civil religion is perhaps better viewed as a calendrical or commemorative ritual.[39]

Closer in style and feeling to festivals in primal and classical religion would be today's music festivals, folk art festivals, classic auto shows, and the like, in which the feasting is done more with eyes and ears than with the mouth. Events such as these usually last for days, as do county and state fairs that celebrate modern crafts and industries. Mardi Gras in New Orleans and Carnival in Latin America originated as festive preparations for fasting during the liturgical season of Lent, but today they are almost completely secular in tone. Annual gatherings for family reunions and occasional gatherings for class reunions could also be considered festivals from the perspective of anthropology. Summer church festivals and Lenten fish fries are festive in nature, and they celebrate community life to some extent, but their primary purpose seems to be fund-raising.   □

Wedding festivals, which sometimes lasted for days in earlier times, have been reduced to today's wedding reception, which lasts for only a few hours but is expected to contain a number of ritual elements such as cutting the cake, toasting the newlyweds, and tossing the garter and bouquet. Senior proms and other dances, which once were an important element of socializing for young people, have become less significant and less mandatory than in the past. Today some sporting events such as college bowl games (like the Rose Bowl and the Orange Bowl), games between classic rivals (like the Army-Navy game), auto racing in the United States (like the Indianapolis 500), and bicycle racing in Europe (especially the Tour de France) take on the flair of religious festivals in bygone eras. But religious festivals

38. See ibid., 35–164.
39. For Bell's treatment of this genre, see *Ritual: Perspecives and Dimensions*, 120–28.

have not disappeared completely, and Catholic fiestas can still be found in Central and South America, as well as in many of the Catholic parts of Europe. Orthodox churches participate in religious festivals from Russia to Greece, as do Eastern Rite Catholics in many countries. And religious festivals are still common occurrences in many places where Islam, Hinduism, and Buddhism are the primary religions.

Fasting has likewise virtually disappeared from Catholicism, and it was never very important in Protestantism. Prior to the liturgical reforms of Vatican II, Catholics were expected to fast during Lent and Advent, eating only one full meal a day except on Sundays. In addition, Catholics were supposed to abstain from meat on Fridays and on certain other days during the year. Today, however, the requirements are much more relaxed. Jews are expected to fast on Yom Kippur (the Day of Atonement), and more observant Jews may fast on as many as five other days during the year, not eating or drinking from sunrise to sundown. Muslims practice a similar complete fast during the holy month of Ramadan, which can be difficult during summer months when the days are long and the weather is hot. Religious fasting is often accompanied by abstaining from ordinary work, praying special prayers, and doing works of mercy such as almsgiving, which heightens people's religious awareness and provides fasting with a richer context of ideals and beliefs. For the general purpose of fasting is to turn people's thoughts away from mundane concerns and help them to focus on things that are of greater importance and more lasting value.

Clearly none of the Catholic sacraments directly involve feasting and fasting, although celebrations of baptism, confirmation, marriage, and ordination are often accompanied by parties and banquets. Catholics had been required to fast from all food and drink from midnight whenever they intended to receive Communion, but this requirement was reduced to three hours by Pope Pius XII in 1953 and then to one hour by Pope Paul VI in 1973, in part to facilitate the reception of Communion during afternoon and evening Masses. Since the one-hour fast coincides with much of the time at the liturgy before the communion rite, it is hardly felt as a restriction by most Catholics today, and some proposals have been made to lengthen the pre-Communion fast in order to increase devotion to Christ in the Eucharist.

f. Political or Governmental Rites

The unique feature of rites of power, as these rituals may also be called, is that they not only celebrate authority but also create authority in the eyes of the beholders. Some of these may be transition rituals, when power and authority are bestowed on individuals, but most of them are purely celebrative, symbolizing authority and ritualizing power for others to see.[40]

In American civil society there are many fewer such rituals than there may have been in Elizabethan England and other countries ruled by monarchs and nobles before the rise of democracy in Europe and America. Nonetheless, every four years, the United States celebrates a presidential inauguration with much pomp and circumstance, and every official appearance of the president is also surrounded by symbols of power and authority: motorcades, military escorts, flags, sirens, crowd control, and so on. Governors, mayors, and other officials often enjoy these same prerogatives on a somewhat reduced scale. Rituals of power and the dynamics of power are highly visible in military forces whose members wear symbols of their rank and medals of accomplishment, give or receive salutes according to their status, and are accorded positions of honor in parades and reviews.   ☐

Interestingly, the holy orders of the Catholic priesthood were originally modeled on the military ranks of the Roman army, since *ordo* in Latin means rank. Ancient Rome had its military orders and governmental orders (like administrative levels in government service today), so as the institutional church grew larger and more complex, it created holy or sacred orders for different levels of ministry. In the Middle Ages there were in fact seven such orders, but these were simplified by the Second Vatican Council, which reduced the number to three: deaconate (the order of deacons), presbyterate (the order of priests), and episcopate (the order of bishops). Men are invested with these orders through transition rituals called ordinations, but their power and authority is reinforced in a variety of ritualistic ways: by wearing distinctive liturgical vestments, by playing central roles in liturgical celebrations, and by being honored with special titles such as Father, Monsignor, and Your Excellency. The papal election and elevation are matters of elaborate ceremony, but the papacy itself is not a separate order. The pope's highest order is that of bishop (as the bishop of Rome) but the papal office carries with it special honor and dignity. Weekly general audiences in St. Peter's Square are as much celebrations of the pope's position in the church as are his visits abroad, cavalcades in the "pope mobile," papal addresses, and pontifical liturgies.   ☐

Somewhat parallel to the different branches of military service are the different religious orders in the Catholic Church: ancient monastic orders such as Benedictines and Carthusians, medieval mendicant orders such as Dominicans and Franciscans, and modern apostolic orders such as the

40. See ibid., 128–35.

Society of Jesus (Jesuits), the Sisters of Charity (of which there are many), and literally hundreds of others. The ceremony through which one enters a religious order and vows fidelity to Christ and the community is not called an ordination and is not one of the church's seven sacraments, but it is sacramental in the broader sense of being a symbolic ritual that celebrates sacred realities such as religious commitment and values. Like deacons, priests, and bishops, the women and men in these orders wear distinctive dress (optional since Vatican II) as a sign of their standing in the church, and when they do, it is perceived as a symbol of spiritual authority.

3. Characteristics of Ritual

Almost everything that human beings do is a matter of routine or ritual. When we wake up in the morning, each of us has a little routine that we follow with some regularity. For many, it looks something like this: get out of bed, head to the bathroom, use the toilet, look in the mirror, comb hair, brush teeth, shave (if necessary), go back to bedroom, and get dressed. If we think about our activities during the day, we can see that they usually follow a certain pattern, and very often the pattern of our workday activities is different from the patterns of our behavior on Saturday and Sunday, when we might fall into different routines such as cleaning the house, or engage in different rituals such as going to church. Even something as commonplace as talking is a matter of patterned behavior: if people did not make sounds in recognizable patterns, they could never communicate. Speech that is not ritualized is gibberish.

Once we recognize the ritual-like nature of human life, we can begin to look for similarities and differences in the many types of ritual activities. Some of these have just been examined in the previous section, classifying different types of rituals in the categories suggested by Catherine Bell. Rituals in every category, however, have certain characteristics, and in *Ritual: Perspectives and Dimensions* Bell discusses six principal characteristics of ritual activity: formalism or formality, traditionalism, invariance, rule governance, sacred symbolism, and performance.[41] Examining each of these characteristics can provide greater insight into the Catholic sacraments and their role in the life of the church.

41. See ibid., chap. 5. Bell does not claim that her set of characteristics is definitive. Not only is the field of ritual studies still developing but, like most social sciences, its terminology is much more fluid than that of the physical sciences such as physics or chemistry. For a similar list of characteristics, see Roy A. Rappaport, *Holiness and Humanity: Ritual in the Making of Religious Life* (New York: Cambridge University Press, 1999), chap. 2.

a. Formalism or Formality

Not all rituals are characterized by formality, but religious ceremonies such as the sacraments display this characteristic to some degree. Deliberate, formal behavior draws attention to what is being done, provides a heightened sense of seriousness, and is more difficult to interrupt.[42]

The distinction between formal and informal can be illustrated by the difference between breakfast on the go and supper around the dinner table, the difference between supper at home and dinner in a fine restaurant, and the difference between dining out with friends and attending a state dinner in the governor's mansion. In each of these examples, the second of the two alternatives has a greater level of formality. Formal dress is more stylized and elegant than informal attire. A formal lecture delivered at a podium and read from a prepared text is quite different from spontaneous talk among friends; and somewhere between these two extremes is a presentation at a business meeting. ☐

As formality increases, the differences among participants in an activity are heightened, and as formality decreases, the opposite is true. In a court of law, there is a sharp distinction between the judge, the plaintiff, and the defendant, but the situation is quite different when someone is trying to mediate a disagreement between two friends. In church, only a designated minister can lead the service, but at home anyone around the table can be asked to say the grace before a meal. In matters of ceremony, action that is methodical and deliberate is perceived as more formal and serious than action that is spontaneous and unscripted. During informal conversation, it is usually acceptable to interrupt the speaker, whereas interrupting a formal lecture or address is considered inappropriate and rude. ☐

All the Catholic sacraments have elements of formality because they are scripted, that is, their words are to be memorized or read from a book and their actions are dictated by the directions in the rite, which is the written version of the ritual. Nonetheless, the degree of formality is variable. In the Latin liturgy before Vatican II, there was little room for spontaneity: every word and action prescribed in the rite had to be performed as directed. During the implementation of liturgical reforms in the 1970s, the pendulum swung in the opposite direction with sometimes rampant creativity in vestments, music, decorations, and locations for Masses, baptisms, and weddings. Since the 1990s there has been a return to more formality in the Catholic liturgy, but individual priests and parishes still

---

42. See Bell, *Ritual: Perspectives and Dimensions*, 139–44.

have some latitude in deciding the degree of formality to be observed in sacramental celebrations, especially at the weekly Eucharist. In general, smaller parishes where people know one another tend to be more informal in their worship, while larger parishes with more financial resources tend to invest more time and energy in liturgical formalism.

b. Traditionalism

By traditionalism is meant a perceived link to the past that invests a ritual with historical weight and importance. At university commencement exercises, the procession of faculty and administrators in their academic gowns links this event to a long educational tradition. Likewise, liturgical vestments worn in church link the wearer and the ceremony to a long ecclesiastical tradition.[43]

When people see or hear traditional elements in a ritual, they feel connected not only to the ritual's past but to their own past as well, for the traditional elements remind them that they have been there before. Even when people are unfamiliar with a ritual's tradition, as may happen when they visit a foreign country, they can be very impressed by rituals that appear traditional even if they are not. In contrast, when recently created rituals do not contain traditional elements, people sometimes have difficulty relating to them or feeling at home in them. Take all the traditional music out of a Christmas service, and to many people it just wouldn't feel like Christmas. By the same token, changing traditional elements in a familiar ritual can sometimes occasion protest, as when a creative cook tries serving something other than roast turkey for Thanksgiving dinner.

When the Catholic sacraments were revised after Vatican II, people for whom tradition meant a lot felt that something important had been lost, and some self-styled Catholic traditionalists do not accept the revised rites as valid. For most people at the time, however, the new Mass contained enough traditional elements for them to feel at home even though much had changed. And for Catholics who never experienced the older rites, the new ones appear to be quite traditional.

c. Invariance

Invariance would seem to be closely related to traditionalism, but in fact it is not, for a ritual can have an aura of tradition about it even if one is attending it for the very first time. Invariance, by contrast, is a character-

---

43. See ibid., 145–50.

istic that can only be perceived over the course of time, across many repetitions of a ritual.[44]

Strict invariance is not necessarily ideal, except in some complex rituals such as the Japanese tea ceremony. Indeed, for many people, a ritual that is 100 percent identical to the last time it was performed might be somewhat less interesting, and after numerous repetitions it might even become boring. In most cases, some variation is allowable and even desirable.

Invariance is more important with regard to ritual structure than with regard to ritual content. Eating a meal in a restaurant is something of a ritual, beginning with being seated and receiving the menu, moving through appetizers and the main course, and concluding with dessert and paying the tab. It is important that the structure remain relatively invariant, but one wouldn't want to eat the same food in the same establishment all the time. Likewise, most Sunday church services (not just the Catholic Mass) maintain a relatively stable format even though hymns, prayers, and scripture texts vary from week to week—and one could imagine some protests if the same sermon were delivered every week! ☐

Invariant structure provides a sense of comfort derived from knowing what to do and knowing what comes next. Invariance also makes it possible to enter more deeply and purposefully into the meaning of the ritual because one no longer has to pay attention to what is happening at every moment. Like driving over a familiar road, invariance makes it possible to focus on the destination rather than on every twist and turn. The repetition of a somewhat invariant ritual also makes it possible to discover symbolisms and discern meanings that had previously escaped one's notice. The receiving of Communion at Mass is a relatively invariant ritual within the eucharistic liturgy, and this invariance can enhance the experience of communion with Christ. ☐

d. Rule Governance

Religious rituals are obviously not the only human activities that are governed by rules. Amateur and professional sports, card games, and board games (and now also computer games) are loaded with rules, driving is governed by the rules of the road, and writing is supposed to follow rules of grammar and spelling. (Even text messaging has its rules.) Indeed, any ritual-like behavior can be codified into a set of rules even if the rules are not written down. Daily habits and weekly routines can be observed and described as though they were a set of rules, even if the rules are followed

44. See ibid., 150–53.

without thinking. Most people learn the rules of how to behave in public
without ever reading a book about etiquette.[45]

If all patterned behavior can be thought of as being governed by rules,
and if ritual is a form of patterned behavior, then certainly it can be thought
of as following written and unwritten rules. But who makes the rules, who
enforces the rules, and how do the rules change? Questions such as these
can arise with regard to religious ritual, and in an organization such as the
Catholic Church, they can sometimes be important.

Perhaps not surprisingly, there are rules governing the implementation
of rules. Every culture has its own way of understanding laws and social
norms, of evaluating their binding force, and for interpreting their application. There are many cultures in the world, and in the Western culture alone
there are two broad approaches to laws and rituals. One derives from the
southern European tradition of Roman law; the other derives from the north-
ern European tradition of English law. At the risk of oversimplification, one
can say that the Roman approach regards rules as general norms to be
adapted to local circumstances, whereas the English approach regards rules
as binding and obligatory regardless of local circumstances. Thus in Italy
(a country in the Roman law tradition) drivers may disregard red lights if
there is no cross traffic, but in the United States (a country in the English
law tradition) drivers will usually stop for a red light even at a deserted
intersection in the middle of the night.

As its name suggests, the Roman Catholic Church is an institution in the
Roman tradition, and church law (usually referred to as canon law because
each law is called a canon or rule) is properly understood as a set of norms
that should be adapted to local circumstances. But the Catholic Church is
also an international institution, and in countries where the English approach
to law is customary, church laws are liable to be understood as binding and
obligatory regardless of local circumstances. This can lead to a legalistic
enforcement of liturgical norms that diminishes rather than enhances the
experience of worship. For example, kneeling during the liturgy where kneeling is not a cultural norm may not symbolize reverence to people, and it may
even evoke feelings of subservience. Legalistic limitations on liturgical expression also often prevent cultural adaptations that allow people to take
ownership of worship and not experience it as foreign.

The Roman Catholic Church is not the only church that has to wrestle
with rules of worship. Orthodox churches (Greek Orthodox, Russian Orthodox,
etc.) translated the liturgy into local languages centuries before the Catholic

45. See ibid., 153–55.

Church did so after Vatican II, but for the most part they are unable to change the form of their public worship, which derives from the ceremonial style of the Roman Empire in the fifth century. On the one hand, this makes Orthodox worship rich in traditionalism, but on the other hand it leads many to abandon what they perceive as archaic formalism. In an attempt to slow down the loss of church membership in Russia, Protestants are forbidden by law from proselytizing people who were baptized in the Orthodox Church. Despite the law, however, Russians continue to join Protestant churches.   □

Even in nonliturgical Protestant churches, rule governance can be an issue. Although there is no central authority dictating the rules of public worship, local custom can itself become somewhat dictatorial. A pastor who changes a congregation's customary worship too drastically, or who introduces innovation without consultation, can quickly find himself or herself out of favor, if not out of a job.   □

Not all rules of public worship are written down. Rules that are printed in books of rites are sometimes called rubrics because in medieval Mass books the directions for what the priest should do were written in red ink (the Latin word for red is *ruber*) while the words he was supposed to say were written in black ink. Church laws about the performance of the sacraments are for the most part rubrical in nature: they give directives about what is to be done. There are additional ranges of rules, however, that never appear in liturgical books, and these might be termed rules of ritual enhancement. When should music be used in liturgical worship, how should it be used, which pieces should be selected, how should they be played or sung, and who should participate by singing, moving, and possibly dancing? Liturgical musicians would say there are rules that should be followed in order to enhance the experience of worship. Not to belabor the obvious, one rule is that liturgical music should be simple enough to be singable yet complex enough to be interesting. Likewise, professional liturgists (not necessarily priests, unless they have a degree in liturgy) would argue that there are rules of ritual performance that should always be observed. For example, one rule is that symbols should be large enough to be seen, and symbolic gestures should be dramatic enough to convey their meaning. Rules such as these are explicitly known only to experts, but their effects can be felt by all those who participate in church rituals.   □

e. Sacred Symbolism

As already noted in chapter 1, section 3, symbols differ from signs because they have multiple meanings, carry covert as well as overt messages, and evoke feelings as well as thoughts. Very often, symbols refer to something that is especially meaningful or sacred for an individual or group, and so the sacredness of the referent becomes associated with the symbol. Symbols are often said to be sacred signs, but it is more accurate to call them signs of the sacred or signs of sacred realities.[46]

It matters little whether the reality in question is known to be sacred by others than those who recognize—and indeed experience—its importance. Sacredness (otherwise known as sacrality, preciousness, importance, significance, meaningfulness, or holiness) is not a physical quality but a spiritual quality. A saint may be described as holy, but it is only a believer—and a devout one at that—who can perceive the saint's sanctity. This is true not only of Christian saints but of Hindu saints and Buddhist saints as well. Nor does this account of sacredness make it "purely subjective" as though it existed only in the mind. Spiritual realities such as truth, honesty, compassion, sanctity, and so on are not objectively real because they are measurable objects but because their existence can be verified on the basis of publicly available evidence.[47] Thus they have the same type of objectivity as a verdict of guilty or innocent returned by a jury on the basis of testimony and other evidence presented at a trial.

When spiritual realities are perceived as sacred, the symbols that represent them are imbued with sacrality. When a personal relationship is sacred, a photograph of the person can enliven one's awareness of that relationship. When a past event in one's life is still personally significant, a souvenir can reawaken one's appreciation for the meaningfulness of that event. We perceive spiritual realities and their importance or sacredness *through* physical symbols, as it were, just as we perceive the meaning of what someone is saying through the words they use, whether spoken or written.

This being said, we can understand why Americans revere their country's flag and consider abuse of it as unpatriotic and sacrilegious, for disrespect to the flag is perceived as disrespect to the country and its sacred values. Physically, a flag (of the United States or elsewhere) is a piece of colored cloth, but what it represents is a spiritual reality or, more properly, a conglomerate of spiritual realities such as history, culture, identity, beliefs, ideals, and values. An attack on the flag is perceived as an attack on all of these—at least by those for whom they are sacred realities, for people of other nationalities would not perceive the attack as threatening and sacri-

---

46. See ibid., 155–59.

47. On objectivity, see Bernard Lonergan, *Insight: A Study of Human Understanding* (New York: Philosophical Library, 1957), 375–84.

legious. For Catholics, the destruction of crucifixes and statues; for Orthodox, the mutilation of icons; for Jews, the defacing of synagogues; and for Muslims, the caricaturing of the prophet Mohammed are always seen not as physical actions but as attacks on sacred realities.   □

As Catherine Bell points out,[48] when symbolic objects are regarded as sacred, they get surrounded with rituals that signify and enhance their sacrality. Thus the national flag is raised and lowered with ceremony, and it is folded in a special triangular fashion. Thus the cross and the scriptures are carried aloft in procession. Thus shrines and monuments are erected to national heroes, and pilgrimages are made to battlefields and other sacred sites. But the reverse is also true. One way of introducing children and foreigners to the ideas and ideals sacred to Americans is to have them participate in the sacred rituals of the U.S. civil religion: visit the U.S. capitol building, stand inside the Lincoln Memorial, view the original handwritten Constitution, and so on. Likewise, one way to introduce children and the uninitiated to the beliefs and values sacred to Christians is to have them visit holy places and observe rituals in which the cross and other sacred symbols, the Bible and other sacred texts, the church and other sacred places can speak their spiritual meaning.   □

The opposite holds as well. When rituals put participants in touch with sacred realities, the objects and actions within the ritual get perceived as sacred and special. In the Catholic sacraments, for example, ordinary objects such as water, oil, bread, and wine, and ordinary actions such as touch become holy by being taken up into ritual actions. Through the sacred rituals, people can encounter and experience acceptance and belonging (baptism), affirmation and strengthening (confirmation), personal presence (Eucharist), forgiveness and reconciliation (penance), caring and healing (anointing of the sick), fidelity and commitment (marriage and ordination). Moreover, since these spiritual realities are understood to be graces or gifts from God, they are simultaneously experienced as God's presence, God's love, God's power, God's forgiveness, God's strength, and so on. For spiritual realities such as these are always precious and meaningful, and attributing them to God is one way to acknowledge their importance.   □

f. Performance

Like a stage play, a sacramental ritual is something of a performance: it has a beginning, a middle, and an end, or if you will, a development, a

---

48. See Bell, *Ritual: Perspectives and Dimensions*, 156–58.

climax, and a dénouement; it is done in costume; it is scripted and the participants play assigned roles. Not all rituals are ceremonies, and ritual studies examines the performative nature of other rituals such as parades, pageants, rallies, sports events, political demonstrations, and so on; but the Catholic sacraments are all rituals that are also ceremonies.[49]

When each of them originated, the sacraments were understood to be powerful performances—effective signs, as they were later called. Baptism was a lengthy process of immersion in the Christian community and the Jesus way of life that culminated in a life-changing ritual of immersion in water. Eucharist was an actual meal in which people shared the food they brought, and in doing so experienced oneness in community and the presence of their Lord. Penance began as a performance of public repentance, culminating in a dramatic reconciliation with Christ and the church. Anointing of the sick originated in healing practices performed by saintly persons and ordinary Christians before it was adopted as a church ritual to be performed by priests.[50] During the Middle Ages, however, scholastic theologians looked for the essence of each sacrament and canon lawyers asked about the minimum that had to be done to preserve their essential validity. Although the issue was still one of performance, sacraments came to be viewed as magical rituals in which words and actions had to be said and done just right in order to produce their promised supernatural effects.[51] It was only after the reforms of Vatican II that Catholic liturgists began to insist on ceremonial performance as important for the experience of worship.

Two qualities of worship that can be observed in plays as well as in liturgical rituals are multisensory communication and dynamic framing.

A play is a dramatic experience of sight and sound; sacramental ceremonies entail sight and sound, but sometimes also smell (scented oils, fragrant incense) and even touch (the laying on of hands in ordination, anointing in a number of sacraments). Both the totality of the dramatic action and the individual elements within it can speak to participants and communicate a more intense awareness of spiritual realities.

Framing is a performance quality that is created by boundaries of time and space, which in a way define the edges of the performance. A play, for example, begins when the curtain rises and ends when the curtain falls on the last act; but a play also takes place on a stage or in a performance area that psychologically defines the boundaries of the imaginary world in which

49. See ibid., 159–64.
50. For examples, see Martos, *Doors to the Sacred*, chap. 2 and sec. 2 of chaps. 6–12.
51. For examples, see ibid., chap. 3, esp. sec. 5, and sec. 3 of chaps. 6–12.

the action takes place. Likewise, a sacramental ritual begins with an opening hymn or procession or invocation, and it concludes with a closing hymn or recession or prayer of thanks and blessing. These opening and closing elements form the temporal parameters of the ceremony and frame the sacred time within which the significant action takes place. Likewise, the church building and designated places within it (primarily the areas around the altar and around the baptismal font or pool) frame the sacred space within which the sacramental action occurs.   □

In recent decades (and especially since the implementation of the Rite of Christian Initiation of Adults in 1985), liturgical scholars and liturgical ministers have become increasingly insistent on the importance of ritual performance. They, as well as pastors and parishioners, recognize that while the theological effects of sacraments may depend solely on meeting the requirements of canon law, their spiritual effects depend largely on how well they are performed.   □

4. Ritual Sensibility

The sacraments are more or less public ceremonies. Private baptisms and weddings with few in attendance are still possible, private confession can take place apart from a liturgical penance service, and anointing of the sick can also be done in private, especially in the case of a sudden and severe accident. For the most part, however, sacraments are supposed to be church ceremonies attended by many people. And wherever there are many people, there are going to be many kinds of people with different attitudes and levels of understanding. At a Catholic wedding, the friend who happens to be an atheist is not going to view the ritual in the same light as the relative who is very religious.

Ronald Grimes refers to such attitudes as modes of ritual sensibility. They can be thought of as the attitudes of individuals or as the attitude that seems to predominate in a ritual performance. They might therefore be thought of as modes of awareness or modes of consciousness that can be found in individuals and groups during a ritual performance. Grimes distinguishes six such modes: ritualization, decorum, ceremony, magic, liturgy, and celebration.[52]

---

52. See Grimes, *Beginnings*, 40–57.

a. Ritualization

Ritualization can be understood as the biological foundation of ritual, for it is a term used in studies of animal behavior to designate "stylized, repeated gestures and postures of animals" in such functions as mating and self-defense.[53] The tail display of the male peacock and the chest thumping of a stressed gorilla are familiar examples of ritualized animal behavior.

Among human beings, then, a ritual activity falls into the mode of ritualization when it is performed unconsciously and automatically. Psychologists call human behavior ritualistic when it is done repeatedly without any need to do so, for example, washing one's hands or examining one's appearance, or arranging the items on one's desk. Daily chores are often done ritualistically, such as setting the table or washing the dishes. Addictions can also be a cause of ritualistic behavior, as when one smokes cigarettes or chews gum without thinking about it.

As we have already seen, invariance and rule governance are basic characteristics of ritual action, and these characteristics have a biological basis in ritualistic behavior. But when church rituals are performed ritualistically, they lack the intentionality and awareness that make rituals meaningful. They can be, or can be perceived as being, empty and meaningless.

b. Decorum

One step up from ritualistic behavior is decorum or polite behavior. Our lives are filled with rituals of decorum:

> We social animals say "good morning" when it is not, and "come again" when we mean only "goodbye." We brush our teeth twice a day, get off at five every afternoon, and, without thinking, kiss our children at every departure and arrival. . . . Our speech is filled with stock phrases, and our gestures repeat themselves endlessly without significant variation. With little conscious intention, we sit and dress in such a manner as to display our national origin, economic status, psychological state, and occupation.[54]

Social conventions and manners are somewhat like ritualistic behavior, but they are approved by society and carry cultural meaning. "Decorum is civilized behavior."[55] Yet at the same time, it is semiconscious, almost unconscious behavior, because we engage in it without thinking about it.

53. Ibid., 42.
54. Ibid., 45.
55. Ibid., 46.

Walking to the right on a sidewalk (or to the left in some countries), properly handling a fork and knife, apologizing after bumping into someone—these are all habits that are learned early in life and that continue rather automatically thereafter. □

Worship in real life always contains elements of decorous behavior that are not adverted to in ecclesiastical law or theology. Vestments may be prescribed for the presider, but their appearance and how they are worn are not; nor is the presider's attentiveness, body language, and eye contact, all of which affect the worship experience for the participants. Some churches expect people to wear their Sunday finest, while others are much more casual, but all churches have an unwritten dress code that would be violated if, for example, someone showed up with no clothes at all. Likewise, the congregation's behavior before, during, and after the service are subject to rules of decorum that are noticed only when they are broken. In general, the experience of worship can be enhanced by encouraging appropriate behavior and it can be worsened by inappropriate behavior. □

c. Ceremony

Ceremony is both a type of ritual and a dimension of ritual. The seven sacraments are ecclesiastical ceremonies, but so also are other Catholic ceremonies such as Benediction of the Blessed Sacrament and entrance into a religious order. Civil ceremonies such as the dedication of buildings and the inauguration of officials, sports ceremonies such as the bestowal of medals and trophies, commercial ceremonies such as announcing new products, and family ceremonies such as singing "Happy Birthday" and blowing out candles on a cake—these are all rituals that follow certain principles such as those described in the previous section (formalism, tradition, invariance, symbolism, etc.) and that therefore make them recognizable as ceremonies.[56]

Whereas decorous behavior is largely unconscious, ceremonious behavior is deliberate. The rules of decorum are already established, but ceremonies can be designed anew and old ceremonies can be adapted to new situations. Decorum is self-effacing but ceremony is self-assertive— asserting the existence, beliefs, and values of society or a social group. Whereas decorous behavior is polite, ceremonial behavior is insistent on what it stands for and what it celebrates. □

56. Ibid., 47–48.

Among other things, ceremony often symbolizes and asserts power—either the power of a group or organization, or the power of some over others, or both. This is obviously the case in military parades and award ceremonies, but it is also usually the case in civil ceremonies on national holidays and state occasions. All Christian rituals except for the most informal (such as studying the Bible or praying the rosary in a small group) are presided over by appointed leaders who sometimes exercise power during the ritual (for example, initiating new members, forgiving sins, ordaining new clergy).

Because ceremonies intentionally symbolize the beliefs and values of society or a social group, they can mask contradictions between the symbols and social reality. Public officials can swear to uphold the law even though they disregard the law when it suits them. Church leaders can celebrate Christ's love and compassion even though they are legalistic and judgmental in their leadership style. State ceremonies can celebrate liberty and human rights even though state institutions incarcerate the innocent and torture the guilty. When this happens too obviously or too often, a loss of credibility can precipitate institutional decline or even set the stage for revolt.

d. Magic

Christianity has long been opposed to magic and witchcraft, understood as an attempt to manipulate God or control spiritual forces of good or evil. This is not the only understanding of magic that is found in the human sciences today, however, and so it is possible to use a more neutral definition of magic to name and explain what sometimes goes on in rituals, both secular and religious. In some respects, the recent rehabilitation of the term "magic" parallels the earlier rehabilitation of the term "myth."

Magic can be defined as the perception of cause and effect without understanding all the connections between them, that is, without understanding how the cause produces the effect. A stage magician waves his wand and pulls a rabbit out of a silk hat. We do not know how he did it, but we saw the cause (waving the wand) and the effect (the appearance of the rabbit) and so we call it magic. Other feats of illusion may be more complex, but they are still magical because an effect is produced and we do not know how it is done.

Magical perception is a type of thinking that we all develop early in childhood. No one is born with the ability to perceive cause and effect, but between the ages of six months and eighteen months, children develop the ability to connect two apparently unrelated activities (for example, a wall switch is flipped and lights come on) as being causally related.[57] Once we develop this cognitive structure, we can use it for the rest of our lives. We turn appliances on and off without understanding switches or electricity, we collect interest on our deposits without understanding the banking system, we tap the keys on our computer without understanding word-processing programs, and we click buttons on the mouse without knowing very much about the inner workings of the internet. As adults, our lives are filled with magical perceptions, and because we do not understand the connections between causes and effects, we rely on those with arcane and esoteric knowledge (that is, mechanics and technicians) to rescue us when things in our world do not respond the way we want them to.   □

Interacting with technology, however, is not the only way we use magical thinking. Someone gives us expensive tickets to a Broadway play, we present them at the door, and we are admitted to the theater. It's magic! We don't have any money in our wallet so we put an impulse purchase on a credit card. It's magic! It is clear that even the use of currency is magic, when we think about what can be taken out of a store in exchange for some pieces of paper and metal that are practically worthless in themselves. We do not understand the intricacies of the financial system or of the other systems on which our society depends, but we can interact with them with a minimum of effort, using only magical thinking.

Consider the following, as well. We are handed a high school diploma or a college degree and we can suddenly get jobs from which we were previously barred. We get sworn in as a police officer or firefighter and we suddenly have authority we did not have before the ceremony. We get elected to public office but we cannot exercise official power until after our inauguration as mayor or governor or what have you. Moving from the secular to the religious sphere, people are fully initiated into the Catholic Church only after they have been baptized and confirmed. Men and women are married only after they have been through a wedding ceremony (this holds in the secular sphere as well), and in order to become priests in the Catholic Church men need to be ordained, although women in other churches can become ministers (and even priests) also by being ordained. Rites of passage work (in part) because people are willing to regard rituals as causes of changes in social status. There are complex social dynamics behind these

---

57. See Jean Piaget, *The Construction of Reality in the Child* (New York: Basic Books, 1954), 219–319, esp. 229ff. Also Monique Laurendeau and Adrien Pinard, *Causal Thinking in the Child: A Genetic and Experimental Approach* (New York: International Universities Press, 1962).

culturally conditioned perceptions, but we do not have to understand these social dynamics in order to see people as changed or different as a result of participating in a transition ritual.

Magical thinking can also be taken a step further, however, which is when it moves into the realm of attempted manipulation.[58] We can notice that we bought a winning lottery ticket at a certain convenience store, and if we suspect a causal connection there, we may want to buy all our future lottery tickets at the same store. At the race track, we may see a horse (or greyhound or stock car) with our lucky number on it, so we place a bet in the hope that the number will make us lucky again. We have a disease that conventional medical treatment cannot cure, so we seek out alternative medicines, or we go to a faith healer, or we make a pilgrimage to Lourdes in the hope that doing this will effect a cure.[59] Making promises to God in exchange for divine assistance, carrying secular or religious objects (like a four-leaf clover or a St. Christopher medal) in the hope of avoiding mishaps, and lighting candles in the hope that a prayer will be answered are all exercises in this type of magical thinking.[60] (They are also examples of exchange rituals described earlier in this chapter.)

Even if religious ceremonies such as the sacraments are not meant to be magical rituals in this second sense of the term, people can and do perceive them as such. Parents can want to have a baby baptized so that its soul can go to heaven, and they may want to have their child confirmed so that he or she will be spiritually prepared for the moral battles to come. Likewise, people will go to confession in order to avoid going to hell, and they can perform spiritual good works in order to shorten their stay in purgatory. They can call on a priest to do the last rites for a dying parent in the hope of a speedy entrance into heaven for their loved one.

There is also a third sense of magic that comes into play when an event has such an effect on us that we are tempted to call it magical.[61] Everything

58. Actually, in children this type of causal perception occurs first. That is, infants learn to perceive connections between their exertions and changes in their perceptual field (e.g., the connection between crying and being picked up, or between shaking a rattle and hearing a sound) before they learn to perceive such connections between objects in the world around them. See Piaget, *The Construction of Reality*, 229–56, 293, 315.

59. According to research on the placebo effect, the unconventional treatment of physical ailments is effective about a third of the time, which is a large enough success rate to build up people's faith in such treatments. Much is still not known about how the placebo effect actually works, so from the perspective of the discussion in this book, it is magic.

60. Grimes' discussion of magic in *Beginnings*, 48–50, is primarily of this second type of magical thinking and ritual.

61. See ibid., 50.

comes together just right on an important date, and afterward we tell others about that magical evening. We attend a musical performance and find ourselves transfixed and transposed into a different state of consciousness, and one way we can describe it is to say it was magical. We remember last year's beautifully prepared and executed Christmas liturgy, enhanced with a children's choir and our favorite carols, and so we decide to attend the same service this year in hopes of experiencing the same magic. But magic in this sense is close to what can be called a peak experience or a hierophany or an experience of sacred space and time, so this phenomenon is better treated in the next section, on liturgy.

e. Liturgy

In Ronald Grimes' taxonomy, "Liturgy is a symbolic action in which a deep receptivity, sometimes in the form of meditative rites or contemplative exercises, is cultivated."[62] In terms of what has been discussed earlier in this book, we can say that liturgy is a ritual activity that fosters spiritual experiences or religious experiences, that can trigger hierophanies or peak experiences, that tries to open up sacred space and time, that makes one receptive to important spiritual realities, that can heighten awareness of significant ideas and ideals, that can deepen the appreciation of mystery, or that can lead to an encounter with the transcendent Other, however it is conceived or imagined. ☐

What is experienced, discovered, or encountered in this mode of ritual sensibility is literally not of this world, if by "this world" one means the physical universe. We may be embodied beings, but we are not just our bodies. We may be part of the material universe, but we are not just matter. An X-ray photo can see our spine, but it cannot see our moral backbone or ethical principles. A CAT scan (computerized axial tomography) can see our heart, but it cannot see our love, our commitment, or our courage. MRI technology (magnetic resonance imaging) can inspect our brain, but not our ideas, our ideals, or our aspirations. Yet these nonphysical or spiritual realities are, when we think about it, the most important aspects of human life: they are precious, they are sacred. ☐

Spiritual realities of this sort—things that are experienced as real and important even though they are not experienced with the five senses through which we interact with the physical world—are always both known and unknown. They are known inasmuch as we experience them, and they are

---

62. Ibid., 52.

unknown inasmuch as we never fully understand them. An old song asks, "What is this thing called love?" and one reason why there is no end to love songs and love poems and love stories is that the experience of love can never be adequately described or completely articulated. Yet we all know what love is when we fall in love and experience it ourselves.

Such spiritual realities have every right to be called mysteries in the basic sense of the Greek *mysterion*, meaning hidden from view. Mysteries of this sort cannot literally be seen even though they can be experienced and, in this sense, known. Even though they are elusive realities, we are keenly aware when they are absent from our lives: without friendship and belonging, love and acceptance, meaning and purpose, honesty and justice, our existence can feel empty and aimless.

Human beings have always felt the need to connect and reconnect to spiritual realities such as these. In fact, the etymology of the word "religion" is suggestive of this, for it comes from two Latin roots: *lig*, meaning connection (a ligament connects muscle to bone), and *re*, meaning again (as in rework, reapply, etc.). In a very basic sense, then, religion is a way of getting connected and reconnected with fundamental spiritual realities that are necessary for human living and needed for living humanly. Religious rituals are therefore ritual means of establishing and reestablishing a felt connection to such mysteries, of intensifying awareness of them, and of increasing appreciation for them. They are, in other words, liturgical in the way that Grimes uses the word: "it refers to any ritual action with an ultimate frame of reference and the doing of which is understood to be of cosmic necessity."[63]

Does this mean that all religions are equal? No, for some religions emphasize some ideals (for example, compassion in Buddhism) while other religions emphasize other ideals (for example, submission to God in Islam). Does this mean that religion is only about human mysteries, or that there are no transcendent mysteries such as God or heaven, angels or devils, Christ or the Holy Spirit? Is the divine totally reducible to the human? Not at all. But in the human sciences, of which ritual studies is one, all that can be dealt with is what is available to human experience, whether through external observation or self-awareness. It can say nothing about what is beyond, for that is the realm of faith and theology. But it can provide valuable insight into what is in fact accessible to human investigation, it can help make religious rituals more meaningful and relevant to people's lives, and it can prevent religious rituals—even Christian rituals—from pretending to be only about things of which we have absolutely no experience.

63. Ibid., 51.

f. Celebration

Ronald Grimes reserves the term "celebration" for a festive, playful ritual modality. "For example, carnivals, feasts, and festivals contain the most concentrated expressions of celebration. Celebration is ludic. Thus it is distinguished by its root in play and its seeming to be unmotivated and spontaneous."[64] On this definition, Mardi Gras in New Orleans and Carnival in some Latin American countries would be close to being pure examples of celebration. But so also would be Fourth of July festivities in the United States, Bastille Day in France, and independence day celebrations in other countries. On a smaller scale, birthday and anniversary parties, urban block parties, church picnics and county fairs would be counted as celebrations. Even a TGIF get-together after work would fit. "A celebration rite is one in which there is no bargaining, no gain, no pursued result, and no magic. Celebration is expressive ritual play."[65]

There is a dimension of celebration, however, that this analysis leaves out. Celebrations are always *about* something. In a genuine celebration, something is being celebrated, even if it is only the end of another work week. There is, if you will, an *occasion* for the celebration; otherwise it is as arbitrary as happy hour in the neighborhood bar every afternoon.

Sacraments are sometimes called celebrations, but if they are, they are more in line with commencement exercises, Easter pageants, state dinners, and Martin Luther King Day celebrations. Celebrations such as these publicly ritualize important events and significant realities past and present. They ceremonialize and make visible meaningful happenings that would otherwise be invisible: completing a program of education, Christ's paschal mystery, international détente, the impact of a courageous individual on civic life. Catholics also sometimes use the phrase, "celebrating the sacraments," but this is a mistake. If sacraments are celebrations, it makes little sense to talk about celebrating celebrations. It makes more sense to talk about sacramental celebrations or liturgical celebrations.

As celebrations, sacraments are more ceremonial than spontaneous, more liturgical than ludic, more serious than playful. They are celebrations in the sense that a baptism could be said to celebrate someone's becoming a member of the church, or in the sense that a wedding could be said to celebrate a marriage. Like other celebrations, however, they are always about something, they always refer to something, they always point to

64. Ibid., 53.
65. Ibid., 54.

something that is being celebrated. Without a point of reference, a celebration is literally pointless. It is a party just for the sake of partying.

What then do celebrations celebrate? To what do they refer? Certainly they refer to something in the present. A birthday party celebrates the completion of another year of life, but it also celebrates friendships and relationships with those in attendance. One would hardly celebrate one's birthday with complete strangers, and a solitary birthday party would hardly be a celebration. Independence Day parades celebrate our country's independence from foreign domination. Thanksgiving dinner has become a celebration of family ties, even if it once was a harvest festival. Graduation celebrates the completion of four (or more) years of education. Ordination celebrates the beginning of a priestly ministry. A wedding celebrates the beginning of married life. Reconciliation celebrates God's forgiveness. Anointing of the sick celebrates God's compassionate concern.

Sometimes more clearly and sometimes less clearly, celebrations also have a referent in the past. Certainly there would be no birthday today if someone had not been born some years before, and certainly it would not be a party if friendships and relationships had not been formed some years before. So the party celebrates a key event in the past, as well as a history of cherished relationships. Likewise, Independence Day in the United States celebrates and refers to the signing of the Declaration of Independence on July 4, 1776. Thanksgiving Day refers to the first harvest festival shared by Pilgrims and Native Americans, as we all learned in school. Graduation refers to the years of work it took to earn a diploma or degree. Ordination refers to years of preparation in a seminary and, before that, coming to awareness of a vocation to the priesthood. A wedding celebrates the love that has woven two people's lives together. Baptism and reconciliation, each in their own way, celebrate a process of conversion. Anointing of the sick celebrates a life of faith and hope that is not abandoned in time of illness.

There is, moreover, another past referent for each of the Christian sacraments. The Baltimore Catechism (based on the 1566 Catechism of the Council of Trent) made the claim that the sacraments were "instituted by Christ," and for centuries Catholics took this to mean that Jesus himself gave his followers instructions on how to do the seven church rituals. Today most Catholics recognize that those words cannot be taken literally because historical research has shown that most of the seven did not become church rituals until long after the first century. Still, Catholics have a sense that what they celebrate in their sacraments has some reference to Jesus himself, that the sacraments point back to the teachings of the New Testament, that they are somehow grounded in the life and ministry of Christ. And they are not wrong. One needs only to look at what the sacraments are about (that is, what they celebrate) and to look at what Jesus was about (that is, the gospel accounts of what he said and did) in order to see this.   □

The two sacraments for which this is the clearest are reconciliation and the anointing of the sick. Many of the gospel stories show Jesus healing and forgiving people, and Jesus also told his followers to do the same,[66] so the past referents for these two sacraments are easy to establish. The central meaning of baptism is entrance into the Christian community and immersion in a Christlike life, and Jesus in the New Testament draws a community of followers around him and invites them to be his disciples, that is, to learn from him how to live. Confirmation is a problematic sacrament for reasons already explained, but if we grant that the Holy Spirit and the spirit of Christ are one and the same (as the New Testament indicates), then we can say that Jesus tried to communicate his spirit to his listeners so that they would behave as he did. The gospels point out that the disciples never really caught on to this during Jesus' lifetime, and the book of Acts shows that once they were filled with the spirit of their teacher, they started to behave like him.[67] In the Eucharist, Christians share a symbolic meal in the presence of their Lord, just as the apostles did at the Last Supper and just as many others did in the gospels,[68] so the past referent of this sacrament is well established. Ordination celebrates a life of ministry, and it is obvious that Jesus' life was one of ministry. The past referent for the sacrament of marriage is not so clear because Jesus was never married, he had something to say about divorce but not about marriage, and the story about him attending a wedding reception is not really about marriage. But if Christian marriage is about mutual caring and self-giving, as is taught in the Epistle to the Ephesians, this ideal of marriage is clearly rooted in Jesus' command to love as he loved and to lay down one's life for others.[69]   □

In any celebration, the reference to the future is the vaguest of the three because people do not have the future uppermost in their minds. Yet awareness of the future is always tacitly present, as can be demonstrated by imagining a setting without a future. If a man were going to be executed

66. On forgiving others, see Matt 6:14-15; 18:21-35; Mark 11:25; Luke 6:37; 17:3-4; John 20:23. On the ministry of healing, see Luke 9:1-6; Acts 3:1-10; 1 Cor 12:4-11, 28-31.
    67. See Acts 2–5.
    68. For accounts of the Last Supper, see Matt 26:17-29; Mark 14:12-25; Luke 22:7-20; 1 Cor 11:17-27. For other meals in the presence of Jesus, see Matt 9:10-11; 14:13-21; 15:29-39; Mark 2:15-17; 6:30-44; 8:1-10; Luke 5:29-30; 7:36-50; 9:10-17; 11:37-38; 14:1-14; 24:28-32; John 6:1-13; 21:4-14.
    69. Eph 5:21-33; John 13:34-35; 15:13.

the day after his birthday, or if a woman were close to death from breast cancer, a birthday party would hardly seem appropriate. Likewise, if a country were on the brink of being invaded and losing its independence, independence day festivities would be out of place if not absurd. Every celebration therefore implicitly refers to a future in which the celebrants will continue to enjoy what is being celebrated. At weddings, commencements, and other celebrations of beginnings, references to the future are more explicit.

When Christians envision the future, they often refer to it as the kingdom of God or the reign of God. Some early Christians believed that God's kingdom on earth would arrive quickly with the second coming of Christ, but when that expectation went unfulfilled, the kingdom of God became a symbol or metaphor for the goal of history, understood from a Christian perspective. The New Testament speaks of the kingdom as being already but not yet, as somehow present but not yet fully realized, and Christians who are optimistic about the future believe that God's reign is slowly being established on the earth. Christians intent on social reform speak of working toward the kingdom, or of trying to bring about God's kingdom in this world.

Although the meaning of the metaphor is somewhat elusive (in past centuries, the kingdom of God was at times identified with heaven and at times with the church), the referent becomes clearer when one understands that the original Greek phrase, *ta basileia tou theou*, can also be translated as God's dominion or the place where God rules. The kingdom (or reign, or realm) of God is therefore anywhere that God's rules are being followed—not only God's rules of justice, such as the principles embodied in the Torah and the writings of the prophets, but also God's rules of love and compassion, such as the principles behind the teachings of Jesus. Were God's rules for humankind being obeyed around the world, the kingdom of God would be present in its fullness, and life on earth would be paradise. It would be heaven on earth.

If each of the seven sacraments looks backward to the life and ministry of Jesus, they also look forward to the kingdom of God, or some aspect of it. What if everyone in the world were immersed in a Christlike community (baptism), filled with the spirit of Jesus (confirmation), fully forgiven and totally forgiving of others (reconciliation), healed of all physical and emotional pain (anointing of the sick), caring for one another (marriage), and ministering to one another's needs (ordination)? Would that not be the kingdom of God in its fullness? Would that not be like living in paradise? Would that not be like heaven on earth? One of the New Testament images of God's kingdom is a banquet to which all are invited and all have their fill. If all the world were spiritually satisfied and sharing food so that no one went hungry, wouldn't that be the future to which the eucharistic meal points?

The sacraments therefore celebrate spiritual realities in the present (as do all celebrations), they celebrate the Christian foundation of those mysteries in the life and ministry of Jesus, and they celebrate the hope and expectation that the world is moving ever closer to the full realization of those ideals in the kingdom of God.

Additional Reading

Ritual Studies

Bell, Catherine. *Ritual: Perspectives and Dimensions*. New York: Oxford University Press, 1997.

————. *Ritual Theory, Ritual Practice*. New York: Oxford University Press, 1992.

Bradshaw, Paul, and John Melloh, eds. *Foundations in Ritual Studies: A Reader for Students of Christian Worship*. Grand Rapids, MI: Baker Academic, 2007.

Gane, Roy. *Ritual Dynamic Structure*. Piscataway, NJ: Gorgias Press, 2004.

Grimes, Ronald L. *Beginnings in Ritual Studies*. Rev. ed. Columbia: University of South Carolina Press, 1995.

————. *Readings in Ritual Studies*. Upper Saddle River, NJ: Prentice Hall, 1996.

Gruenwald, Ithamar. *Rituals and Ritual Theory in Ancient Israel*. Leiden, The Netherlands: Brill, 2003.

Harvey, Graham, ed. *Ritual and Religious Belief: A Reader*. New York: Routledge, 2005.

Rappaport, Roy A. *Holiness and Humanity: Ritual in the Making of Religious Life*. New York: Cambridge University Press, 1999.

Rothenbuhler, Eric W. *Ritual Communication: From Everyday Conversation to Mediated Ceremony*. Thousand Oaks, CA: Sage Publications, 1998.

Schilderman, Hans. *Discourse in Religious Studies*. Leiden, The Netherlands: Brill, 2007.

Christian Ritual

Anderson, E. Byron. *Worship and Christian Identity: Practicing Ourselves.* Collegeville, MN: Liturgical Press, 2003.

Daly, Robert J. *The Origins of the Christian Doctrine of Sacrifice.* Philadelphia: Fortress Press, 1978.

Dietering, Carolyn. *Actions, Gestures and Bodily Attitudes.* Saratoga, CA: Resource Publications, 1980.

Giles, Richard. *Creating Uncommon Worship: Transforming the Liturgy of the Eucharist.* Collegeville, MN: Liturgical Press, 2004.

Lukken, Gerard. *Rituals in Abundance: Critical Reflections on the Place, Form, and Identity of Christian Ritual in Our Culture.* Leuven, Belgium: Peeters, 2005.

McCall, Richard. *Do This: Liturgy as Performance.* Notre Dame, IN: University of Notre Dame Press, 2007.

McGuckian, Michael. *The Holy Sacrifice of the Mass: A Search for an Acceptable Notion of Sacrifice.* Chicago: Liturgy Training Publications, 2005.

Penn, Michael Philip. *Kissing Christians: Ritual and Community in the Late Ancient Church.* Philadelphia: University of Pennsylvania Press, 2005.

Post, Paul, Gerard Rouwhorst, Louis van Tongeren, and Anton Scheer, eds. *Christian Feast and Festival: The Dynamics of Western Liturgy and Culture.* Leuven, Belgium: Peeters, 2001.

Smith, Dennis E. *From Symposium to Eucharist: The Banquet in the Early Christian World.* Minneapolis: Fortress Press, 2003.

CHAPTER 4

The Sacraments in History

The sacraments did not fall from heaven, fully formed. They have a history through which they took shape and were reshaped by successive generations of Catholic practice, canonical regulation, and theological interpretation. As rituals they went through periods of development and even decline. As occasions for religious experience they have been affected by the psychological dispositions of those who participated in them. As events in the religious life of a believing community they have been altered by the social style of the cultures through which they were handed down. And like the sacraments themselves, sacramental theology has also undergone changes in both form and content during the Christian centuries.

1. Historical Investigation into the Sacraments

In response to the Protestant Reformation, the Council of Trent called for a Catholic Counter-Reformation, a major focus of which was the Mass and the sacraments. To refute the reformers' allegations that ecclesiastical worship was an unbiblical medieval invention, church historians and liturgical scholars began the first comprehensive search through archives and libraries for evidence that linked the sixteenth-century liturgy to its patristic and apostolic beginnings. What they found was far from complete, but it seemed enough to demonstrate that major elements in Catholic worship were indeed quite ancient, and it was enough to give liturgists a sound basis on which to develop the missal and sacramentary that the church then used for the better part of four centuries.[1]

---

1. For a more complete history of liturgical studies, see William J. O'Shea, "Liturgiology," *New Catholic Encyclopedia*, vol. 8 (New York: McGraw-Hill, 1966), 919–27; also

Despite the liturgical stability that came out of these reforms, historical inquiry into the ancient and medieval periods of Christian worship continued in the seventeenth and eighteenth centuries, but for the most part the fruits of that research were known only to scholars with antiquarian interests. Theologians and canonists made little use of these findings in trying to understand the sacraments and in deciding how they were to be properly performed. The general Catholic consensus seemed to be that the sacramental system had reached its apex, and so further change was unnecessary.

In the nineteenth century, however, Prosper Guéranger founded the monastery of Solesmes in France and through his inspiration the Benedictines in Europe sparked a renewed interest in Christian worship and Gregorian chant. Their major concern, however, was not antiquarian but pastoral, for they wanted to reawaken people's appreciation for the liturgical life of the church. It was the beginning of what today we call the modern liturgical movement. Even though their interests were ultimately pastoral, their initial efforts were largely historical, for they believed that a sound liturgical piety could only be based on a solid foundation of liturgical scholarship.[2]

Even before the First World War, a great deal of historical foundation laying had been accomplished. Texts of the *Didachē* (second century), *The Apostolic Tradition* (third century), the *Anaphora of St. Serapion* (fourth century), and *The Apostolic Constitutions* (fifth century), as well as other ancient liturgical documents were discovered (or rediscovered) and published; new editions of the Gelasian, Gregorian, and Leonine sacramentaries (Roman, fifth and sixth centuries) as well as Eastern rite liturgies (Greek, Armenian, Syrian) were issued; voluminous collections of ancient and medieval texts were begun; academic encyclopedias systematized what was being discovered; scholarly journals were founded in France, Belgium, Holland, and Germany to publish the results of liturgical research. Some of the books of that period that attempted to summarize the history of the liturgy on the basis of what was then becoming known have remained classics in the field.[3]

Virgil C. Funk, "The Liturgical Movement (1830–1969)," in *The New Dictionary of Sacramental Worship*, ed. Peter E. Fink (Collegeville, MN: Liturgical Press, 1990), 695–715. For more recent developments, see German Martinez, "History of Liturgical Reform" in Fink, esp. 1068–72.

2. See Louis Soltner, *Solesmes and Dom Guéranger, 1805–1875* (Orleans, MA: Paraclete Press, 1995).

3. Louis Duchesne, *Christian Worship: Its Origin and Evolution* (London: SPCK, 1902); Edmund Bishop, *Liturgica Historica: Papers on the Liturgy and Religious Life of the Western Church* (Oxford: Clarendon Press, 1918) collects articles written earlier; Ludwig Eisenhofer and Joseph Lechner, *The Liturgy of the Roman Rite* (New York: Herder and Herder, 1961) is based on research begun by Valentin Thalhofer in the nineteenth century.

On this solid and expanding base of historical documentation, scholars during the period between the two great European wars began to reconstruct the history of Christian worship in all its aspects: the Mass and the sacraments, the liturgical year, the Liturgy of the Hours (the Divine Office), monastic and religious music and art, liturgical vestments, and sacred vessels. Slowly but surely the edifice began to take shape, now under the leadership of Lambert Beauduin at the monastery of Mont-César in Belgium and Ildefons Herwegen at the abbey of Maria Laach in Germany. The results of these historical and liturgical investigations continued to be published in scholarly journals, but in addition, the less technical and more pastoral aspects of these studies began to be made more widely available through periodicals generally read by seminary and college teachers, bishops, and priests.

It was not until after the Second World War that the work begun almost a century before began to take final form. At last it was possible to see how all the elements of the church's worship had come together and assumed their place in the Tridentine rites.[4] And at last it was possible to publish rather complete histories of the Mass and each of the seven sacraments. Almost simultaneously, two scholars working independently drew together decades of earlier investigations to produce thorough accounts of the history of the Eucharist.[5] Inspired by their success, similar studies of the other sacraments began to appear in Herder's *Handbuch der Dogmengeschichte*[6] and in Edition du Cerf's series, *Lex Orandi*.[7] It was not until somewhat later, however, that comprehensive historical treatments of marriage[8] and ordination[9] became available.

What showed clearly through all these histories, moreover, was that the development of the Mass and the sacraments had been neither simple nor uniform, and that the Tridentine missal and sacramentary had excluded much of the variety in the church's liturgical tradition. In their efforts to

4. See Mario Righetti, *Manuale di Storia Liturgica*, 4 vols. (Milan: Editrice Àncora, 1946–49), which covers almost all aspects of church worship.

5. Gregory Dix, *The Shape of the Liturgy* (London: Dacré Press, 1946); Josef Jungmann, *The Mass of the Roman Rite*, 2 vols. (New York: Benziger, 1951, 1955).

6. The first volume on the sacraments appeared in 1951. Two of these have been translated into English: Burkhard Neunheuser, *Baptism and Confirmation* (New York: Herder and Herder, 1964); Bernhard Poschmann, *Penance and the Anointing of the Sick* (New York: Herder and Herder, 1964).

7. The series was begun in 1944, but few of these books have been translated into English and none of the sacramental histories.

8. Edward Schillebeeckx, *Marriage: Human Reality and Saving Mystery* (New York: Sheed and Ward, 1965); Theodore Mackin, *What Is Marriage?* (New York: Paulist Press, 1982).

9. Bernard Cooke, *Ministry to Word and Sacraments: History and Theology* (Philadelphia, PA: Fortress Press, 1976).

make Catholic worship more truly catholic by recovering dimensions of public worship that had existed prior to Trent, leaders of the liturgical movement began to suggest changes that would increase people's participation in and appreciation for ecclesiastical prayer.[10] These suggestions were based on sound liturgical scholarship,[11] but they were also based on solid biblical research and recent developments in sacramental theology.[12] The movement gained additional momentum through yearly liturgical conferences in a number of countries, which brought together scholars and pastors to discuss new ideas and possibilities, as well as through periodic international meetings for liturgical experts to share their discoveries about the past and hopes for the future. This momentum culminated in the liturgical reforms approved by the Second Vatican Council, but the effects of the liturgical movement are still being felt in the recent revision of the church's Code of Canon Law, in the growing desire for more regional autonomy in ecclesiastical worship, and in other ways.

Even from this sketch of modern liturgical research and its implications, it is clear that a full history of the sacraments cannot be presented in a single chapter of a short book.[13] What can be presented, in a way that provides a bridge between the sociological history of religion discussed in the second chapter and the current theological interpretations of the sacraments to be discussed in the next chapter, is a brief history of Catholic *sacramentality*. For beneath the visible changes in the church's sacraments over the past twenty centuries, there have been underlying changes that have shown in different phases of what might be called sacramental form or style.[14]

2. The Apostolic Period

Even secular historians must admit that Jesus of Nazareth was a charismatic individual. During his brief ministry he drew crowds of people who

10. See, for example, Godfrey Diekmann, *Come, Let Us Worship* (Baltimore, MD: Helicon Press, 1961).

11. See William J. O'Shea, *The Worship of the Church: A Companion to Liturgical Studies* (Westminster, MD: Newman Press, 1957); Cyprian Vagaggini, *Theological Dimensions of the Liturgy* (Collegeville, MN: Liturgical Press, 1959); Aimé Georges Martimort, *L'Église en Prière* (Tournai, Belgium: Desclee, 1961).

12. See the next chapter in this book, on sacramental theology.

13. For a more complete history of the sacraments, see Joseph Martos, *Doors to the Sacred: A Historical Introduction to Sacraments in the Catholic Church* (Liguori, MO: Liguori/Triumph, 2001).

14. For a somewhat different but illuminating approach to changes in Christian sacramentality through seven historical periods, see Marion J. Hatchett, *Sanctifying Life, Time and Space: An Introduction to Liturgical Study* (New York: Seabury Press, 1976).

were sincerely interested in or merely curious about him, he attracted a band of faithful followers who traveled with him and afterward preserved the memory of what he had said and done, and he aroused enough antagonism among the religious and political leaders of Palestine that they had him put to death. But his charismatic presence returned to his disciples shortly after his crucifixion, and even after those vivid appearances ceased, it remained in a spiritual form that could be experienced by those who had never met him in the flesh.

Jesus' personal charisms were many. He spoke with an authority that commanded attention, and the things he said struck people as a revelation rather than as a repetition of what they already knew. He touched people both physically and spiritually, and through that touch their bodies were healed and their spirits were lifted. He acted sometimes decisively and sometimes enigmatically, seemingly sure of what he was doing but not always understood, even by his disciples. His lifestyle testified to a transcendent richness that more than compensated for its worldly poverty. His behavior bore witness to a depth of reality that was not disturbed by the surface events of daily life. His prayer seemed to both grow out of and intensify his intimate relation with the God he addressed as *Abba*. Even his personality was charismatic, for to his followers it was obvious that the Spirit of God and the spirit of Jesus were one and the same.[15]   □ *

In this broad sense, then, Jesus was a sacramental person. His preaching announced that the reign of Satan was over and the reign of God had begun, and his life was a sign that this was true. What he said spoke God's word in the hearts of his hearers, and what he did revealed God's action in a world that often seemed anything but sacred. Jesus' concern for others was a sign of God's care for his people; his miracles were a sign of God's power and providence; his forgiveness of their sins was a sign of God's love, even—or, rather, especially—for sinners. Thus Jesus was a living symbol of salvation. To the poor he promised wealth; to the sorrowing he revealed reasons for joy; to the blind he gave sight; to the discouraged he brought good news. The ultimate symbol of that salvation was Jesus' resurrection by the Father,

---

*This symbol in the margin indicates an interactive question that can be found at http://www.TheSacraments.org.

---

15. See, for example, Donald Senior, *Jesus: A Gospel Portrait* (Dayton, OH: Pflaum/Standard, 1975); Bruce Vawter, *This Man Jesus: An Essay toward a New Testament Christology* (New York: Doubleday, 1973).

for through his being raised he became a sign that those who lived in God had nothing to fear from death.[16]

We can say, therefore, that the first phase of Christian sacramentality was the *personal sacramentality* of Jesus himself: both the incarnate sacramentality of Jesus of Nazareth during his lifetime, and the transcendent sacramentality of Jesus the Christ after his resurrection. Moreover, Jesus' many charisms continued to be incarnated in the community of those who accepted his lordship over their lives. His disciples preached the good news of salvation from sin and death. Their fellowship was a living symbol of freedom from alienation and antagonism. Their ministering to each other's needs was a sign of how Christ wanted them to live, and their forgiveness of each other's faults was a sign of how he wanted them to love one another. This is not to say that the early Christian community was a perfect sacrament of Christ, either for its own members or to the society in which it found itself. In both the Acts of the Apostles and the epistles of St. Paul, for example, we see not only the ideal sacramentality to which Christians were committed but also the failure of Christians to live up to that ideal.[17] But the ideal was nonetheless real in the minds and hearts and actions of those for whom Jesus was the way, the truth, and the life.

This second phase of Christian sacramentality can be designated as a *charismatic sacramentality*, and this for a number of reasons. It was charismatic in Max Weber's sense that it was inspired by the charisma of Jesus, and that it began to routinize or repeat the types of charismatic behavior that characterized Jesus' life and made him a sacrament of God. It was also charismatic in the sense that the apostolic church did many things that are typical of modern Pentecostal churches and that were also found in the Catholic charismatic renewal in the sixties and seventies: laying on of hands, speaking in tongues, prophesying in God's name, and so on.[18] But the sacramentality of the earliest Christian community was also charismatic in the sense that it tended to be spontaneous and "moved by the Spirit" rather than highly structured and organized. People were preached to wherever they were encountered; needs were met as they arose; ministers were sometimes chosen by lot, while at other times they were designated because they had

16. See "Jesus as Figure and Person, Symbol and Sacrament" in Ann and Barry Ulanov, *Religion and the Unconscious* (Philadelphia, PA: Westminster Press, 1975), 97–117; Gerald O'Collins, *The Resurrection of Jesus Christ* (Valley Forge, PA: Judson Press, 1973).

17. See, for example, Acts 4:32–5:16; Rom. 6:1-4; 1 Cor 11:17-34; Eph 17:6-9.

18. See Acts 8:14-17; 10:44-48; 1 Cor 12:8-11, 28-30; 14:1-40. John Koenig, *Charismata: God's Gifts for God's People* (Philadelphia, PA: Westminster Press, 1978), esp. chap. 2; Wade H. Horton, ed., *The Glossolalia Phenomenon* (Cleveland, TN: Pathway Press, 1966), 23–82.

the needed gifts (charisms) for the job. Jewish Christian communities tended to organize themselves in ways that Jews were used to; Hellenistic communities chose patterns that Greeks were more comfortable with. And through the course of the first century, church structures and practices changed and evolved, not always in the same direction, and not always at the same pace.[19]   ☐

3. The Patristic Period

Even from the very beginning, however, there were a few ritual actions that seemed to be common to all Christian communities even though the apostolic church was not concerned with ritualism as such.[20] Those who became believers in Jesus were almost always initiated into their new life through a ritual immersion in water, or baptism. Christians often had hands laid on them while others prayed that they might receive the Holy Spirit, or that they might be spiritually strengthened or physically healed, or that they might worthily perform a ministry to which they were being called. And every community regularly shared the Lord's Supper, commemorating Jesus' last meal with his disciples, symbolizing the messianic banquet in the kingdom (or reign) of God, and signifying the unity that they both desired and to some extent already experienced.   ☐

In these ritual routinizations of the charismatic spirit of Christ can be seen the emergence of a third type or phase of Christian sacramentality. It can be designated as a *communal sacramentality* because it was common to all the small and scattered Christian communities that were appearing around the Roman Empire, and because it began to form a focus for the communal life of those churches. Instead of baptisms being performed on the spot at the time of an individual's conversion, they came to be performed regularly at Easter or Pentecost, in the company of others who had accepted the Christian message, and in the presence of the head of the local congregation. Likewise the Lord's Supper by the third century was no longer a meal with other food besides bread and wine, but a more strictly symbolic meal that could be shared by the whole community even when the threat

---

19. See Edward Schillebeeckx, *Ministry: Leadership in the Community of Jesus Christ* (New York: Crossroad, 1981), chap. 1; Eduard Schweizer, *Church Order in the New Testament* (London: SCM Press, 1961); James A. Mohler, *The Origin and Evolution of the Priesthood* (New York: Alba House, 1970).

20. "Ritualism is taken to be a concern that efficacious symbols be correctly manipulated and that the right words be pronounced in the right order" (Mary Douglas, *Natural Symbols: Explorations in Cosmology* [New York: Random House Vintage Books, 1973], 28).

of persecution made meeting times short, and even when groups grew large enough that they could no longer fit around a common table for a full dinner. As these rituals took shape, therefore, both the yearly baptism and the weekly Eucharist became socially institutionalized forms of Christian sacramentality through which people were received into and celebrated their life within the church.[21]

It was not until the fourth century that the next phase of Christian sacramentality began to appear as a distinct sacramental style. When Christianity was legalized and later made the official religion of the Roman Empire, it became necessary to move beyond the loosely structured rituals that had been characteristic of the earlier times. Besides having a more or less set pattern, Christian rituals began to be given definite contents in the form of words to be repeated and actions to be performed in one way and not another. Prayers started to be written down and reused, and rubrics began to be established as legal norms. When Sunday was declared an official day of rest (it had been just another weekday) the eucharistic meal developed into an elaborate liturgy lasting up to three or four hours. Similarly, baptism moved from private homes and rain cisterns to basilicas and baptisteries, and in doing so it became a more lengthy and formal process that began with prayers and exorcisms six weeks before Easter, continued with instructions and examinations during Holy Week, and culminated in the washing and anointing on the night of the Paschal Vigil.[22]

By the start of the patristic period, other charisms of Christ had already become routinized to some extent: healing, forgiveness, and service to others. Now, at the height of Mediterranean Christianity these too became connected with rituals of the institutional church. Oil, water, and other substances that were used for healing were sometimes blessed expressly for this purpose. The need to readmit repentant Christians who had renounced their faith during persecution led to the development of a "second baptism" or penitential discipline. When the persecutions were over, this ecclesiastical ritual was also made available to notorious sinners who wanted to be reconciled with the community, and public penance became a process as lengthy as baptism but even more rigorous. Finally, certain forms of service became increasingly institutionalized as the church grew in numbers and complexity. There developed specialized ministries of local church

21. See Arthur McCormack, *Christian Initiation* (New York: Hawthorn Books, 1969), chap. 3; Edward Kilmartin, *The Eucharist in the Primitive Church* (Englewood Cliffs, NJ: Prentice-Hall, 1965).

22. See O. C. Edwards Jr., *How It All Began: Origins of the Christian Church* (New York: Seabury Press, 1973); Martos, *Doors to the Sacred*, 151–54; 221–26.

leadership (bishop), advising the bishop and later acting for him at Eucharist (presbyter), administration of ecclesiastical and social services (deacon), secretarial duties (acolyte), caring for the needs of women (widows), instructing new converts during their preparation for baptism (teachers), and so on. And initiation into some of these services, especially the ministries of church leadership and liturgical worship, developed into institutional rituals that usually included a laying on of hands and a prayer over the candidates.[23]   □

During the period from the second through the sixth centuries, then, the Christian gifts of conversion and worship, forgiveness and service became not only routinized but also institutionalized in formal, set rituals. The patristic period may therefore be designated as the period of *institutional sacramentality*, for it was characterized by the establishment of repeated, authoritatively sanctioned actions that were instituted to continue certain charismatic activities of Christ within the world. This does not deny that there were also other nonritualized ways of continuing the work of Christ (for example, teaching and preaching) and even noninstitutionalized ways of doing this (for example, caring for the poor or forgiving one another). Nor does it suggest that at this phase in the development of Christian sacramentality ritualism (in the technical sense of close attention to fixed rituals) was paramount. True, ritualism was growing, but through most of the patristic period there was still a great deal of regional diversity in ecclesiastical practices, and there was still much creative adaptation of church rituals to express the Christian mysteries and to meet the people's spiritual needs.

4. The Medieval Period

The time between the fall of Rome (around 500) and the end of the Viking raids on southern Europe (around 1000) is sometimes called the Dark Ages because it was not a time of great intellectual enlightenment. It was nevertheless a time of cultural transition and many practical changes in the church. With the loss of North Africa and the Middle East to the Islamic Empire, and with its growing isolation from the Greek churches, European Christianity became Germanic rather than Mediterranean in culture. Moreover, the Germanic tribes that overran and pillaged Europe were preagricultural peoples whose religion was of the primal rather than the

23. See Margaret Hebblethwaite and Kevin Donovan, *The Theology of Penance* (Notre Dame, IN: Fides Publishers, 1979), chap. 2. Paul Edwards, *The Theology of the Priesthood* (Notre Dame, IN: Fides Publishers, 1974), chaps. 3 and 4.

classical type. And so even when they settled down and accepted Christianity as their religion, they brought into it many of their own cultural attitudes and practices. Principal among these, from the viewpoint of a history of sacramentality, was a belief in the automatic effectiveness of ritual.

To some extent all rituals are automatically effective. Like signs or symbols of any sort, rituals seem to signify things and bring about changes without any deliberate effort on the part of the participants. Moreover, people are not ordinarily aware of how their personal commitments and social presuppositions contribute to the effectiveness of their rituals. Thus even in the institutional sacramentality of the patristic world there was a tendency to speak about rituals having certain effects quite independently of the ministers and the recipients. Theologically, it was understood that God caused the effects and that the rituals were just the means through which God acted on the soul in a hidden yet real way.

The prime example of this was baptism. Initially it had been a process of personal conversion and commitment, symbolized and finally effected by a ritual of bathing, anointing, dressing in new clothing, and sharing food with one's new community. By late patristic times it had become a brief ritual for infants symbolizing the washing away of original sin and effecting one's entrance into the church. Then, when this abbreviated ritual was used to symbolize a tribe's acceptance of Christianity, sometimes hundreds of adults were baptized with little or no preparation, and they were told that as a result of this ritual all of their past sins were forgiven. Likewise they were told that their children, in order to join the church and be saved, had to be dipped in or sprinkled with water while certain words in a strange language (Latin) were recited.[24]

Also illustrative of this attitude toward sacraments was what happened when confirmation became a separate sacrament. Following the practice of Rome, Germanic bishops commonly reserved to themselves the rite of anointing after baptism, but this meant that children were regularly baptized by local priests and not anointed until some time later when the bishop could visit their locality. The existence of this separate ritual naturally led some to wonder about its effects. Since this anointing had no obvious experiential or social effects, theologians looked to the scriptures for clues about possible hidden, spiritual effects. Eventually it was agreed that the Holy Spirit was received more fully than in baptism, and that

---

24. On this period and on baptism in particular, see Martos, *Doors to the Sacred*, 151–63; also Alexander Ganoczy, *Becoming Christian* (New York: Paulist Press, 1976).

through the ritual Christians were strengthened to overcome the trials of adult life.[25]

Much the same can be seen in the evolution of the sacrament that was formerly called extreme unction. Even before the Middle Ages both priests and laypeople had anointed the sick in the hope that God's healing power might be communicated through the oil and bring about recovery. Around the ninth century, however, this anointing came to be administered only in cases of very severe illness. But if this anointing no longer effected physical recovery, it seemed that its effects must be purely spiritual. Gradually both the prayers that accompanied the ritual and the theology that explained it reflected the growing belief that its hidden effect was to prepare the soul of the person for heaven. And since the subjects of the sacramental rite were sometimes at the point of death and even unconscious, it seemed natural to believe that the ritual had to be automatically effective.[26]

For a long time those who oversaw the church's penitential practices resisted this tendency toward automatic effectiveness. Until the ninth century harsh penances had to be performed *before* a sinner would be readmitted to Communion, and after the penance was done the priest prayed, *asking* that God would forgive the penitant's sins. By the eleventh century, however, it was becoming common for people to perform less severe penances *after* being readmitted to the altar, and it was becoming customary for priests to *declare* that the sins had been absolved. Thus from the twelfth century onward penance was considered to be automatically effective, with God's grace coming through the priestly ritual—even though in this case (as also with the other sacraments) people had to be predisposed to accepting that grace and cooperating with it.[27]

During the medieval period, therefore, *ritual sacramentality* became the dominant mode or style of Christian religious practice. Ordination quite easily lent itself to this interpretation since it had always been true that the ceremony marked the beginning of a man's priestly ministry.[28] Quite literally, the ordination ritual made a man a priest. And when matrimony became

---

25. See Austin P. Milner, *The Theology of Confirmation* (Notre Dame, IN: Fides Publishers, 1972), chap. 2; Jean-Paul Bouhot, *La Confirmation: Sacrament de la Communion Ecclésiale* (Paris: Éditions du Chalet, 1968), 66–90.

26. See James L. Empereur, *Prophetic Anointing: God's Call to the Sick, the Elderly, and the Dying* (Wilmington, DE: Michael Glazier, 1982), chap. 1; Claude Ortemann, *Le Sacrement des Malades* (Paris: Éditions du Chalet, 1971), 27–57.

27. See Monika Hellwig, *Sign of Reconciliation and Conversion: The Sacrament of Penance for Our Times* (Wilmington, DE: Michael Glazier, 1982), chaps. 4–5.

28. On the shift from institutional to ritual sacramentality regarding ordination, see Nathan Mitchell, *Mission and Ministry: History and Theology in the Sacrament of Order* (Wilmington, DE: Michael Glazier, 1982), chap. 4.

an ecclesiastical ritual around the twelfth century (before this, it had been either a private agreement between the man and woman, or a family ceremony usually presided over by the father of the bride) it was easy to perceive the bond of marriage as a hidden effect resulting from the performance of the wedding ceremony.[29]

By the later Middle Ages this attitude so pervaded the Catholic sacraments that even the Mass was commonly regarded as having a number of automatic effects. Chief among these, of course, was the confecting (as it was sometimes called) of Christ's body and blood out of bread and wine. But the Mass was also regarded as a sacrifice that took place every time the Eucharist was offered to God, and the spiritual merits of this sacrifice were believed to be applicable to whomever the priest intended. In addition, popular superstition attributed magical powers to the consecrated host and magical effects to its worship.

Ritual sacramentality was becoming divorced from institutional sacramentality and connected to individual initiative on the part of both the ministers and the participants. Similarly, the sacraments became only tenuously attached to any aspect of communal sacramentality while becoming more and more associated with personal piety. Finally, insistence on the notion that God guaranteed the effectiveness of the rituals, regardless of whether any effects were felt, led to an almost total loss of the charismatic dimensions of the sacraments. Nevertheless, the sacraments were still theologically related to the sacramentality of Jesus through the understanding that Christ acted in the sacraments and had personally instituted all seven of them.

5. The Tridentine Period[30]

Although there were in fact many reasons why Martin Luther and the other reformers rejected the ritual sacramentality of medieval Catholicism, theologically it can be said that they found unintelligible and intolerable a style of sacramentality that had little or no inner effect on people, that was separated from the communal life of the church, and that was even lacking

29. On the development of the medieval wedding ritual and scholastic theology, see Schillebeeckx, *Marriage*, 272–332.

30. In *Doors to the Sacred* I refer to this as the *modern* period, following the usage of literature and the arts. Following Bellah's usage of the term, however, Christianity began to develop a modern cultural style with early Protestantism, but Catholicism began to enter the modern phase of religion only in the second half of the twentieth century. Many refer to the present as a postmodern period, but it may also be thought of as late modernity.

proper institutional regulation. They accepted, however, the Catholic belief in the sacraments' institution by Christ, and using the Bible rather than custom as a guide for determining which of the sacraments actually came from Jesus, they acknowledged baptism and Eucharist (which are both explicitly mentioned in the scriptures) as genuine sacraments and regarded the other five as ecclesiastical inventions. They also accepted the traditional belief that Christ acted through these sacraments, even though they came to disagree among themselves as to how the divine activity was accomplished in these two cases.[31]

Within the Protestant vision of Christian sacramentality can be seen the beginning of a shift toward a more modern mentality. By and large it grew out of a dissatisfaction with the ritualism of the Middle Ages and expressed a desire for a more integrated personal involvement in sacramental actions. On the one hand, Protestantism insisted that God's action in the world could not be confined to ecclesiastical rituals; but on the other hand, it equally insisted on the importance of an active faith and a personal response when God did act through the sacraments. To some extent the pluralism of Protestant practices and interpretations of the sacraments came out of a constant search by various denominations to find new sacramental forms that would allow God's presence and power to be experienced, acknowledged, and lived. □

In response to the Protestant Reformation, the Council of Trent (1545–63) initiated a Catholic Counter-Reformation that first of all insisted on the traditional numbering of the sacraments as seven. It believed it found references in the New Testament to all of them, and even though it could not find an explicit record of Christ having instituted each of them, it reasoned that God need not have given the church a written record if they were divinely approved church practices. Second, the council reaffirmed the medieval theology of the sacraments as an intellectually valid way of explaining what they were and how God acted through them. Even though this scholastic theology was sometimes misunderstood, the council reasoned, it provided a sound philosophical framework for understanding their place in the life of the church and their role in effecting the salvation of individuals. Third, the council acknowledged the truth of the reformers' charges that the church's sacramental system was open to many practical abuses, and it initiated a series of reforms designed to eliminate most of them. By insisting on better theological training for priests, by eliminating much of the laxity

---

31. See G. W. Bromiley, *Sacramental Teaching and Practice in the Reformation Churches* (Grand Rapids, MI: William B. Eerdmans, 1957).

in church government, and by tightening the regulations for the proper performance of the sacramental rituals, the Council of Trent and the popes who came after it were able to ensure that there was a closer correspondence between sacramental theology and sacramental practice.[32]

During the Tridentine period, therefore, the Catholic Church developed what might be called *a purified or stabilized ritual sacramentality*. It was a purified sacramentality because it was purged of many practices that had obscured the theological meaning of the sacraments and that had often vitiated their spiritual value. But it was also a stabilized sacramentality because for the first time in Christian history the sacraments were given a uniform set of rites that were to be used in the entire church and that were not to be altered without explicit permission from Rome. In this way Catholicism reintroduced and reinforced the institutional dimension of sacramentality in its liturgical worship, and in authoritatively sanctioning the specific rituals the magisterium guaranteed that these were indeed instruments of salvation and channels of grace. But as a church Catholicism did not retrieve the communal or charismatic aspects of the sacraments, for there is not much evidence of these in either the theology or the canon law of this period. This is not to deny, however, that there were communal dimensions to eucharistic celebrations,[33] or that there were charismatic ministers of the sacraments.[34] But it does affirm that the main emphasis in both theology and practice was on the institutional and ritual aspects of the sacraments.

6. The Contemporary Period

Since the Second Vatican Council in the 1960s, the church has entered a new phase in its sacramental life. Most Catholics associate this new phase with the liturgical reforms of the 1970s (liturgy in vernacular languages, a variety of rites for a number of sacraments, and so forth). Some also associate it with new theological outlooks (based on personalism, existentialism, and phenomenology) that replaced scholasticism (based on ancient Greek philosophy and medieval metaphysics) during the same period. Both the

---

32. See Philip Hughes, *The Church in Crisis: A History of the General Councils 325–1870* (New York: Doubleday, 1961), chap. 19; Henri Daniel-Rops, *The Catholic Reformation* (London: J. M. Dent, 1962), 79–104.

33. I am thinking of the role that daily Mass would play in the community life of a convent, for example, and of parish celebrations such as baptisms, First Communion, and weddings.

34. For example, the Curé of Ars was renowned as a holy and insightful confessor; others could also be mentioned.

liturgical reforms and the theological shift, however, are merely part of a vast transformation of Catholicism that is just beginning. The present cultural transformation of the Catholic religion is more sweeping than changes in sacramental rituals, and it runs deeper than changes in sacramental theology.[35]

In regard to the sacraments, however, it encompasses a retrieval of all the previous phases of Christian sacramentality, a recognition that they are all important for worship, and a projection of all of them simultaneously into the future. Just as developmental psychology recognized that each succeeding stage in personal development incorporates, modifies, and builds upon the preceding stages of individual growth, so also sociology and history recognize that each succeeding stage in cultural evolution builds upon the preceding stages of social development. Normally, as we look back at our past life or our collective history we notice only the new things that emerged at each step along the way, but modern psychology, sociology, and history make us aware that the past is still with us. And insofar as we can rediscover the past and affirm that it is truly part of us (instead of denying it the way an adolescent denies his childhood or the way "liberal" Catholics reject the "conservative" church), we can be more fully aware of what we have become and allow ourselves to be any or all of them in the future.

This kind of self-awareness and self-consciousness involves both differentiation and integration. The differentiation is a matter of discovering and distinguishing the various components that make up the present reality (whether that reality is our individual personality, or secular society, or the church). The integration is a matter of acknowledging the contribution and worth of the various components and then approving their successive or simultaneous interaction (as individuals, for example, we alternate between different emotional states, realms of meaning, and so forth; as a society we tolerate ethnic diversity, encourage occupational diversification, allow for political differences, and so forth).

It can be anticipated, then, that the modern phase of Catholic sacramentality, as it unfolds in the future, will not be a new culturally uniform type of spirituality, for the church is moving out of a period of cultural uniformity (that is, identification with European culture) and into a period of cultural diversity (that is, identification with many regional cultures around the globe). Even less will it be a reversion to one of the previous phases of Christian sacramentality (despite the sometimes narrow enthusiasm of

---

35. On this point, see Martos, *Doors to the Sacred*, chap. 5, and section 5 of chaps. 6–12.

liturgical purists, legalistic bishops, traditionalist movements, and so on). Rather, modern Catholicism will embrace all the previous phases as dimensions of its own catholic sacramentality: a sacramentality that in the past spanned centuries of change and development but that in the future will encompass continents of cultural diversity.

Modern Catholic sacramentality can therefore be designated as *pluralistic sacramentality*, for it both acknowledges the sequential pluralism of the past and looks forward to the simultaneous pluralism of the future. The period in which we find ourselves is therefore still a transitional stage, for although the differentiation of the various aspects of sacramentality is well under way, its integration has only just begun.

Individually that integration will ultimately mean less dissociation between religious beliefs and our everyday lives, and more connectedness between what we live from day to day and what we celebrate in the sacraments. Communally that integration will mean less alienation between individuals and more cooperation in a unity that is both expressed and fostered in group worship. Ecclesiologically that integration will mean less cultural hegemony and ritual uniformity at the expense of other cultures and other possible ritual forms, and more tolerance, appreciation, and encouragement for a sacramental pluriformity fitted to the needs of diverse cultures and specialized groups. Theologically that integration will mean less of an attempt to develop a single overarching sacramental theology and more attempts by individuals and groups to develop sacramental theologies that are integral with their own experience of themselves, God, and the church, and with their own understanding of the scriptures, the world, and history.

Even though recently the church's leadership has attempted to slow down the process of transformation, the social and cultural forces that are at work are so vast that nothing can stop it in the long run. Just as the Renaissance had an impact on medieval Christendom, splitting it into an array of Protestant denominations on the one hand and a monolithic but reformed Catholicism on the other, contemporary innovations are having an impact on Christianity today. Social mobility is introducing Hispanic culture to North America, African culture to Europe, and Islamic culture to both. Air travel makes it possible for Catholics to enjoy cultural diversity in some countries and to address economic disparities in others. Electronic communications media, especially the internet, make it possible for national and world events to shape the consciousness of individuals and groups in ways that are beyond the control of political and religious leaders. The changes have been so profound in recent decades that ours is sometimes called a postmodern era, but a more long-term perspective suggests that what is happening is the expansion and acceleration of cultural dynamics that began in the Renaissance, the Enlightenment, and the Industrial Revolution. Still, the environmental effects of modern consumerism may reshape the global climate, reverse centuries of population growth, and cause the collapse of modern capitalism. Then, if a truly postmodern situation emerges, the church is likely to adapt as it has in the past, celebrating the Christian mysteries in rites that are culturally appropriate and individually engaging.

Additional Reading

Liturgical Worship

Bausch, William J. *A New Look at the Sacraments*. Rev. ed. Mystic, CT: Twenty-Third Publications, 1983.

Bouley, Allan, ed. *Catholic Rites Today: Abridged Texts for Students*. Collegeville, MN: Liturgical Press, 1992.

Botte, Bernard. *From Silence to Participation: An Insider's View of Liturgical Renewal*. Washington, DC: Pastoral Press, 1988.

Bradshaw, Paul F. *Early Christian Worship: A Basic Introduction*. Collegeville, MN: Liturgical Press, 1996.

Bugnini, Annibale. *The Reform of the Liturgy 1948-1975*. Collegeville, MN: Liturgical Press, 1990.

Champlin, Joseph M. *The Proper Balance: A Practical Look at Liturgical Renewal*. Notre Dame, IN: Ave Maria Press, 1981.

Klauser, Theodor. *A Short History of the Western Liturgy: An Account and Some Reflections*. 2nd ed. New York: Oxford University Press, 1979.

Lang, Bernhard. *Sacred Games: A History of Christian Worship*. New Haven, CT: Yale University Press, 1997.

Larson-Miller, Lizette, ed. *Medieval Liturgy: A Book of Essays*. New York: Garland, 1997.

Martos, Joseph. *Doors to the Sacred: A Historical Introduction to Sacraments in the Catholic Church*. Liguori, MO: Liguori/Triumph, 2001.

Stevenson, Kenneth. *First Rites: Worship in the Early Church*. Collegeville, MN: Liturgical Press, 1989.

White, James F. *A Brief History of Christian Worship*. Nashville, TN: Abingdon Press, 1993.

Christian Initiation

Brockett, Lorna. *The Theology of Baptism*. Notre Dame, IN: Fides Publishers, 1971.

Dujarier, Michel. *A History of the Catechumenate: The First Six Centuries*. New York: Sadlier, 1979.

Jeremias, Joachim. *Infant Baptism in the First Four Centuries*. Philadelphia: Westminster Press, 1962.

McDonnell, Kilian, and George T. Montague. *Christian Initiation and Baptism in the Holy Spirit: Evidence from the First Eight Centuries*. Collegeville, MN: Liturgical Press, 1991.

Milner, Austin P. *The Theology of Confirmation*. Notre Dame, IN: Fides Publishers, 1972.

Neunheuser, Burkhard. *Baptism and Confirmation*. New York: Herder and Herder, 1964.

Eucharistic Liturgy

Dix, Gregory. *The Shape of the Liturgy*. New York: Seabury Press, 1982.

Foley, Edward. *From Age to Age: How Christians Have Celebrated the Eucharist*. Collegeville, MN: Liturgical Press, 2008.

Jungmann, Josef A. *The Mass: An Historical, Theological, and Pastoral Survey*. Collegeville, MN: Liturgical Press, 1976.

Koenig, John. *The Feast of the World's Redemption: Eucharistic Origins and Christian Mission*. Harrisburg, PA: Trinity Press International, 2000.

Rubin, Miri. *Corpus Christi: The Eucharist in Late Medieval Culture*. Cambridge, England: Cambridge University Press, 1991.

Sacraments of Healing

Dallen, James. *The Reconciling Community: The Rite of Penance*. Collegeville, MN: Liturgical Press, 1992.

Dudley, Martin, and Geoffrey Rowell, eds. *The Oil of Gladness: Anointing in the Christian Tradition*. Collegeville, MN: Liturgical Press, 1993.

Gusmer, Charles W. *And You Visited Me: Sacramental Ministry to the Sick and Dying*. New York: Pueblo Books, 1984.

Hebblethwaite, Margaret, and Kevin Donovan. *The Theology of Penance*. Notre Dame, IN: Fides Publishers, 1979.

Kelsey, Morton T. *Healing and Christianity: A Classic Study*. 3rd ed. Minneapolis: Augsburg Fortress, 1995.

Poschmann, Bernhard. *Penance and the Anointing of the Sick*. New York: Herder and Herder, 1964.

Marriage

Haughton, Rosemary. *The Theology of Marriage*. Notre Dame, IN: Fides Publishers, 1971.

Mace, David, and Vera Mace. *The Sacred Fire: Christian Marriage through the Ages*. Nashville, TN: Abingdon, 1986.

Mackin, Theodore. *What Is Marriage?* New York: Paulist Press, 1982.

————. *The Marital Sacrament*. New York: Paulist Press, 1989.

Martin, Thomas M. *The Challenge of Christian Marriage: Marriage in Scripture, History, and Contemporary Life*. Mahwah, NJ: Paulist Press, 1990.

Reynolds, Philip Lyndon. *Marriage in the Western Church: The Christianization of Marriage during the Patristic and Early Medieval Periods*. Leiden, The Netherlands: Brill, 1994.

Ministry and Ordination

Brown, Raymond E. *Priest and Bishop: Biblical Reflections*. New York: Paulist Press, 1970.

Cooke, Bernard. *Ministry to Word and Sacraments: History and Theology*. Philadelphia, PA: Fortress Press, 1976.

Edwards, Paul. *The Theology of the Priesthood*. Notre Dame, IN: Fides Publishers, 1974.

Osborne, Kenan B. *Priesthood: A History of Ordained Ministry in the Roman Catholic Church*. Mahwah, NJ: Paulist Press, 1988.

Warkentin, Marjorie. *Ordination: A Biblical-Historical View*. Grand Rapids, MI: William B. Eerdmans, 1982.

CHAPTER 5

The Sacraments in Theology

The sacraments did not always have a theology. If sacramental theology is a sustained reflection on sacramental practice and experience in the light of scripture and tradition, then we must admit that that sort of product did not exist in the early church. This is not to say that the early Christians did not understand what they were doing when they shared the Lord's Supper, when they baptized, or when they laid hands on people. But it was not until later in the patristic period that some of the church fathers began to offer somewhat theoretical explanations of what the sacraments were and how they worked.

Moreover, it was not until the Middle Ages that Catholic theologians developed a single, systematic way of understanding what today we call the seven ecclesial sacraments. The sacramental theology of the scholastics, based on the philosophical system of Aristotle, gave Christianity a more or less unified sacramental theory that, despite differences among the doctrines of Thomas Aquinas, Hugh of St. Victor, John Duns Scotus, and others, provided a common framework for understanding the nature and function of the sacraments.[1]

Scholastic concepts provided the only acceptable Catholic explanation for the sacraments until the mid-twentieth century. Today, scholasticism is one possible philosophical system among many, and so instead of there being a single Catholic sacramental theology there is a growing variety of sacramental theologies.

---

1. For a handy sketch of the history of sacramental theology, see J. R. Quinn, "Sacramental Theology," *New Catholic Encyclopedia*, vol. 12 (New York: McGraw-Hill, 1966), 789f. Scholastic presentations of sacramental theology can be found in Clarence McAuliffe, *Sacramental Theology: A Textbook for Advanced Students* (St. Louis, MO: B. Herder, 1958); and Ludwig Ott, *Fundamentals of Catholic Dogma* (Cork, Ireland: Mercer Press, 1955).

1. Theological Developments Affecting the Sacraments

The idea that there can be different ways of understanding the sacraments seems strange to Catholics who grew up with a Tridentine mentality. The Council of Trent in the sixteenth century and the church's magisterium since then repeatedly warned Catholics against entertaining explanations of the sacraments other than those provided by scholastic theology.[2]

It is important to remember, however, that even within our own tradition (that is, not including the Orthodox and Protestant traditions) there is indeed a pluralism in Catholic theology. It may be called a *sequential pluralism* since there has been a succession of theologies and theological styles through the course of the centuries. The ways that the apostolic community understood its sacramental actions was somewhat different from the ways that the fathers of the church understood them. The first Christians had an implicit understanding of what they were doing and what God was doing in their sacramental practices, and this implicit understanding was expressed both in the prayers and other words that accompanied the physical gestures, and—to some extent, at least—in the gospels and epistles of the New Testament. This implicit understanding was also expressed in sermons and essays that bishops wrote to explain the sacramental rituals for converts, for their congregations, and for the sake of refuting heresies. At the start, these explanations were very scriptural in tone and language, but eventually they became more metaphysical, adopting the language of the Greek philosophers Plato and Plotinus. Still, the fathers' explicitness of their implicit understanding of the sacraments was often more practical than theoretical in intent, and it was often more pastoral than systematic in approach.[3]

Even in scholasticism there is sometimes a noticeable difference between the interpretations of sacraments given by the early schoolmen and those given by the later schoolmen and the neoscholastics. In discussing penance, for example, Peter Abelard in the twelfth century gave much more importance to psychological factors such as shame and remorse than did John Duns Scotus in the thirteenth century in his more legalistic approach to the sacraments. Early scholasticism still mentioned physical healing as a possible effect of extreme unction, but late scholasticism regarded the sacrament

2. For excerpts from conciliar and papal documents on the sacraments, see *The Church Teaches: Documents of the Church in English Translation* (St. Louis, MO: B. Herder, 1955), 257–344; also Ott, *Fundamentals*, part 4, 2.

3. A standard reference work for patristic sources is Johannes Quasten, *Patrology,* 3 vols. (Westminster, MD: Newman Press, 1963). On the sacraments specifically, see J. N. D. Kelly, *Early Christian Doctrines* (London: Adam and Charles Black, 1958), chap. 16.

almost exclusively as a preparation for death. Some of the earliest schoolmen even doubted whether marriage should be classified as a sacrament.[4]

In addition, the more historians learned about earlier periods of Catholic history, the more they realized that prior to the period of Tridentine uniformity, there was a greater variety in the sacramental theories of patristic and medieval writers than had been previously recognized. The relative isolation of cultural centers and the slowness of copying and transporting theological works resulted in a high degree of intellectual individualism even when the basic style of theologizing was fairly uniform.[5]

The essential difference, then, between the present period of Catholic theology and the previous period is not that in the past there was agreement and today there is disagreement. Rather, it is first of all that in the past there was a sequential pluralism of approaches whereas today we have entered a period of *simultaneous pluralism*. And second, it is that in the past the slowness of communication and the relative isolation of regions ensured that theological differences often went unrecognized,[6] whereas today's differences are quickly recognized and met with responses ranging from approval to tolerance to disapproval.

One of the first persons to offer an alternative to the standard scholastic approach to the sacraments was Dom Odo Casel, a Benedictine monk in the monastery of Maria Laach early in the twentieth century. Casel was a leading figure in the liturgical movement in Germany who tried to develop a sacramental theology that deliberately took active participation in the liturgy and the experience of mystery in Christian worship as its foundation. His ideas, though never condemned by the magisterium, were long regarded with official suspicion and unofficial skepticism, and it was not until the late 1950s that his originality began to be fully appreciated.[7]

---

4. For these and other examples, see Joseph Martos, *Doors to the Sacred: A Historical Introduction to Sacraments in the Catholic Church* (Liguori, MO: Liguori/Triumph, 2001).

5. For a glimpse of this variety, see Paul F. Palmer, ed., *Sources of Christian Theology* (Westminster, MD: Newman Press), vol. 1, *Sacraments and Worship: Liturgy and Doctrinal Development of Baptism, Confirmation, and the Eucharist* (1955); vol. 2, *Sacraments and Forgiveness: History and Doctrinal Development of Penance, Extreme Unction, and Indulgences* (1959).

6. Heretical differences were of course recognized, but these were not included *within* orthodox theology. The general tendency was either to ignore the divergent views of other theologians or to harmonize what they wrote with one's own position. A good example of this latter practice is the way St. Thomas Aquinas used quotations from patristic writers in his own *Summa Theologiae*.

7. For summaries of Casel's contribution, read the articles by Burkhard Neunheuser and Charles Davis in *Worship* 34 (1960): 120–27 and 428–38; see also Odo Casel, *The Mystery of Christ, and Other Writings* (Westminster, MD: Newman Press, 1962).

As was noted in the first section of the previous chapter, it was also during this period following the Second World War that the liturgical movement began to gain momentum, partly as a result of the research that had been going on into the history of Catholic worship. That research made it clear that Christian sacramental life had been understood in other ways before the advent of medieval scholasticism, and so it opened Catholic thinkers to the possibility of explaining the sacraments in nonscholastic terms. And the desire to do this was heightened still further by the rapid expansion of Catholic biblical studies during the 1950s. Scripture scholars were discovering that scholastic philosophical categories were often ill-suited for interpreting what the Bible was saying, and so systematic theologians began to search for other philosophical systems that might provide a better intellectual framework for their discussion of revelation.[8]

They found what they were looking for, at least initially, in contemporary existentialism and phenomenology, two sometimes overlapping philosophical methods that emphasized the examination of particularly human realities and focused on the experience of being a person. Although neither philosophy was explicitly religious (some of their leading proponents were avowedly agnostic or atheistic), Catholic theologians discovered that they could use existential thinking and phenomenological analysis to explore the experience of being a Christian and to examine specific religious realities such as faith.

Foremost among the Catholic scholars who began to use these philosophical methods as an intellectual foundation for their own theologizing about the sacraments were Edward Schillebeeckx in Holland and Karl Rahner in Germany. In 1952 Schillebeeckx published *De sacramentele Heilseconomie* (*The Sacramental Economy of Salvation*), in which he examined the traditional scholastic theology of the sacraments from a historical, doctrinal, and theological perspective. He was careful, moreover, not to deny the validity of the traditional explanation of salvation and the sacraments, and in 1957 he showed the compatibility of existentialist and scholastic categories in *Christ, the Sacrament of the Encounter with God*. Rahner's broad philosophical framework may be termed neoscholasticism or transcendental Thomism, but it grew partly out of a thoroughgoing attempt to integrate the valid insights of scholasticism with the philosophical analyses of Martin Heidegger. In his short work *The Church and the Sacraments*,

---

8. See Elmer O'Brien, *Theology in Transition: A Bibliographical Evaluation of the "Decisive Decade," 1954–1964* (New York: Herder and Herder, 1965), esp. 174–211. Also, T. M. Schoof, *A Survey of Catholic Theology, 1800–1970* (Glen Rock, NJ: Paulist Newman Press, 1970) presents the broader context for these developments, 121–224.

Rahner showed that he too, like Schillebeeckx, was concerned with providing a more contemporary philosophical foundation for traditional sacramental theology.

As the work of scripture scholars, church historians, liturgical experts, and philosophical theologians found its way into Catholic thinking about the sacraments, there occurred what can only be called a massive shift in sacramental theology. Scriptural studies forced a reexamination of the belief that Christ had personally instituted each of the sacraments, but more importantly, they suggested that the sacraments should be studied not within abstract treatments of supernatural grace but within the concrete context of salvation history and the redemption wrought by Christ's death and resurrection.[9] Patristic and other historical studies suggested that sacraments had to be understood not as isolated acts of individuals but as communal events in the life of the church and as ecclesial participations in the priesthood of Christ.[10] Liturgical studies indicated that a more adequate appreciation of the sacraments necessitated a whole series of shifts from attendance at Mass to participation in the liturgy, from administration and reception of sacraments to celebrations of the Christian mysteries, and from a focus on rubrics and validity to an awareness of dynamics and appropriateness.[11] Finally, both neoscholasticism and modern philosophies insisted that it was better to speak of sacraments as signs rather than causes of grace, in personalistic rather than mechanistic fashion, using experiential rather than metaphysical categories.[12]

For a while in the 1960s it seemed as though Catholic theologians had succeeded in combining the old and the new into a stable and satisfactory synthesis. In 1963 the council's Constitution on the Sacred Liturgy called for an updating of the church's sacramental life, based in large measure on this broadened understanding of sacramental theology. For the remainder of the decade and well into the 1970s, great efforts were put into the practical

---

9. See François-Xavier Durrwell, *The Resurrection: A Biblical Study* (New York: Sheed and Ward, 1960), esp. chap. 8; and *In the Redeeming Christ* (New York: Sheed and Ward, 1963), esp. part 2.

10. See Aimé Georges Martimort, *The Signs of the New Covenant* (Collegeville, MN: Liturgical Press, 1963); Colman E. O'Neill, *Meeting Christ in the Sacraments* (New York: Alba House, 1964).

11. See Massey H. Shepherd, ed., *The Liturgical Renewal of the Church* (New York: Oxford University Press, 1960), chaps. 1 and 2; Lancelot Sheppard, ed., *The People Worship: A History of the Liturgical Movement* (New York: Hawthorn Books, 1967).

12. See John H. Miller, *Signs of Transformation in Christ* (Englewood Cliffs, NJ: Prentice-Hall, 1963); J. Stephen Sullivan, ed., *Readings in Sacramental Theology* (Englewood Cliffs, NJ: Prentice-Hall, 1964).

work of liturgical reform and the educational task of informing both clergy and laity about the nature and purpose of the revised rites.[13] And while these practical tasks were absorbing most of Catholicism's liturgical energies there seemed to be little forward movement in sacramental theory.

Unfortunately, however, neither the liturgical renewal nor the educational efforts of theologians and catechists had uniformly happy results. In many ways the liturgy became more meaningful, but Mass attendance dropped. The sometimes legalistic practice of penance became a more interpersonal process of reconciliation, but confession lines dwindled. Seminary and clerical life became less monastic, but vocations to the priesthood fell off. Marriage became viewed less as a contract and more as a covenant, but the divorce rate among Catholics increased.[14] So it was not long after the reforms had been put into effect that liturgists and theologians themselves began to wonder about the theology on which the reforms were based, and to look more deeply into the nature and purpose of sacraments.

The result is that alternative sacramental theologies began to be examined more seriously. It is not that any one of them was regarded as the new sacramental theology that would eventually replace the synthesis of the 1960s; rather, in a culturally more modern fashion, they were looked upon as diverse ways of interpreting the sacraments within a variety of theological contexts.

From the current variety of sacramental theologies we can of necessity take only a sampling. We shall begin with the scholastic approach since it has held such a central place in Catholic thought since the Middle Ages, and even though it is no longer used as a philosophical base by most sacramental theologians, it is still found in the 1983 revision of canon law and in parts of the 1994 Catechism of the Catholic Church. After that, we shall take a brief look at the beginning of the shift away from this scholastic perspective toward a more pastoral approach taken by the bishops at the Second Vatican Council. Finally, we shall examine five contemporary approaches that illustrate the diversity of Catholic thinking in recent decades.

---

13. For the complete texts and official introductions, see *The Rites of the Catholic Church*, 2 vols. (Collegeville, MN: Liturgical Press, 1990). For commentaries on the new rites, see James D. Crichton, *Christian Celebration: The Sacraments* (London: Geoffrey Chapman, 1973).

14. Of course the changes in sacramental theology and practice did not in themselves cause these things to happen, but they did in some ways enable them to happen by suggesting that if official change is possible then unofficial change is also possible, and they certainly did not prevent these things from happening. For a good sampling of what theologians were thinking about the changes, one can read many of the articles in the liturgical journal *Worship* written during the 1960s and '70s.

2. The Scholastic Approach

The traditional theological context for understanding the sacraments in the Roman Catholic Church has been that of scholasticism, a system of ideas developed by men who taught in medieval universities and schools of theology. These schoolmen or scholastics (as they came to be known) used the writings of the Greek philosopher Aristotle as a basis for their systematic approach to understanding all of reality.[15] In areas such as physics and astronomy, biology and anatomy, logic and psychology, ethics and politics, and so on, they often borrowed from Aristotle's ideas in a fairly straightforward manner, developing as they did so their own scholastic philosophy. But in discussing the Christian mysteries of the Trinity, grace, redemption, the church, and the sacraments, they had to rethink much of what they found in Aristotle's metaphysics and integrate it with what they derived from the Christian tradition, to develop what became known as scholastic theology.[16]

Traditional scholasticism, however, was not a homogeneous synthesis of conclusions that all Catholic thinkers agreed to, for there were many details over which theologians disagreed. Rather, it embraced a unified set of assumptions about the way to approach theological questions and about how to bring the scriptures, the writings of the fathers, established doctrines, canon law, and church practice into the task of developing a theoretical understanding of the Christian mysteries. The basic soundness of this theological method is attested to by the way it provided a foundation for Catholic theology for over seven centuries. Medieval thinkers such as Thomas Aquinas and John Duns Scotus, and later ones such as Francis Suarez and Cardinal Cajetan, all worked within the scholastic framework, as did lesser-known Catholic theologians. This framework was also adopted by the Council of Trent in the sixteenth century, which was convened to counteract the Protestant revolt, and which ushered in a long period of relative stability in all □ * of Catholic theology, including sacramental theology.[17]

*This symbol in the margin indicates an interactive question that can be found at http://www.TheSacraments.org.

15. As an introduction to this period, see Richard E. Rubenstein, *Aristotle's Children: How Christians, Muslims, and Jews Rediscovered Ancient Wisdom and Illuminated the Dark Ages* (Orlando, FL: Harcourt, 2003); Frederick Copleston, *A History of Medieval Philosophy* (London: Methuen, 1972); Josef Pieper, *Scholasticism: Personalities and Problems of Medieval Philosophy* (London: Faber and Faber, 1960).

16. See Yves Congar, *A History of Theology* (New York: Doubleday, 1968), chaps. 3 and 4; also Martos, *Doors to the Sacred*, chap. 3, and sec. 3 of chaps. 8–12.

17. Because of the implicit approval that the council gave to this approach, scholastic theology is sometimes referred to as Tridentine theology.

Despite differences in detail, then, the scholastic approach to the sacraments sanctioned by the Council of Trent worked with a fundamental set of key concepts that were developed during the Middle Ages, and that provided an intellectual framework for explaining the meaning and purpose of the church's sacramental worship. From an Aristotelian point of view, the church is a "perfect society," which is to say that it has within it everything that is needed for its existence and for the fulfillment of its ends.[18] As a human society, the church needs members and it needs order; but as a society whose ends are supernatural, the church needs the means to bring its members, and indeed the whole world, to salvation. Thus Christ in founding the church also instituted the sacraments as the means by which individuals become members of the church (baptism), are strengthened by the Holy Spirit (confirmation), enter into communion with Christ (Eucharist), are forgiven for their sins (penance), and prepare for life hereafter (extreme unction). In addition, Christ provided two sacraments whose purpose is social rather than individual, one for the preservation of the family and the propagation of offspring (matrimony), and one for the governance of the church and the continuation of the sacramental economy of salvation (holy orders). As can be easily imagined, this is a view of the sacramental system that made great sense in the relatively stable and simple life of the Middle Ages.

Moreover, if one uses Aristotelian categories to understand the essential nature of sacraments, they quite obviously fall under two categories, signs and causes. That they are signs is clear from the fact that they are not realities in themselves but indicators of unseen supernatural realities such as divine grace and forgiveness. That they are causes is equally clear from the fact, attested to by official doctrine and by the rites themselves, that they effect certain changes in the souls of individuals and have definite consequences for the life of the church.[19] The sacraments are thus signs that have supernatural effects: they are effective or efficacious signs.

But what is it that the sacraments cause? It is at this point that we reach the limits of Aristotelian metaphysics and must introduce a distinctly Christian category, namely, grace.[20] In one sense, all good things are gifts from God, or graces, but more specifically Christian theology uses the term grace to refer to the gift of divine life that makes people morally good and able

---

18. See Ott, *Fundamentals*, 275f.

19. I have tried to give a more complete account of why the sacraments were regarded as causes in the Aristotelian sense of that term in *Doors to the Sacred*, 62–64.

20. For a thorough treatment of sacraments and grace within a scholastic context, see Bernard Leeming, *Principles of Sacramental Theology* (Westminster, MD: Newman Press, 1956), chaps. 1–3.

to lead holy lives. For this reason it is called sanctifying grace. It comes from God, either directly or through certain channels such as the sacraments. Sacraments are thus instrumental causes of grace, and evidence of this can be seen in the fact that the basic way that Christians achieve holiness is by being baptized and confirmed in the church, by going to confession and Mass regularly, and by entering into a particular state of life through matrimony or holy orders. All sacraments therefore confer sanctifying grace, but in addition each sacrament confers a supernatural strengthening that enables the recipient to be holy in a specific way, such as avoiding a confessed sin (penance) or being a devoted spouse (matrimony).

Now if sacraments are instrumental causes of grace (God being the primary cause), it follows that the sacramental rituals themselves, not the ministers who perform them, are the channels through which the effects are received. All sacramental effects are thus received *ex opere operato*, through the performance of the ritual (literally, by the work worked), and not *ex opere operantis*, through the minister of the sacrament (literally, by the work of the worker). It matters little, therefore, whether a person is baptized by one priest or another, or whether a person goes to one confessor or another; what matters is that the ritual be properly performed, for it is the ritual itself through which the effect is communicated. If the rite is properly performed in all its essentials, it is said to be valid, and grace is bestowed *ex opere operato*. If the rite is improperly performed, then it is invalid, which is to say it is not a true sacrament at all.[21]

This simple schema, however, is complicated by the fact that grace is not the only effect that results from sacramental rituals. In the Mass, the effect of the words of consecration is the Blessed Sacrament, as the Eucharist came to be known. Moreover, baptism, confirmation, and holy orders cannot be repeated more than one time for the same individual because they are said to confer an indelible character. But neither the Eucharist nor the character is simply a sign (*sacramentum tantum*) or simply the reality (*res tantum*) of grace. In fact, the Eucharist seems to be something of both, for it is both a sign of Christ's presence and the reality of his body and blood. Likewise, the sacramental character is both a sign that one has been baptized, confirmed, or ordained, and a supernatural reality because it makes one permanently a member of the church, a confirmed Christian, or a priest. It is therefore both a sign and a reality (*sacramentum et res*), a sacramental reality that is produced by the valid performance of the ritual, either on the altar at Mass or in the soul of the individual for whom the rite is performed.

21. On sacramental efficacy and validity, see ibid., chaps. 1 and 8.

Once the theological schema is complete in this way—so that one can speak about the sacramental ritual as a sign (*sacramentum tantum*), the effect of grace as a supernatural reality (*res tantum*), and the other effect as both sign and reality (*sacramentum et res*)—one can legitimately and coherently speak of "administering" and "receiving" sacraments. Note, however, that the sacrament that is administered and received in and through the ritual is the *sacramentum et res*, the sacramental reality. In the Eucharist it is the Blessed Sacrament, given and received in Communion. In the three sacraments that can be performed for a person only once, it is the sacramental character. In matrimony it is the marriage bond, a sacramental reality that lasts until the death of one of the spouses. In penance and extreme unction the precise sacramental reality is harder to determine (this being one of the details over which the scholastics came to no firm agreement).[22] Viewed thus within the scholastic framework, each sacramental ritual has not one but two effects, the sacramental reality and grace, and this second effect can be further subdivided into sanctifying grace and the particular grace of each sacrament.   □

If all this sounds rather objective and mechanical, it is partly due to the fact that the Aristotelian-scholastic system was a static one that could not easily account for variability or individual differences. As an intellectual method it tried to find the unchanging nature of things, or their "essence"; and although it acknowledged the existence of incidental differences, or "accidents," it did not deal with them in any systematic fashion. In sacramental theology, this meant that scholasticism sought to determine the essential nature of sacrament in general, and the essence of each of the seven sacraments, but it did not pay attention to the particulars of actual performance, the dynamics of social interaction in the sacraments, or the changes in the rituals over the course of time. It was a static system, which is precisely the type of intellectual system that one would expect to find in the medieval world, which had a stable culture and a stratified society. Nevertheless, the scholastics did recognize that there were, in the administration and reception of the sacraments, certain subjective and personal elements that had to be taken into account.   □

Regarding the administration of the sacraments, even though the minister does not have to be holy in order to perform a ritual that is an instrumental cause of grace, at the very least he has to have the right intention. That is, he has to intend to perform a valid sacramental action in accordance with the regulations of the church, so that it will have the effects ascribed to it in

22. See ibid., 265.

the church's teachings. Regarding the reception of the sacraments, what is likewise needed is the right intention, which here means the willingness to receive the appropriate sacramental effects. With at least a minimal intention, then, a person can receive the sacramental reality, but to receive the fullest effects of a sacrament—namely, all the grace that is offered through it by God—a more positive preparation and receptive disposition is required.[23]

In this way, therefore, scholastic theology attempted to account for the basic objective and subjective elements that medieval Christians were aware of in their sacramental rituals. As already noted, the fundamental soundness of the scholastic approach is attested to by its ability to provide an intellectual foundation for Catholic reflection on the sacraments until well into the twentieth century. At the same time, however, its fundamental weakness was its inflexibility, attested to by its inability to be swayed by Protestant charges of spiritual malaise and popular superstition in sacramental practices, and attested to by its inability to admit the insights of modern philosophies into its system. Thus it was perhaps inevitable that once Catholics themselves began to voice some dissatisfaction with the Tridentine sacraments, and once scriptural and historical studies began to contribute insights that could not easily be handled within scholasticism, Catholic thinkers began to look for alternative ways of understanding and explaining the sacraments.

3. The Approach of Vatican II

What is remarkable about the achievement of the Second Vatican Council in calling for a renewal of the church's sacramental and liturgical life is that the Catholic bishops did so without appealing to any explicit theology of the sacraments, such as that of scholasticism. In this respect the council fathers were like the early fathers of the church, who preached and wrote about Christian worship in a pastoral rather than speculative manner, using biblical rather than metaphysical language. The bishops' appeal for reform was therefore based not on philosophical presuppositions but on their own experience of the inner dynamics of worship and their own awareness of the social need for more modern forms of sacramental practice. Recent studies in church history and liturgiology enabled the bishops to see that changes in the past sanctioned the possibility of further changes in the present, and even to perceive the direction that such changes should take.

---

23. A rather clear exposition of this aspect of sacramental theology is given in Joseph Pohle and Arthur Preuss, *The Sacraments: A Dogmatic Treatise*, vol. 1 (St. Louis, MO: B. Herder, 1943), 161–203.

Nevertheless, in the early 1960s the bishops could not foresee the full impact that loosening the bonds of ritual rigidity would have on the church's liturgical and intellectual life. What the Second Vatican Council gave the church, therefore, was not a new theology of the sacraments but a new attitude toward sacramental worship. It was an attitude that was biblical rather than scholastic, and pastoral rather than academic.   □

The council's biblical attitude toward worship is clearly expressed in the introductory section of the Constitution on the Sacred Liturgy:

> The liturgy daily builds up those who are in the church, making of them a holy temple of the Lord, a dwelling-place for God in the Spirit (see Eph 2:21-22), to the mature measure of the fullness of Christ (see Eph 4:13). At the same time it marvellously enhances their power to preach Christ and thus show the church to those who are outside as a sign lifted up among the nations (see Is 11:12), a sign under which the scattered children of God may be gathered together (see Jn 11:52) until there is one fold and one shepherd (see Jn 10:16). (SC 2)[24]

Especially in the opening paragraphs of chapter 1 of the constitution, the council fathers again and again use the language of the scriptures to describe the nature and importance of liturgical worship. For example, they observe that "by Baptism men and women are implanted in the paschal mystery of Christ; they die with him, are buried with him, and rise with him (see Rom 6:4; Eph 2:6; Col 3:1; 2 Tim 2:11). . . . Similarly, as often as they eat the Supper of the Lord they proclaim the death of the Lord until he comes (see 1 Cor 11:26)" (SC 6). They invoke the image of Christ the high priest developed in the Epistle to the Hebrews and connect it to the concept of the church as the body of Christ presented in the letters of St. Paul. "The liturgy, then, is rightly seen as an exercise of the priestly office of Jesus Christ," which is both "an action of Christ the priest and of his body, which is the church" (SC 7). And from this unity of Christians with each other and with their Lord in their worship, especially eucharistic worship, they conclude that

> the liturgy is the summit toward which the activity of the church is directed; it is also the source from which all its power flows. For the goal of apostolic endeavor is that all who are made children of God by faith and Baptism should come together to praise God in the midst of his church, to take part in the sacrifice and to eat the Lord's Supper. (SC 10)   □

---

24. See Austin Flannery, ed., *Vatican Council II: The Basic Sixteen Documents* (Northport, NY: Costello Publishing Co., 1996).

Likewise, the bishops' pastoral attitude is evident from the opening lines of the document itself:

> The sacred council has set out to impart an ever-increasing vigor to the Christian lives of the faithful; to adapt more closely to the needs of our age those institutions which are subject to change; to encourage whatever can promote the union of all who believe in Christ; to strengthen whatever serves to call all of humanity into the church's fold. (SC 1)

This pastoral rather than doctrinal perspective is also apparent from the beginning of chapter 3, which is on the sacraments and sacramentals:

> The purpose of the sacraments is to sanctify people, to build up the body of Christ, and, finally, to worship God. Because they are signs they also belong in the realm of instruction. They not only presuppose faith, but by words and objects they also nourish, strengthen, and express it. That is why they are called sacraments of faith. (SC 59)

Finally, the broadness of the bishops' perspective on the liturgy is clear from the range of issues with which they deal in discussing renewal and reform: attention to liturgical language, vestments, and ceremonies; education for both clergy and laity; the importance of liturgical leadership and active participation; the influence of art, architecture, and music on worship; the redesign of all the church's sacramental rites, with allowances made for regional differences and even individual preferences.

The same pastoral attitude toward the sacraments pervades the other conciliar documents as well. In the Constitution on the Church (*Lumen Gentium* 42), Christians are exhorted to grow in the love of God and of one another through prayer and service, through scripture and the sacraments. In the Decree on the Bishops' Pastoral Office in the Church (*Christus Dominus* 30), pastors are reminded that they should encourage frequent sharing in the sacraments and intelligent participation in the liturgy. And in the Decree on the Ministry and Life of Priests (*Presbyterorum Ordinis* 5), the sacraments are described in pastoral terms rather than defined in dogmatic ones: "By Baptism priests make men and women part of the people of God; by the sacrament of Penance they reconcile sinners with God and the church; by the anointing of the sick they console those who are ill; and especially by the celebration of Mass, they offer Christ's sacrifice sacramentally."[25]

---

25. This same descriptive and scriptural language is also found in the more lengthy section on the sacraments in the Constitution on the Church (LG 11).

It should also be noted that, despite repeated references to earlier church documents in footnotes, and despite occasional language reminiscent of doctrinal formulas, the Constitution on the Sacred Liturgy makes a strong effort to balance the traditional notion of sacraments as causes of grace with the reminder that they are, above all, signs of grace: "In the liturgy the sanctification of women and men is given expression in symbols perceptible by the senses and is carried out in ways appropriate to each of them" (SC 7). The sacraments "do, indeed, confer grace, but, in addition, the very act of celebrating them is most effective in making people ready to receive this grace to their profit, to worship God duly, and to practise charity" (SC 59). In a similar way the document repeatedly tries to correct the implicit individualism of scholastic sacramental theology by stressing the fact that the liturgical sacraments are communal celebrations, stating that the church's leaders earnestly desire "that all the faithful should be led to take that full, conscious, and active part in liturgical celebrations which is demanded by the very nature of the liturgy" (SC 14).   □

In a very real sense, the bishops of the Second Vatican Council did as much for sacramental theology in what they did not say as in what they did say, for they did not speak about the sacraments in traditional scholastic terminology. Without denying the legitimacy of such a conceptual framework for interpreting the nature and function of sacraments in the Christian, they refused to endorse it as the only possible framework, and they introduced correctives to time-honored imbalances when they did use it. Moreover, by extensively employing the language of the Bible in speaking about the sacraments, they used a language that is fundamental to any theology of the sacraments, and therefore a language that is open to many theological contexts. For the task of sacramental theology is not only to relate liturgical worship to the scriptures and to Christian living but also to examine it critically and interpret it within a coherent intellectual framework.

4. Existential and Phenomenological Approaches

In the decades after Vatican II, the most popular sacramental theology was the one developed by Edward Schillebeeckx and Karl Rahner in the fifties and sixties. As already noted, it provided the first philosophical alternative to scholasticism in the modern church, and for years it provided the intellectual framework for sacramental theology courses taught in Catholic colleges and seminaries.[26]   □

26. The principal work of Schillebeeckx on the sacraments that is available to English-speaking readers is *Christ, the Sacrament of the Encounter with God* (New York: Sheed and

This approach may be termed existential because it tries to deal with the sacraments concretely rather than abstractly, that is, it seeks to understand what goes on in actual liturgies and what actually results from participating in sacramental rituals. The approach may also be termed phenomenological because the method it uses to reach this existential understanding is one of attending to the phenomenon of sacramental religion, describing what is revealed in and through religious acts, and providing a theological interpretation of them. It may even be called an experiential approach to the sacraments because the basic phenomena that it attends to are religious experiences, both the personal experiences of individual participants in the sacramental rituals and the social experience of believers whose religious lives are centered on the sacraments. Although the interpretations that Schillebeeckx and Rahner each give to sacramental experience are slightly different, their approaches are similar enough that they may be regarded as using the same basic method in developing their sacramental theology.[27]

Both theologians regard sacraments basically as symbols or symbolic activities, and so underlying their sacramental theory is a philosophical interpretation of symbolism. Understood phenomenologically, any reality that we experience is a symbolic reality in the sense that its outward appearance (the phenomenon) is a sign (a symbol) of what it actually is (its existential being). One can even turn this analysis around and say that "all

---

Ward, 1963). The central ideas in this work are summarized in his article "The Sacraments: An Encounter with God," in *Theology Digest* 7 (Spring 1960): 117–21. Other works on the sacraments include *Marriage: Human Reality and Saving Mystery* (New York: Sheed and Ward, 1965); *The Eucharist* (New York: Sheed and Ward, 1968); and *Ministry: Leadership in the Community of Jesus Christ* (New York: Crossroad, 1981).

Karl Rahner's main contribution to sacramental theology first appeared in English as *The Church and the Sacraments* (New York: Herder and Herder, 1963), but many of the ideas it contains are given a more contemporary treatment in chapter 8 of *Foundations of the Christian Faith: An Introduction to the Idea of Christianity* (New York: Seabury Press, 1978). Rahner has also published numerous articles on the sacraments that have been collected in the volumes of his *Theological Investigations* (New York: Crossroad Publishing Company), the principal ones on the general subject of sacraments being: "Concerning the Relationship between Nature and Grace," vol. 1, 297–317; "Personal and Sacramental Piety," vol. 2, 109–33; "Reflections on the Experience of Grace," vol. 3, 86–90; "The Theology of the Symbol," vol. 4, 221–52; "The Sacramental Basis for the Role of the Layman in the Church," vol. 8, 51–74; "The Presence of the Lord in the Christian Community at Worship," vol. 10, 71–83; "What Is a Sacrament?" vol. 14, 135–48; "Introductory Observations on Thomas Aquinas' Theology of the Sacraments in General," vol. 14, 149–60; "Considerations on the Active Role of the Person in the Sacramental Life," vol. 14, 161–84. Also helpful is his more popular treatment, *Meditations on the Sacraments* (New York: Seabury Press, 1977).

27. I have given separate treatment to Schillebeeckx and Rahner in *Doors to the Sacred*, 110–14.

beings are by their nature symbolic" because they necessarily "express themselves in order to attain their own nature."[28] That is, the existential nature of any being is both embodied in and manifested through something that is a sign of its inner reality. "The symbol strictly speaking (symbolic reality) is the self-realization of a being in the other, which is constitutive of its essence."[29]

Although this general analysis applies to all the beings of our experience, its most important application in sacramental theology is to personal beings. For human beings, the body and physical acts incorporate and thus make real what they are as persons and what they are becoming. "The body is not only the manifestation of the human person who [is revealed]; it is also the medium in which the soul externalizes its personality development. Thus corporeity becomes a sign of the innermost acts of the person."[30] For example, people become athletes and scholars, saints and sinners, by choosing to perform different sorts of bodily acts; the result is both that they become incarnations of those various types of persons and that they reveal what they have become in what they do. Thus, existentially and phenomenologically, any person is a symbolic reality, an incarnate sign of what he or she really is.[31]

Moreover, it is only in physical, experienceable activities that persons meet other persons: "The mutual encounter of persons takes place in and through the body."[32] Therefore, if people are to meet God as a person, the meeting must take place in and through physical signs, that is, symbols or sacraments. "From God's viewpoint, the encounter is revelation; from [the human being's] viewpoint, religion. Both revelation and religion then, as the mutual encounter of the created [being] with the uncreated God, are essentially . . . sacramental."[33] Just as we meet other human beings, reveal ourselves to and learn about each other through our bodily presence and physical gestures, so also we meet the divine being, embodying our existential attitude toward God in religious acts and discovering what is revealed

28. Rahner, "The Theology of the Symbol," 224.
29. Ibid., 234.
30. Schillebeeckx, "The Sacraments," 118. See also the almost identical (but philosophically more abstruse) statement by Rahner in "How to Receive a Sacrament and Mean It," *Theology Digest* 19 (Summer 1971): 232.
31. For a fuller exposition of this analysis of symbolism and its application to sacramental theology, see John R. Sheets, "Symbol and Sacrament," *Worship* 41 (1967): 194–210; Piet Fransen, "Sacraments, Signs of Faith," in *Intelligent Theology*, vol. 1 (Chicago: Franciscan Herald Press, 1969), 126–48.
32. Schillebeeckx, "The Sacraments," 118.
33. Ibid., 117.

to us in those same acts. And such acts are sacraments, for they are "a living, personal encounter with God."[34]

In the Christian economy of salvation, however, these individual sacramental acts are secondary or, more precisely, tertiary. The first or primordial sacrament is Jesus Christ, the incarnate Word of God. As Rahner puts it, "the incarnate Word is the absolute symbol of God in the world, filled as nothing else can be with what is symbolized."[35] As Son of the Father, Christ is the Logos, the second person of the Trinity, and as such he is the complete and perfect manifestation of the Godhead within the Godhead itself. But the Logos became flesh in the humanity of Jesus of Nazareth. Therefore, Jesus in his humanity "is the self-disclosure of the Logos itself, so that when God [moves toward external self-expression], that very thing appears which we call the humanity of the Logos."[36] Thus, "Christ in his historical existence is both reality and sign of the redemptive grace of God," which is the inner life of the Trinity.[37]

But Christ as the human externalization of the Trinity was not meant to be a sign of God only to those who lived twenty centuries ago; he is also a revelatory symbol of God for all ages. "The man Jesus, as the personal visible realization of the divine grace of redemption, is *the* sacrament, the primordial sacrament, because this man, the Son of God himself, is intended by the Father to be in his humanity the only way to the actuality of redemption."[38] Jesus was not only the Truth, the true symbol of the Father; he was and still is the Way, the means to the Father. "Human encounter with Jesus is therefore the sacrament of the encounter with God."[39] It is in and through Christ that believers meet God and experience the presence and power of his saving grace. "The encounter of the believer with Christ, the primal sacrament (*Ursakrament*) remains the fundamental act of the Christian religion as a personal communion with the three divine Persons."[40]

But where do people encounter Christ and through Christ come into contact with the saving grace of God? The most important place that this happens is in the church, the body of Christ, now existent in time and space. "The Church is the abiding presence of that primal sacramental word of definitive grace, which is Christ in the world, effecting what is uttered by

34. Ibid.
35. Rahner, "The Theology of the Symbol," 237.
36. Ibid., 239.
37. Rahner, *The Church and the Sacraments*, 15.
38. Schillebeeckx, *Christ, the Sacrament*, 15.
39. Ibid.
40. Schillebeeckx, "The Sacraments," 118.

uttering it in sign."[41] A second but fundamental sacrament in the Christian economy of salvation is therefore the institutional church, the church that was instituted by Christ to continue his work of bringing people into existential contact with God the Father, just as Jesus did. "When we say that the Church is the persisting presence of the incarnate Word in space and time, we imply at once that it continues the symbolic function of the Logos in the world."[42] Thus the church is the fundamental sacrament, the foundational reality that lies at the basis of all the visible acts of the church that manifest Christ to the world and open a channel between individuals and God's saving grace. "As the ongoing presence of Jesus Christ in time and space, as the fruit of salvation which can no longer perish, and as the means of salvation by which God offers salvation to an individual in a tangible way in the historical and social dimension, the church is the basic sacrament."[43]

It is within this context that we can situate the seven ecclesial sacraments (as well as the sacramentals and other "sacraments broadly defined," such as the sacred scriptures[44]). According to Rahner, the sacraments are "acts of the Church, as the basic sacrament of the world's salvation, realizing itself concretely in the life-situation of the individual."[45] In Schillebeeckx's words, "A sacrament, that is an act of the primordial sacrament which is the Church, is a visible action proceeding from the Church as a redemptive institution."[46] Remembering the theory of the symbol that states that the inner nature of any being becomes an existing reality by becoming embodied in something that symbolizes its own inner nature, we can say that just as the Word of God came to real existence in our world by becoming incarnate in the person and deeds of Jesus, so also the risen Lord continues his real existence in history by being embodied in the institution and acts of the church. And the sacraments are essentially acts of the church. "The sacraments make concrete and actual, for the life of the individual, the symbolic reality of the Church as the primary sacrament and therefore constitute at once, in keeping with the nature of the Church, a symbolic reality."[47]

---

41. Rahner, *The Church and the Sacraments*, 18. See Schillebeeckx, *Christ, the Sacrament*, 41.

42. Rahner, "The Theology of the Symbol," 240.

43. Rahner, *Foundations of the Christian Faith*, 412.

44. See Rahner, "The Theology of the Symbol," 221f.; "What Is a Sacrament?" 140; "Introductory Observations on Thomas Aquinas' Theology of the Sacraments in General," 152.

45. Rahner, "How to Receive a Sacrament and Mean It," 233.

46. Schillebeeckx, *Christ, the Sacrament*, 52.

47. Rahner, "The Theology of the Symbol," 241.

Looked at from God's side, therefore, "the seven sacraments are fundamentally an operation of the heavenly Christ that is sacramentalized in the
visible, authorized operation of the Church."[48] Looked at from the believer's
side, however, the sacraments are occasions for encountering that supernatural
operation of the heavenly Christ (another word for which is grace) within
the natural world of human experience.[49] Phenomenologically, then, authentic
sacramental celebrations have what Schillebeeckx calls a "dialogue structure,"
for they are moments of meeting between God and persons, they are occasions of interplay between the divine and the human. Existentially understood,
"the sacraments are not things, but rather personal, living encounters with
the glorified Jesus and, in him, with the living God."[50]

In some ways, this new way of understanding sacraments was a radical
departure from the scholastic method that had been used by Catholic theologians for centuries. In another way, however, it was a return to the way
that theology was done by the best scholastic thinkers such as St. Thomas
Aquinas and St. Bonaventure. In the thirteenth century, the schoolmen took
the non-Christian philosophies of ancient Greeks and used them to better
understand Christian doctrines and practices. Analogously, in the twentieth
century, Rahner and Schillebeeckx took the non-Christian philosophies of
existentialism and phenomenology and used them to interpret not only
traditional beliefs and sacramental practices but also the innovations of the
Second Vatican Council. Although their writings were sometimes regarded
as heretical by ultraconservatives who felt that only scholastic theology
could be authentically Catholic theology, both Rahner and Schillebeeckx
were steadfastly loyal to the magisterium and went to great lengths to show
that what they wrote did not contradict Catholic doctrine. Because of this
loyalty, and because of their intellectual brilliance and painstaking scholarship, neither was ever condemned by the Vatican and both continue to be
highly regarded today.

5. A Liberation Approach

The same cannot be said for liberation theology. At the same time that
existentialism was popular in Europe, Marxism was becoming increasingly
popular among socialists and leftists in Central and South America. For if
the primary philosophical question in the developed world was "What is

48. Schillebeeckx, "The Sacraments," 119.
49. See Rahner, "Reflections on the Experience of Grace," 86–90; also, Aidan Kavanagh,
"Sacrament as an Act of Service," *Worship* 39 (1965): 92–94.
50. Schillebeeckx, "The Sacraments," 119.

the meaning of my existence?" the burning issue in the underdeveloped world was "Why are we poor and oppressed?" The writings of Karl Marx, who sought to understand the reasons for poverty and oppression in nineteenth-century Europe, seemed to offer valuable insights for understanding the politics and economics of twentieth-century Latin America. The problem was that the writings of Marx had also been used to justify Communism in the Soviet Union, Eastern Europe, and China.[51]

☐

After the bishops at the Second Vatican Council set aside the scholastic approach to Catholic teaching in favor of a more biblical and pastoral approach, however, and after Schillebeeckx and Rahner demonstrated that it was possible to use modern philosophies to understand Christian beliefs and practices, the door had been opened to the process of rethinking theology even further. In Central and South America, the need for a radically new style of Catholic theology was first felt by priests and seminarians who saw that the church had, for the most part, identified itself with the ruling class, the "power elites" in their countries. At the same time, the Latin American church had for centuries done little to alleviate the misery of the rural peasants and the urban poor, the "powerless masses" who constituted perhaps nine-tenths of the population. They sensed that the situation of these Christians was not unlike that of the Israelites enslaved in Egypt, and they saw that the Jesus of the gospels was primarily concerned with the weak and the poor; and yet traditional theology seemed to tell people to accept their suffering and wait patiently for heaven. Moreover, these (mostly young) theologians had learned from sociology and political philosophy (especially Marxism) that the symbolic images that people accept as the basic structures of reality largely determine the way they think and react to the world around them. Thus these theologians saw a need to rebuild Christian theology from the ground up, to begin with their intuition that any authentic theology had to be concerned about the oppressed, and that the images that it presents of God, church, salvation, and so on must enable people to recognize and liberate themselves from oppression.[52]

☐

Among the theologians who attempted to rethink the meaning of Christianity in the light of their politically oppressive social situation, only Juan

---

51. For the historical background, the work of Enrique Dussel is especially helpful. See his *History and the Theology of Liberation: A Latin American Perspective* (Maryknoll, NY: Orbis Books, 1976); *Philosophy of Liberation* (Maryknoll, NY: Orbis Books, 1985); and *Beyond Philosophy: Ethics, History, Marxism, and Liberation Theology* (Lanham, MD: Rowman and Littlefield, 2000).

52. For an introduction and overview of liberation theology, see Hugo Latorre Cabal, *The Revolution of the Latin American Church* (Norman: University of Oklahoma Press, 1978);

Luis Segundo dealt extensively with the nature and purpose of the church's sacraments.[53] Segundo argued that for centuries the sacraments in the Latin American church (and by extension, the rest of the church) have been for all practical purposes magical rites and instruments of political oppression. What they ought to be, however, are signs that raise awareness of moral responsibility and encourage social liberation. He therefore proposed that the old magical theology of the sacraments should be discarded in favor of a new and more critical sacramental theology.[54] To appreciate how Segundo arrived at this radical conclusion, however, we need first to look at some of his theological premises.

Like many other liberation theologians, Segundo contends that authentic Christianity is "this-worldly" and not "other-worldly." For untold millennia, religion assumed that the sacred was separate from the profane, that the gods lived in a world outside history. Along with this, religious morality was fundamentally a reflection of the existing social order, and so myth and ritual taught people to accept that order as sacred and to conform their behavior to it. Even ancient Judaism, he believes, did not free itself entirely from this religious mentality, for it still saw God as utterly transcendent and morality as an unimaginative conformity to the divine will.[55] With the coming of Christ, however, this outlook was exactly reversed. God's revelation in Jesus is that the transcendent reality is radically immanent in human

---

Thomas M. McFadden, ed., *Liberation, Revolution, and Freedom: Theological Perspectives* (New York: Seabury Press, 1975); Rosemary Radford Reuther, *Liberation Theology: Human Hope Confronts Christian History and American Power* (New York: Paulist Press, 1972). For some basic writings by liberation theologians themselves, see Gustavo Gutierrez, *A Theology of Liberation: History, Politics, and Salvation* (Maryknoll, NY: Orbis Books, 1973); Leonardo Boff, *Liberating Grace* (Maryknoll, NY: Orbis Books, 1979); Jon Sobrino, *Christology at the Crossroads: A Latin American Approach* (Maryknoll, NY: Orbis Books, 1978).

53. See Juan Luis Segundo, *A Theology for Artisans of a New Humanity* (Maryknoll, NY: Orbis Books), vol. 1, *The Community Called Church* (1973); vol. 2, *Grace and the Human Condition* (1973); vol. 3, *Our Idea of God* (1974); vol. 4, *The Sacraments Today* (1974); vol. 5, *Evolution and Guilt* (1974). For his understanding of the task of theology today, see *The Liberation of Theology* (Maryknoll, NY: Orbis Books, 1976). For a comprehensive introduction to Segundo's work, see Alfred T. Hennelly, *Theologies in Conflict: The Challenge of Juan Luis Segundo* (Maryknoll, NY: Orbis Books, 1979).

54. For a summary of these points, see Hennelly, *Theologies in Conflict*, 96–98; Segundo, *The Liberation of Theology*, 40–43. Segundo is of course thinking primarily of scholastic sacramental theology and the sort of sacramental ritualism that it is sometimes used to justify.

55. Many scripture scholars and contemporary theologians, it should be noted, would not agree with this; it seems that on this point Segundo's use of the Old Testament is rather one-sided. Of course there are also other theologians who would disagree with him on other points as well.

history, and the good news of Jesus is that people have the God-given power to love one another creatively in shaping their own destiny. Thus grace is simply "[God's very being] made into our existence"; it is the human spirit, "the Spirit that dwells in us."[56] Seen in this light, salvation is a work of liberation, a work of people freeing themselves with God's help from domination by physical, psychological, and social forces. "God has no plan for us except to associate us with the divine creative work in the history of the universe."[57] But this implies that Christianity is fundamentally secular rather than religious in the traditional sense of the word. "At bottom, secularization means that everything in the Church, absolutely everything, must be translated from 'religious' terms into [the human] task in history."[58]

But what about Jesus? Didn't Christ come to establish a new religion and to give human beings the sacraments as a means of salvation? No, says Segundo, if by religion you mean the worship of a transcendent God outside history, and if by sacraments you mean cultic rituals by means of which individuals can get to heaven. Although one can find isolated texts in the scriptures to prove that the church should have religious rituals, "a complete reading of the New Testament does not suggest, at first glance, that Jesus meant to establish any sacred rites—in the strict sense of the term."[59] Religious rites before the time of Christ were strictly magical, for magic in tribal and other religions is intrinsically an attempt to produce supernatural effects through human actions.[60] Furthermore, "one of the essential elements of the gospel seems to be that the community formed to succeed Jesus is not going to have sacred rites, gestures or words endowed with divine power. In short it is not going to have magic signs that lead people to salvation."[61] On the contrary, Segundo's "complete reading of the New Testament" forces him to conclude that "the overall context indicates that [everyone's] whole destiny depends on just and cordial relations with [one's] neighbor. This is so true that the necessity of righting these relations takes precedence over strictly religious functions."[62] Arguing from Hebrews 10, which describes

---

56. Segundo, *Grace and the Human Condition*, 169.
57. Ibid, 169f. See also 30–35.
58. Segundo, *Our Idea of God*, 78.
59. Segundo, *The Sacraments Today*, 22.
60. "Magic, reduced to its essential elements, consists of the quest for an efficacy that goes beyond [human] powers. It achieves this by recourse to superior powers, whom it tries to get to operate in a specific way through symbolic gestures. These gestures, taking on superhuman power but nevertheless controlled by [humans] through symbolism, will produce the proper effect directly" (Segundo, *The Community Called Church*, 37f.).
61. Segundo, *The Sacraments Today*, 22.
62. Ibid. To support this contention, he cites Matt 5:21-24 and John 4:20-24.

how Christ's unique priesthood did away with the need for temple sacrifice, Segundo reasons that "human beings, then, no longer need sacred intermediaries or sacred mediations."[63] And he analyzes John 6, Ephesians 2, and Colossians 1 and 2 to show that the commonly accepted interpretation of these passages is mistaken: salvation does not come through faith *and* baptism but through faith *or* baptism, for Christian baptism intrinsically assumes the presence of active faith; and so it is always faith, not the ritual of immersion in water, that effects the saving transformation of people's □ lives.[64]

This does not deny the fact that Jesus used the common ritual gestures of his culture and that some of these (such as sharing a meal of fellowship) were picked up and repeated by his followers. But it does deny that these gestures were intended by Jesus or experienced by his followers as anything more than communal signs of social realities. "So far as we know, the Christian living in the primitive Church saw these distinctive signs of his community" not as "something useful or even necessary for eternal life" but as "spontaneous gestures in a community that was [already] in possession of eternal life."[65] What today we call sacraments were at that time ritual expressions of things that were really happening in the Christian community: the sharing of life and goods, the alleviation of physical and emotional suffering, the welcoming of newcomers into a redeemed life through faith in Jesus, the reconciliation of people with one another, the designation of certain individuals to particular tasks in the church, and so on. On the one hand, these communal gestures were consciousness-raising signs through which Christians became aware of what God through his Spirit was doing in human history, and especially in their own lives. But on the other hand, they were also efficacious signs because they made grace tangibly available to the church in its mission of transform □ ing human society, of bringing about God's kingdom on earth.

With the wholesale adoption of Christianity as the religion of the Roman Empire, however, people brought into the church those very same "religious" attitudes that Jesus had deliberately rejected. "In passing from a Christian practice rooted in conversion, in which God's revelation appealed to liberty, to a mass Christianity, the formulas of faith and ritual formulas tended to be simplified and made more immediate."[66] That is, salvation was thought to result immediately from saying the right words and performing the proper

---

63. Ibid., 23.
64. See ibid., 25f. Along these lines, he notes on p. 44 that in 1 Cor 1:11-17, "Paul himself had to fight against the notion that baptism had an almost automatic religious effectiveness."
65. Ibid., 42.
66. Segundo, *The Community Called Church*, 37.

rituals. And this, in essence, is magic. The mass baptism of barbarians during the Dark Ages only perpetuated the magical attitude in the church. Theologians in the Middle Ages and afterward uncritically supposed that this attitude was proper to Christianity, and so they tried to differentiate Catholic rituals from pagan ones on the basis of efficacy, claiming that the Christian rites are "the only efficacious ones. The other rites deceive people; their effect is not truly achieved."[67] In fact, however, Christianity in practice if not in doctrine had become another magical religion. ☐

Segundo says he believes that in its official teachings the church successfully avoided turning Christian magic into dogma, but that at the popular level the *ex opere operato* effectiveness of the sacraments, their conferral of grace and their imparting of indelible marks on the soul were almost always understood magically. Thus in practice the relation between the church and its sacred signs came to be exactly the opposite of what it had originally been: instead of sacraments building up the church and pointing to what had to be done in the world, the church dispensed sacraments for individuals and pointed to a salvation beyond this world. The result was a sort of "bank-deposit" view of sacraments, a belief that a sacrament "communicates something that is assumed to be accumulable" in the soul, namely, grace.[68] ☐

Nor was this view socially benign, for it allowed for the exploitation of the poor while giving them assurances that they were rich in grace, which was much more important than material possessions. The popular conception of sacraments as magic rites thus allowed them to become instruments of domestication through which the ruling class (which included the clergy) kept the poor and uneducated masses in many countries economically enslaved and ignorant of the liberating content of the message of Christ. And Segundo contends that this attitude persists in Latin America, where "the current sacramental system is a pacifying ideological element which helps to maintain the present status quo of society."[69] ☐

Segundo claims that the church itself has recognized the need to separate itself from the magical attitudes of the past, for the bishops at Vatican II said: "A more critical ability to distinguish religion from a magical view of the world and from the superstitions which still circulate purifies religion and exacts day by day a more personal and explicit adherence to faith" (GS 7).[70] In the years following the council, it seemed that the church was listening

67. Segundo, *The Sacraments Today*, 21.
68. Ibid., 92.
69. Ibid., 112.
70. See Segundo, *The Sacraments Today*, 6, 13. The translation of *Gaudium et Spes* cited is in Walter M. Abbott, *The Documents of Vatican II* (New York: Herder and Herder, 1966).

to liberation theology's prophetic call for justice. Pope Paul VI's encyclical *The Development of Peoples* called for a more just world order. At a 1968 conference in Medellin, Colombia, the bishops of Latin America explicitly called for the full emancipation of the poor from every form of servitude. In 1979, at their next regional conference in Puebla, Mexico, the same bishops declared that Christ has a "preferential option for the poor," and they urged all Christians to treat the world's poor with justice and compassion. In Segundo's eyes, these developments showed that the hierarchy had begun to repudiate the easy identification of the church with other-worldly salvation.

If one were to appraise his contribution, one would have to say that Segundo offered no new, fully developed sacramental theology but a new approach to the sacraments based on a radically secular conception of the church. He did not deny the existence of God or the reality of the incarnation or the need for the sacraments or the power of grace, but he did call for a sweeping reinterpretation of Christian doctrines in this-worldly terms. Seen from such a perspective, the church is the community of those who are doing God's will, making Christ present in the world and making grace alive in history through their concern for others. The church's mission is to be a means of salvation for the world by "effectively inserting itself into a love that is already existing, operative and supernatural" so that it "builds up humanity in history."[71] If it does this, then the church is "the sign of [humanity's] fashioning of history in freedom" that God wants it to be; that is, it is a sacrament in a very down-to-earth sense, "a visible community of human beings living in real-life contact with the rest of humankind that, through its existential actions, contains, manifests, and communicates the saving presence of Christ"[72] by contributing toward truly human solutions to economic, political, and social problems.

But a church that is sacramental to the world cannot exist without signs that are sacramental for its members, making God's liberating energy present among them, speaking a prophetic word in their midst, and enabling them to take effective steps toward the establishment of the kingdom.

> On the occasion of each sacrament it should present the Christian people with their present, concrete, existential situation. It should pose this situation as a problem that challenges them and calls for their response. And it should also show divine revelation to be an element capable of helping them to face up to this challenge.

71. Segundo, *The Sacraments Today*, 7.
72. Segundo, *Our Idea of God*, 79.

The community's response, in turn, must take place on two levels: that of intellectual awareness and understanding, and that of action. When the Christian community organizes itself in sacramental terms, it orients itself toward action designed to meet an historical challenge in a reflective and critical way.[73]

For a liberation approach to the sacraments, maintains Segundo, demands that we "conceive and live and reformulate them in function of a community whose liberative action is secular and historical—as the gospel indicates."[74]   ☐

Beginning in the 1980s, however, the church's leadership turned away from the secularizing path charted by liberation theology. Pope John Paul II, who had fought against atheistic Communism in Poland for most of his life, was not convinced that the ideas of Karl Marx could be reconciled with Christianity, and he did not believe that emphasizing a secular interpretation of the gospel was good for an increasingly secular and Godless culture. When bishops who championed liberation theology retired, the Vatican replaced them with more orthodox-minded bishops. Seminaries that promoted liberation theology were closed, professors who taught liberation theology were transferred, and priests were encouraged to return to a more traditional spirituality. But for a while in Latin America, there flourished an alternative not only to scholastic theology but also to the popular European approach to sacramental theology.

6. Foundational/Transformational Approaches

Schillebeeckx and Rahner pioneered new ways of looking at and talking about sacraments, and it was largely because they showed how Catholics could develop new theologies that were in conformity with church teaching that the bishops at Vatican II decided not to endorse scholastic theology but to take a more pastoral and biblical approach. Those two theologians were present at the council and contributed to its deliberations, suggesting (among other things) that one could refer to Christ as a sacrament and the church as a sacrament, and in fact the latter idea was adopted and used in a number of council documents.[75]

After the council, a second generation of theologians continued the effort to speak about the sacraments in ways that were consistent with

---

73. Segundo, *The Sacraments Today*, 104.
74. Ibid., 93.
75. LG 1, 9; GS 42, 45; also Decree on the Mission Activity of the Church (*Ad Gentes*) 1, 5.

traditional beliefs yet contemporary in their language and concerns. Two of these were the Americans Bernard Cooke and Donald Gelpi. As in the case of Schillebeeckx and Rahner, the details of their sacramental theologies were different, but their approaches have enough in common that they can be treated together. Both theologians acknowledge the transformative power of rituals, for the tradition has always held that the sacraments are effective signs, so each in his own way attempts to explain how sacraments work without resorting to Aristotelian analysis or medieval thinking.[76]

Although both writers intentionally bring human experience into their thinking on sacraments, Gelpi's approach is often more deliberately descriptive, presenting in great detail the process of conversion that is envisioned by the Rite of Christian Initiation of Adults (often referred to by Catholics as the RCIA) designed and introduced after the Second Vatican Council. Gelpi describes five different forms of conversion—religious, affective, intellectual, moral, and sociopolitical—and although it is only the first of these that is intentionally fostered during the catechumenate (as the time of preparation for baptism is called), he believes that the others will follow if converts continue to work out the implications of their decision to follow Christ.[77] He shows how marriage and ordination, viewed as sacraments of two different Christian vocations, celebrate decisions in the process of ongoing conversion, confirming and fostering the baptismal call to service.[78] The rite of reconciliation "deepens . . . the experience of repentance and ongoing conversion," while the rite of anointing "transforms the experience

76. Bernard Cooke's extensive writings on the sacraments include *Christian Sacraments and Christian Personality* (New York: Holt, Rinehart and Winston, 1965); *Ministry to Word and Sacraments: History and Theology* (Philadelphia: Fortress Press, 1976); *Sacraments and Sacramentality* (Mystic, CT: Twenty-Third Publications, 1983, 1994); *Reconciled Sinners: Healing Human Brokenness* (Mystic, CT: Twenty-Third Publications, 1986); and (with Gary Macy) *Christian Symbol and Ritual: An Introduction* (New York: Oxford University Press, 2005).

Much of Gelpi's work is both foundational and systematic. His books include *Charism and Sacrament: A Theology of Christian Conversion* (New York: Paulist Press, 1976); *The Divine Mother: A Trinitarian Theology of the Holy Spirit* (Lanham, MD: University Press of America, 1984); *Committed Worship: A Sacramental Theology for Converting Christians*, 2 vols. (Collegeville, MN: Liturgical Press, 1993); *The Turn to Experience in Contemporary Theology* (New York: Paulist Press, 1994); *The Firstborn of Many: A Christology for Converting Christians*, 3 vols. (Milwaukee, WI : Marquette University Press, 2000); *The Gracing of Human Experience: Rethinking the Relationship between Nature and Grace* (Collegeville, MN: Liturgical Press, 2001).

77. The analysis of conversion, its relation to traditional theological concepts, and its application to the sacraments of initiation take up the entire first volume of *Committed Worship*.

78. Gelpi, *Committed Worship*, vol. 1, chaps. 1–4.

of serious illness into an opportunity for converting more deeply to God."[79] Although Gelpi does address traditional questions about the nature of Christ's presence in Communion, his major focus is on the transformative effect of the eucharistic liturgy, first as the ritual culmination of the adult conversion process, and second as an engine of ongoing conversion.[80]

Both Gelpi and Cooke regard conversion as the foundation of the Christian life, but whereas Gelpi extensively describes the process of conversion in relation to participation in liturgical rites, Cooke attempts to explain the process by analogy to other human experiences. First and foremost among these are the experiences of love and friendship.

Many people have had the experience of falling in love—perhaps love at first sight, perhaps a gradual realization, or perhaps after being told that they were loved. Regardless of the initial circumstances, however, entering into a loving relationship is a very down-to-earth example of conversion, and being in a loving relationship brings about a felt change in consciousness: it transforms the way we feel not only about the other person but also about ourselves and the world around us. It gives us a new way of looking at life; in technical terms, it gives us a new hermeneutic of experience. It even affects the way we behave.[81]

Traditional Catholic theology spoke about changes in the soul that were caused by certain sacramental rituals: baptism imprints the image of Christ, confirmation bestows the seal of the Spirit, ordination confers the priestly character, and marriage creates an unbreakable bond. Cooke proposes that these spiritual effects should be understood on the analogy of close friendship and caring love, a relationship that not only changes the way people see things but also gives them the power to do what they are incapable of doing if they have no friends and are feeling unloved. This analogy has a solid basis in scripture, which talks about God's love being poured into our hearts (Rom 5:5; 1 John 4:7), an image that should be taken seriously but not literally. Scholastic theology also spoke of sacraments giving grace, but again, this must not be taken mechanically.

> Insofar as Christian rituals celebrate an active life of charity, they give grace. Insofar as Christian rituals strengthen the sick, pardon sinners, heal the broken, they give grace. Insofar as they celebrate and strengthen the Christian commitment to a life of maturation in selfless love, they give

---

79. Ibid., vol. 2, 249.
80. Ibid., vol. 1, 262–68; vol. 2, 223–47.
81. See Cooke, *Sacraments and Sacramentality*, 30–33, 81–84; also "Love as Grace" in *Christian Symbol and Ritual*, 51.

grace. Insofar as they celebrate and support a loving friendship and caring family life, they give grace.[82]

Love and friendship, like all good things, are gifts from God and can therefore be regarded as grace. They are gifts that save us from loneliness and isolation, despair and depression, selfishness and temptation, addiction and greed, anger and hatred, as well as other sins and shortcomings because they fill our lives with what is truly rewarding and fulfilling. Knowing that God loves us, and allowing the realization of that love to affect our outlook on life, has a real power to make us better than we would otherwise be. "To the extent that this divine love can be accepted into one's life and appreciated for what it is, it has a transforming (that is, saving) effect. This means that God's love for humans is the ultimate humanizing influence in their experience."[83]

Although we cannot experience God directly, we can understand something of God's love by reflecting on human love. In this sense, human love is symbolic, or a sacrament, of divine love. For just loving and caring for others enables people to develop and grow, so also accepting God's love for us enables us to change our lives and become more fully human by caring for others and the world around us. "Perhaps the most basic sacrament of God's saving presence to human life is the sacrament of human love and friendship."[84]

Basing his theology on this central insight, Bernard Cooke does not begin his treatment of individual sacraments with baptism, as is usually done, but with marriage. A Christian marriage of mutual self-giving embodies and exemplifies the transforming effect of grace, as we have already seen. A healthy family also models the acceptance and belonging, support and encouragement that characterize what happens when one is baptized into a Christian community. Loving parents communicate their spirit to their children and strengthen them with their parental gifts, which is what confirmation celebrates in the family of God called the church. In caring families, offenses are forgiven and hurts are mended, paralleling reconciliation and healing in the larger community. In a very real sense, loving family members minister to one another, laying down their lives for one another in many ways, large and small, in the same way that those who are ordained minister to the people of God. And when family life is celebrated around the table—if not always in hurried everyday meals, then at least in special

---

82. Cooke, *Sacraments and Sacramentality*, 52.
83. Ibid., 25.
84. Ibid., 81; see also 82, 86.

celebrations—then the meal is one of thanksgiving (the original meaning of eucharist) in which God's presence can be felt in the family's love and unity.[85]

Human learning occurs in proportion to the intensity or duration of the learning experience. Learning one's native language is not an intense experience, but over the course of a few years all children learn their mother tongue. By the same token, a brief but intense experience such as climbing a mountain or being in a car crash can teach us something that is never forgotten. In the same way, the more involved people are in religious rituals—for example, being baptized as an adult or becoming an ordained minister—the more likely it is that its symbolic words and actions will have a transforming impact on the way they think and feel. But it is also true that sacramental celebrations such as weekly Eucharist or annual feasts such as Christmas can have a slow but cumulative effect on our consciousness, altering our hermeneutic of experience and making us more Christlike, especially when this gradual conversion is supported by an active community of faith.[86] Thus Cooke can say that "sacraments are specially significant realities that are meant to transform the reality of 'the human' by somehow bringing the person into closer contact with the saving action of Jesus Christ."[87]

The new meanings that sacraments communicate to people—and these are also meanings that are communicated through the scriptures, through church teachings, and by the Christlike action of others—are God's gifts for human salvation, and in that sense they are grace. "Grace is the transformation of individuals and communities at the deepest level of their being and meaning; it is also a transformation of their finality, their basic destiny."[88] Given a new hermeneutic of experience, a new way of interpreting what happens to them and what happens in the world around them, Christians are able to think, feel, and behave differently than they otherwise would. Thanks to what has been revealed in the scriptures, what has been accomplished in Christ, and what is communicated in the sacraments, Christians in a very real way are a new creation, bringing new life to a sinful world. "They are a transforming influence; they are creative of a distinctive dimension of human history" by proclaiming the good news that salvation has been accomplished by Christ, that they are loved by God, and that their lives can be transformed by grace.[89] In the end,

85. Ibid., chaps. 7–20.
86. See ibid, chap. 3.
87. Ibid., 8.
88. Ibid., 237.
89. Ibid., 235.

Grace is the transformation of human persons under the impact of God's loving self-gift in Christ. This transformation comes about through the reinterpretation of life's experiences in the light of Jesus' life, death and resurrection. Christian sacraments are those elements of Christians' life experience that mediate this reinterpretation and thereby transform human existence into new and unending life.[90]

7. A Postmodern Approach

After the beginning of modern science (physics, chemistry, biology, geology, etc.) and the invention of modern technologies that put early scientific discoveries to practical use (manufacturing, transportation, communication, medicine, etc.), the Western world was generally optimistic about the prospects for civilization and human betterment. During the second half of the twentieth century, however, some European intellectuals became increasingly disillusioned with modernity's promises of progress and prosperity. In their view, centuries of advancement had culminated in death and destruction—World War I, the Great Depression, World War II, and the Cold War—which they saw as resulting from simplistic thinking that reduced the complexity of reality to ideas that had to be either true or false, right or wrong. Eventually called postmodernists, they preferred ambiguity to clarity, variety to order, individuality to hierarchy, and interconnectedness to structure, claiming that these preferences better reflect the world as it is and life as it is lived.[91]

Postmodern attitudes pervaded many areas of avant-garde art and culture, but it was developments in philosophy, sociology, and linguistics that eventually had an impact on theology. Jean-Francois Lyotard argued that the broad claims of modernity (such as human freedom and objective science) and the grand narratives of Western culture (such as the progress of history) had collapsed in the face of irrational social forces and nonrational emotions that pervade contemporary human existence. Jacques Derrida promoted a literary method known as deconstruction, which analyzed modern beliefs and theories (for example, notions of culture and status) in order to expose hidden dualisms and unconscious assumptions in modern thought and society. Jean Baudrillard blurred distinctions between appearance and illusion,

90. Ibid., 238.
91. For an overview that includes art, architecture, literature, literary criticism, and philosophy, see Hans Bertens, *The Idea of the Postmodern: A History* (New York: Routledge, 1995); also Steven Best and Douglas Kellner, *The Postmodern Turn* (New York: Guilford Press, 1997).

presence and absence, sign and referent, proclaiming that nothing is what it seems to be and everything is other than it is.[92]

Martin Heidegger, although not generally regarded as a postmodern philosopher, approached foundational philosophical concerns such as being and nonbeing in a way that both rejected modern philosophy and influenced many self-avowed postmodernists. In fact, Heidegger's critique of philosophy extended all the way back to Plato and Aristotle, who in his mind focused so much attention on beings or entities that they lost sight of the mystery of being or existence.[93] It was Heidegger's critique of Western metaphysics (also known as ontology) that convinced Louis-Marie Chauvet that it was both desirable and necessary to develop an understanding of sacraments that is not tied to archaic modes of thought and that could speak to Catholics with a postmodern sensibility.

Following Heidegger, Chauvet rejects what he calls "onto-theology," or using metaphysical categories in theology, in favor of an even more radical phenomenological analysis than Rahner's. Unlike the description of scholasticism presented earlier in this chapter,[94] Chauvet sees scholastic theology as an attempt to explain sacraments in terms of "techno-productionist thinking" that regards grace as a "thing" that is "produced" in sacramental ritual[95]—a charge that can more accurately be leveled against nineteenth- and twentieth-century scholastics to whom Chauvet was exposed early in his theological training.[96] Having found this version of scholasticism intellectually wanting, Chauvet sets out to develop an understanding of sacraments that is more in tune with postmodern thought.

---

92. For a sample of writings by and about postmodern authors, see Steven Seidman, ed., *The Postmodern Turn: New Perspectives on Social Theory* (New York: Cambridge University Press, 1994); Walter Truett Anderson, ed., *The Fontana Postmodernism Reader* (London: Fontana Press, 1996); Michael Drolet, *The Postmodernism Reader: Foundational Texts* (New York: Routledge, 2004).

93. Martin Heidegger's major work is *Being and Time* (New York: Harper and Row, 1962), originally published in German in 1927.

94. See also my other summaries of scholastic method in sacramental theology in *Doors to the Sacred*, 51–64, 163–68, 240–43, and other places where Thomas Aquinas and thirteenth-century scholasticism are discussed.

95. See Louis-Marie Chauvet, *Symbol and Sacrament: A Sacramental Reinterpretation of Christian Existence* (Collegeville, MN: Liturgical Press, 1995), chap. 1: "Critique of the Onto-theological Presuppositions of Classical Sacramental Theology," 7–45. *Symbole et Sacrement* was originally published in 1987.

96. See Louis-Marie Chauvet, *The Sacraments: The Word of God at the Mercy of the Body* (Collegeville, MN: Liturgical Press, 2001), xiv–xvii, where he describes what he calls the objectivist model of sacraments, exemplified in the 1947 catechism that he knew as a boy. *Les Sacrements* was originally published in 1997.

While Chauvet accepts many of the conclusions of postmodern thinkers about language and culture, he does not go along with their rejection of grand narratives and their embrace of deconstruction, for to do so would mean rejecting the scriptures and tearing Christian doctrines to pieces. Instead, he accepts the notion that theology is a matter of "faith seeking understanding,"[97] and he employs a very Heideggerian method to understand the church's faith in its sacraments. In doing so, he meticulously analyzes what Catholics see happening in their liturgical rituals, phenomenologically dismantling and reconstructing them in a way that should be satisfying to twenty-first-century believers.

Chauvet begins with the observation, well-established by phenomenology, that the world as we know it is mediated by language. Without denying that there are realities that are unknown (for example, people's secret thoughts and desires) and even unknowable (for example, the inner life of the Trinity), Chauvet points out that, without language, it is not only impossible to speak about reality, but it is even impossible to think about reality because language gives us the ability to name what we perceive and wonder about. Language enables us to interact with the world around us because it is the milieu in which we live. It is a sort of womb in which we are born, a matrix within which we become who we are, know ourselves, and perceive everything else in reality. It is also like a lens through which we look at ourselves and everything else.[98]

In this respect, language is symbolic, for a symbol connects us to what it symbolizes, whether it is something physical like an object or an action, or something nonmaterial like an idea or a value. By thinking in words, we think about the realities behind the words, as it were. Still, there is not a one-to-one correspondence between language and reality, not only because many words have a rich complexity of meaning, but also because it is possible to think about what is only imaginary. On the positive side, the imaginary includes ideals and goals that lead us toward objectives that are not yet real. On the negative side, the imaginary includes falsities and illusions that do not correspond to anything real. The culture and society in which we live, and into whose language world we are born, govern what is real and what is imaginary, and set the rules for both.[99]

Symbolic rituals play a unique role in the cultural environment within which we live, for they too are a type of language. Whether or not they use words, rituals create and maintain the nonmaterial realities they symbolize.

97. Ibid., ix.
98. See ibid., 6–13.
99. See ibid., 14–17.

A simple ritual such as shaking hands both symbolizes and helps bring about a friendly relationship. A more elaborate ritual such as a wedding ceremony makes people married in the eyes of society. Conversely, by denying access to the wedding ceremony, society can deny couples the social standing and legal benefits of marriage. Symbolic rituals thus have important and even powerful social effects, and it is not necessary to appeal to metaphysics to understand or explain those effects. Language itself has hidden power.

By the very fact that Christians live in a community called the church, they have a social identity that comes to them through scripture and ritual, and that is expressed in both ecclesial and secular action. In other words, Christian identity is mediated by the church. But the church is also a sacrament in the sense declared by Vatican II, for it is a symbolic structure that mediates the reality of God to people.[100]

Christian identity (and by extension, Christian existence) therefore has three dimensions—scripture, sacrament, and ethics—and the three are necessarily connected with one another:

> How could the reading of the Scriptures still be genuinely Christian if it were not connected both to the liturgy where the act of proclamation in the church assembly attests preeminently that these Scriptures are the word of God for today and to the ethical life in which they demand to be embodied?
>
> How could participation in the sacraments still be genuinely Christian if it were not connected both to Scripture—which found liturgy not merely as the celebration of God but also as the celebration of the God revealed in the life, death, and resurrection of Jesus—and to the ethical life—by which Christians are called to "veri-fy," that is, "make true" what they have celebrated and received in the sacraments?
>
> How could ethical practice still be genuinely Christian if it was not confronted by the Scriptures, its source, and at the same time rooted in the liturgical celebration? . . . What makes ethical life a Christian reality is . . . not its "matter" but its "form" which is given it by love understood as a response to God's love, which came first (1 Cor 13).[101]

For Chauvet, the ethical dimension of Christian existence is as important as the other two, for "the ethics of dailiness, sanctified by theological faith and charity"[102] is as much a place of Christian worship as the liturgical

---

100. See ibid., 28–31; also *Symbol and Sacrament*, 171–80.
101. Chauvet, *The Sacraments*, 41.
102. Ibid., 63.

assembly. It is in daily life that the world is transformed into the kingdom of God and God's reign is established on the earth. To the extent that they have heard and responded to the challenge of the scriptures, Christians give thanks to God for the gifts they have received, especially the gift of salvation in Jesus Christ. In doing so, they become what the scriptures reveal and what the sacraments celebrate, thus embodying and actualizing in history the gifts they have received.[103]

Having established that Catholics live in a language world mediated by the church, which gives Catholics their Christian identity and mediates the reality of God, Chauvet is able to explain the efficacy of the sacraments without resorting to medieval metaphysics. As we have already seen, language in general and symbolic rituals in particular have the ability to create and maintain spiritual realities that are meaningful to anyone who lives within a given language world. "Baptism, which is precisely the sacrament of entrance into the church"[104] is the ritual action through which individuals become situated in an ecclesial reality that has a definite structure, tradition, and worship. "In order to be a Christian, one must belong to the church. The church is primary."[105] From this follows the famous aphorism, *Lex orandi, lex credendi*, the law of prayer is the law of faith, or more freely translated, the prayer of the church is the faith of the church, or even, what we pray in the liturgy is what we believe. Therefore, what happens in the sacraments is what the church believes happens in the sacraments, and this in turn is spelled out in the rites themselves.[106]

Catholic tradition and theology often speak about the effects of the sacraments in terms of grace, but too often grace has been taken to be something that is able to be quantified (additional grace), used (for getting into heaven), or given a value (as spiritual merit). Chauvet insists, however, that grace is not a thing, not even a spiritual thing. Rather, it is a characteristic of a gratuitous gift, undeserved and freely given by God. For this reason, it is better to speak about God's graciousness rather than about God's grace.[107]

Through baptism, for example, people's relationship to God is radically restructured. They become children of God, brothers and sisters to Christ

---

103. See ibid., 54–66; also *Symbol and Sacrament*, chap. 7. For a valuable summary, see Timothy M. Brunk, *Liturgy and Life: The Unity of Sacrament and Ethics in the Theology of Louis-Marie Chauvet* (New York: Peter Lang, 2007), esp. chap. 2.

104. Chauvet, *The Sacraments*, 32.

105. Ibid., 31.

106. See ibid., 33f.; also *Symbol and Sacrament*, 381, 484.

107. See Chauvet, *Symbol and Sacrament*, 108.

and to one another. Through the performance of a ritual, "the paternity of God, the body of Christ, and the temple of the Spirit are rendered effective in our world."[108] The sacrament truly changes the baptized, but this transformation is not magical. Rather, it is brought about by the power of language, analogous to the way that an inauguration ceremony bestows a new identity on a person being sworn into public office. Whereas the one being sworn in may have earned the office by winning an election, the new relationship of the baptized to God is not in any way earned; it is totally the result of God's graciousness. ☐

It must be understood, nonetheless, that this interpretation of baptismal transformation (or the change effected in any of the sacraments) does not explain everything; indeed, grace is "irreducible to any explanation."[109] And so it is still mysterious, as the Catholic tradition proclaims. Nor can the reception of grace be reduced to "the socio-linguistic mechanism of symbolic efficacy." The reality of grace is more than that, but it is through the church's liturgical and theological language that it can be named and perceived. Furthermore, spiritual effects can be attributed to the church's sacramental rites, and such attribution is valid within the language world of the church even though "this intra-linguistic efficacy" may not be accompanied by "an extra-linguistic efficacy concerning the gift or reception of grace itself."[110] In other words, we never know whether the proclaimed effects really occur in people's lives because we have no way of observing those interior effects. Thus questions about baptizing children of nonpracticing parents, about confirming unprepared adolescents, and so on, remain pastoral problems but they do not present theological problems. ☐

Chauvet introduces the phrase "the presence of the absence" as a way of understanding how Christ is present in the sacrament, especially the Eucharist, even though he is not physically present. The Second Vatican Council spoke of Christ being present not only in the consecrated bread and wine but also in the worshiping assembly, in the minister, and in the proclamation of God's word during the liturgy. In these cases, Christ's presence is an acknowledged presence and maybe even a perceived presence but not a physical presence, which is the way that Catholics too often take the term "real presence." Chauvet points out that in the early centuries of Christianity, "real presence" referred to the presence of Christ in the church, especially the church at worship, and "mystical presence" referred to the

---

108. Ibid., 443.
109. Ibid.; italics removed. The next quotation is taken from the same page.
110. Ibid., 444.

presence of Christ in the Eucharist. During the Middle Ages, however, the consecrated elements came to be called "the real body of Christ" and the church came to be called "the mystical body of Christ." This change in terminology, Chauvet believes, resulted in an overemphasis on Christ's presence in the Eucharist and a misinterpretation of the nature of that presence.[111]

Chauvet notes that an essential characteristic of any symbol is the absence of the symbolized, for if the symbolized were present, there would be no need of a symbol to represent it. The absence of the symbolized is therefore always present in any symbolic activity, whether it be speaking in words or performing a ritual. So the eucharistic ritual—more properly understood as the whole liturgy rather than as the memorial of the Last Supper and the words of consecration—makes Christ present not as one who is physically there but as one who is really there for the believer. Yet this is not a purely subjective presence, for the absence of the symbolized is characteristic of all symbolic activity; so if Christ is a reality, then the Eucharist is a symbol of a real presence.[112]

In both *Symbol and Sacrament* and *The Sacraments*, Chauvet uses the story of Christ and the disciples on the road to Emmaus (Luke 24:13-35) to ground his interpretation of Christ's real presence in the church, in the sacraments, and in the world. In the biblical narrative, two disciples are walking to Emmaus after the crucifixion when they encounter a stranger who reinterprets that event for them and urges them not to be discouraged by the apparently calamitous turn of events. When they get to the town, they invite the stranger to join them for supper, and when he blesses and breaks bread with them, they recognize him as Jesus—and he vanishes from their sight. Following the lead of recent scripture scholarship, Chauvet takes this story not as a narrative of a historical event but as a paradigm of what happens in Christian worship: Christ is really present in the eucharistic meal, but when we recognize him we realize that he is not to be seen. Nonetheless, our hearts are filled and we are motivated to action.[113]

The Eucharist is thus "the symbolic place of the on-going transition between Scripture and Ethics, from the letter to the body," from hearing God's word to putting it into action. As Chauvet puts it,

---

111. See Chauvet, *The Sacraments*, 139f. Also Brunk, *Liturgy and Life*, 62ff. Chauvet relies on the historical interpretation provided by Henri de Lubac in *Corpus mysticum: L'eucharistie et l'Église au Moyen Âge* (Paris: Aubier, 1944).

112. See Chauvet, *Symbol and Sacrament*, 98f., 177f., 404ff.

113. See ibid., 161–70; also *The Sacraments*, 22–28.

The liturgy is the powerful pedagogy where we learn to consent to the presence of the absence of God, who obliges us to give him a body in the world, thereby giving the sacraments their plenitude in the "liturgy of the neighbor" and giving the ritual memory of Jesus Christ its plenitude in our existential memory.[114]

In other words, Christ becomes present in the world when we embody his word in action, loving our neighbor as ourselves according to his command, thus transforming what we remember about Jesus in liturgy into the fullness of what we will later be able to remember about our Christian existence.

8. Liturgical Approaches

As noted at the beginning of this chapter, sacramental theology, as a branch or specialization of Christian theology, has existed only since the Middle Ages, when the schoolmen in the newly founded universities gathered together all the academic knowledge of the time in order to study it systematically. In the ancient world, Christian writers had spoken about baptism, Eucharist, and other church rituals, but there was no discussion of sacraments as a general topic. As late as the twelfth century, in fact, even the issue of how many ecclesiastical rites should be designated as sacraments was an open question.[115]

It should not be entirely surprising, therefore, that another way of looking at church rituals has recently come into existence, this time in the wake of the reforms of Vatican II. The psychology of religion and the sociology of religion had already introduced concepts that could be used to analyze rituals that were now more readily understandable in modern languages. The new field of ritual studies was suggesting ways to observe more carefully what people do during liturgical rituals and to record more accurately the individual and social effects of participating in those rituals. Biblical scholarship was providing new insights into the meaning of Jewish and early Christian religious practices. Historical research was uncovering new information about how the Catholic Church's official rites had varied through the centuries. And ecumenical discussions with Protestant and Orthodox theologians gave Catholic scholars ways to look at church ceremonies from perspectives other than that of scholastic theology.

---

114. This and the earlier excerpt in this paragraph are from Chauvet, *Symbol and Sacrament*, 265; italics removed.

115. See Martos, *Doors to the Sacred*, 48–51.

The scholastic approach to the sacraments (and also the approaches proposed by twentieth-century Catholic theologians) was primarily a reflection on the church's teachings about sacraments—doctrines about the meaning and effects of each rite, popular beliefs associated with them, and of course the words of the rites themselves. Such an approach was clearly generic rather than specific, for it regarded all baptisms as basically alike regardless of their individual differences, and the same could be said of all the other sacraments. This approach was also essentialistic rather than empirical for it sought to discover the essential meaning and purpose of each sacrament regardless of when, where, or by whom it was done. And despite the efforts of modern Catholic thinkers to penetrate the experiential dimension of the sacraments, experience was never a deciding factor in deciding the meaning or value of a particular ritual.

In the 1970s, however, as priests began to talk about the reformed rites from the pulpit, as religious educators began explaining them to adults and children, and as writers began discussing them in articles and books, it became clear that Catholics were starting to talk about their church's practices in ways that were different from the ways they had talked about the Mass and the sacraments before Vatican II. What had been called the Sacrifice of the Mass was now referred to as the eucharistic liturgy, the other six sacraments began to be called liturgical rituals, and less formal church services were suddenly regarded as being nonliturgical. In ecumenical circles, Protestants who attended Sunday worship centered around scripture and a sermon were said to belong to nonliturgical churches, while Orthodox and Catholic believers, as well as Protestants who regularly participated in eucharistic worship or the Lord's Supper, were said to belong to liturgical churches. In colleges and universities, religion departments began offering courses in liturgical studies (history of liturgy, liturgical prayer, and the like), and larger institutions even created departments of liturgy or liturgical studies.

By the 1980s, liturgists and theologians were talking about the emergence of liturgical theology, a new branch of study whose focus was on formal liturgical worship, its structure and contents. Whereas the more familiar sacramental theology was primarily a reflection on and to some extent a defense of Catholic sacramental doctrines, liturgical theology reflected on actual liturgical practice, sometimes explaining it, sometimes critiquing it, and sometimes relating it to matters beyond church teachings and institutional concerns. In the words of liturgical scholar Peter Fink,

> Liturgical theology studies liturgical texts as privileged expressions of the church's faith. It examines as well the inner movements of faith which

ritual action calls forth. It examines the correspondence between what is portrayed in ritual and what is lived by individuals and by the community. It calls on the arts, the human sciences, and pastoral experience as well as the more traditional sources of doctrine, philosophy and liturgical history. . . . It is open to any source and any method which serves to link worship, faith and human life.[116]

Such was the variety of what were called works of liturgical theology, however, that academics in the 1990s began to look for some order in the diversity. All liturgical theologians subscribed to the classic maxim *Lex orandi, lex credendi*, meaning that the church's public prayer is the foundation and expression of its core beliefs, but beyond that there was little unity in the field. Kevin Irwin at the beginning of that decade suggested that writings by those who consider themselves liturgical theologians could be divided into three categories: theology of liturgy, theology drawn from liturgy, and doxological theology.[117] In recent years, however, it has been sometimes difficult to draw a clear line between the first two categories because authors who discuss the theology implicit in liturgical texts and celebrations tend to discuss how those ideas are related to other theological issues such as Christology and ecclesiology, as well as to pastoral concerns such as spirituality and parish life. At the same time, Irwin's third category seems to have developed into a highly specialized endeavor that calls itself liturgical theology but is very different from anything else that goes by that name. For the sake of simplicity we will call it special liturgical theology, and we will refer to everything else in the field as general liturgical theology.   □

Special liturgical theology traces its origins to the work of Alexander Schmemann, a priest and liturgical scholar in the Russian Orthodox tradition. Although born in Estonia and educated in France, he taught for many years at St. Vladimir's Seminary in the United States and also as a visiting professor at other American universities and schools of theology. As an Orthodox observer at the Second Vatican Council in the 1960s, Schmemann came in contact with Catholic theologians and liturgists, impressing some of them with the importance of what he was referring to as liturgical theology. It is very likely that the term itself derives from his writings, especially *Introduction to Liturgical Theology*, first published in 1966 and still in print.[118]

116. Peter E. Fink, "Sacramental Theology after Vatican II," in *The New Dictionary of Sacramental Worship* (Collegeville, MN: Liturgical Press, 1990), 1114.

117. Kevin W. Irwin, "Liturgical Theology," in ibid., 724–25. See also his *Liturgical Theology: A Primer* (Collegeville, MN: Liturgical Press, 1990).

118. Alexander Schmemann, *Introduction to Liturgical Theology* (Portland, ME: American Orthodox Press, 1966; 2nd ed. from Crestwood, NY: St. Vladimir's Seminary Press, 1975).

Schmemann's concept of liturgical theology is both unique and hard to pin down. Its uniqueness is hinted at in the subtitle of *Liturgy and Life*, a collection of articles on Christian development through liturgical experience.[119] The Orthodox tradition places great emphasis on spiritual experiences—one would almost say mystical experiences—that can and indeed should occur when devout believers enter into liturgical worship with their full heart and mind. Such deep participation, over time, transforms one's consciousness and behavior in a way that is directly shaped by the theology embedded in liturgical texts and expressed in actual liturgical celebrations. For Schmemann, *Lex orandi, lex credendi* is literally true because when liturgy plays a deep role in spiritual formation, what is prayed becomes what is believed and indeed what is lived.

Schmemann's works and ideas have had a profound influence on a small but well-respected group of Catholic liturgical scholars, most notably Aidan Kavanagh, a Benedictine monk whose lectures *On Liturgical Theology* espoused Schmemann's approach and introduced it to a wide Catholic audience. *The Shape of Baptism: The Rite of Christian Initiation* greatly affected the understanding and implementation of the Rite of Christian Initiation of Adults in the United States, especially in its insistence that the ceremonies and symbols of the RCIA be allowed to speak directly to catechumens undergoing the initiation process, strictly avoiding the temptation to explain them in advance. Similarly, his *Confirmation: Origins and Reform* was influential in promoting a return to the "original sequence" of the sacraments of initiation instead of placing confirmation after eucharist, as had become common practice in the Catholic Church. Although the confirmation of adolescents is still widely practiced in the United States, many dioceses now prepare children to be confirmed before they receive their First Communion.[120]

Other major works include *For the Life of the World: Sacraments and Orthodoxy* (Crestwood, NY: St. Vladimir's Seminary Press, 1973); *Liturgy and Life: Lectures and Essays on Christian Development through Liturgical Experience* (New York: Department of Religious Education, Orthodox Church in America, 1974); *Of Water and the Spirit: A Liturgical Study of Baptism* (Crestwood, NY: St. Vladimir's Seminary Press, 1974); and *The Eucharist: Sacrament of the Kingdom* (Crestwood, NY: St. Vladimir's Seminary Press, 1988). See also Thomas Fisch, ed., *Liturgy and Tradition: Theological Reflections of Alexander Schmemann* (Crestwood, NY: St. Vladimir's Seminary Press, 1990).

119. See reference in preceding note.

120. See Aidan Kavanagh, *On Liturgical Theology* (New York: Pueblo Books, 1984; reprinted by Liturgical Press in 1992); *The Shape of Baptism: The Rite of Christian Initiation* (New York: Pueblo Books, 1978; reprinted by Liturgical Press in 1991); *Confirmation: Origins and Reform* (New York: Pueblo Books, 1988); also numerous articles in *Worship* and other periodicals.

Another proponent of Schmemann's approach to liturgical theology has been Robert Taft, an American Jesuit who is a Byzantine Rite Catholic[121] and an international expert on Eastern rite liturgies. Although not as widely read as Schmemann and Kavanagh, Taft's works are often cited in support of what we are calling special liturgical theology.[122]

Most helpful for understanding this approach is David Fagerberg, whose 1992 book *What Is Liturgical Theology?* pulled together the key ideas in this approach and articulated them in a somewhat systematic fashion.[123] Like Schmemann and Kavanagh, Fagerberg reserves the term "liturgical theology" to a theological understanding that is implicit in liturgical experience. Like them as well, he redefines both liturgy and theology in showing that the church's *lex orandi* is the foundation of the Christian *lex credendi.*

For most people, the word "liturgy" refers to a type of church service that is formal and ritualized, or one that is designed and promulgated by an ecclesiastical authority for use throughout a particular church or denomination. Thus, worship that is stylized, relatively unchanging, and done "by the book" is generally regarded as liturgical in character, whereas worship in churches that have relative autonomy over the design and implementation of their services (and that could in theory be different in format from one week to the next) is usually called nonliturgical. Fagerberg acknowledges this meaning, but he calls it the "thin" sense of the term: liturgy as stylized or formal ritual.[124] Liturgy in its "thick" sense is richer by far. Liturgy in this latter sense is what happens when formal ritual does what it is supposed to do. □

The Greek word for people is *laos,* from which we get the words "lay" and "laity." From a Christian perspective, *laos* refers to the people of God, the community of the baptized, the faithful, and, by extension, the church. Similarly, the Greek word for work is *ergon,* from which we get the words "energy" and "ergonomic," but *ergon* could also mean business or occupation.

121. Although a member of the Society of Jesus, which is a religious order in the Western church, he is a member of an Eastern rite church whose liturgies are essentially the same as those of the Orthodox churches but that are in political communion with Rome. Such churches are often referred to as uniate churches.

122. See Robert F. Taft, *Beyond East and West: Problems in Liturgical Understanding* (Washington, DC: Pastoral Press, 1984); *The Byzantine Rite: A Short History* (Collegeville, MN: Liturgical Press, 1992); *Liturgy in Byzantium and Beyond* (Brookfield, VT: Variorum Press, 1995); and *Through Their Eyes: Liturgy as the Byzantines Saw It* (Berkeley, CA: InterOrthodox Press, 2006).

123. See David W. Fagerberg, *What Is Liturgical Theology?: A Study in Methodology* (New York: Pueblo Books, 1992); reprinted with new introductory and concluding chapters as *Theologia Prima: What Is Liturgical Theology?* (Chicago: Liturgy Training Publications, 2003). All references are to this second edition of the book.

124. See Fagerberg, *Theologia Prima,* 9f.

The Greek *leitourgia* is a compound word derived from these, it could be translated as the work of the people, and it is the word from which we get the English "liturgy." One could argue, therefore, that the root meaning of liturgy is the work of the people or the people's business.[125]

Theologically, the work of God's people or the essential occupation of the church is to be Christ in the world: it is to enter into the paschal mystery of dying so that others may live; it is to live as Jesus did, in submission to the Father's will and anointed by the Holy Spirit; thus it is to live the life of the Trinity, a life of total self-giving love.[126] "One does more than worship in *leitourgia*; one does the world the way it was meant to be done (Kavanagh) in behavior that is eschatological and cosmological (Schmemann)."[127]

The Christian life of *leitourgia* is thus the foundation for liturgy in this sense of the word. This is why Robert Taft can say, "The purpose of all Christian liturgy is to express in a ritual moment that which should be the basic stance of every moment in our lives."[128] When liturgical experience has this type of richness, then it is true to say:

- [L]iturgy is the place of communion with God.[129]

- Liturgy is the manifestation of the new creation, which is the God-Man perpetuated temporally, personally, sacramentally, and socially.[130]

- Liturgy is not just ritual; it is a way of living and way of thinking, expressed ritually.[131]

- The liturgy doesn't just make the thinker think doxologically or theologize prayerfully; it forms a believer whose life is theological.[132]

- Liturgy is the faith of the church in motion, like listening is friendship in motion, or studying is scholarship in motion, or sitting down at supper together is family in motion, or comforting a child with a skinned knee is parenting in motion, or making love is marriage in motion.[133]

---

125. See ibid., 110.
126. See ibid., 6, 14, 226.
127. Ibid., 114. In his book, Fagerberg often references his two primary mentors, showing how they sometimes write about the same thing in different words, as is the case here.
128. Ibid., 17; quoting Robert F. Taft, *Beyond East and West: Problems in Liturgical Theology* (Rome: Pontifical Oriental Institute, 1997), 52.
129. Fagerberg, *Theologia Prima*, 5.
130. Ibid., 17.
131. Ibid., 22.
132. Ibid., 4. Also said of *leitourgia* on p. 122.
133. Ibid., 219.

Those who enter deliberately and consciously into this sort of liturgy can be called Christians, followers of Christ, members of his mystical body, the baptized, or the faithful. Fagerberg contends that they should also be called liturgists because they are the ones who do liturgy, they participate in liturgical worship, they ritually enter into the experience of *leitourgia*.[134] In this deeper sense, a liturgist is not a student or professor of liturgy (in the thin sense) but someone "who strives for this life of Christ, and who, in the measure he or she attains it, is witness to the world in its final destiny."[135] *Leitourgia* is the work of the church, liturgists perform that work, and liturgy is the ritualization of that work, its symbolic reenactment and re-presentation. "Liturgy celebrates a reality (liturgy is doing the world) by bringing to ritual moment what is steadfastly and pervasively true."[136] ☐

Liturgy of this sort does not happen automatically; it is hard work, just as imitating Christ and loving others is hard work. To say it another way, being a disciple of Jesus entails discipline: self-discipline or asceticism.[137] Such discipline is not primarily practiced in a monastery or convent, however, but in liturgy, and so it can be properly called liturgical asceticism.[138] In the course of deep liturgical worship, liturgists encounter the mystery they are celebrating, they are spiritually affected by it, and they respond accordingly. They hear the word (*logos*) of God (*theos*) spoken in their hearts, and in the discipline of self-surrender they speak that same word.[139] In doing so, they become speakers of God, God-speakers, theo-logians. They speak God's word with their minds and hearts and lives so they can be rightly called theologians even though they do not do so in pulpits, classrooms, or professional journals. ☐

For Schmemann, Kavanagh, and Fagerberg, this response that occurs in and through liturgical experience is rightly called liturgical theology. It is theology that happens in the context of liturgy, implicit in the experience of worship—an understanding of what is going on, what is being said by God, and what the human reply should be. It is theology embedded in the rule of prayer, the *lex orandi*, and when this liturgical theology gets reflected on and expressed in words, it gets articulated as the rule of faith, the *lex credendi*. In other words, the theology that is experienced in liturgy is

---

134. See ibid., 8, 30f.
135. Ibid., 17.
136. Ibid., 143.
137. See ibid., 19–22.
138. See ibid., 30.
139. "Liturgy is encounter with God, yes, but furthermore it is a living adjustment—meaning a theological response—to the Holy One" (ibid., 67; see also 40–42).

the wellspring from which flows theology that is spoken and written in
words.[140]

Liturgical theology in this sense is the primary and foundational theology of the Christian community. It is *theologia prima* (primary theology),
uttered in God's presence before any *theologia secunda* (secondary theology,
or theology in the usual sense of the word) is uttered in human speech.[141]

> The adjustment made by those who encounter God's holy presence is an
> instance of *theologia prima*. . . . It is an instance of corporate theologiz-
> ing which is done in the liturgical community and not in private isolation.
> Thus . . . the corporate theological experience is normative for private
> theology, and this theological experience is found in concrete liturgical
> actions and not in abstracted ideas about liturgy.[142]

This having been said, it is clear that this does not cover the whole field
of liturgical theology. Much that is called liturgical theology does not fit
this specialized, if thought-provoking, definition. It remains that a few words
need to be said about liturgical theology in a more general way.

Broadly speaking, liturgical theology can refer to any theologizing that
is done in relation to liturgy. It can be a theology of liturgy in the sense of
a general understanding of the meaning and purpose of liturgical worship,
such as may be found in the Catechism of the Catholic Church, in the general
instructions for each of the sacramental rites, in Vatican II's Constitution
on the Sacred Liturgy, and in other church documents. It can also be found
in works by individual theologians such as Odo Casel's *The Mystery of
Christian Worship* (originally published in 1932), J. D. Crichton's monu-
mental *Christian Celebration* (Geoffrey Chapman, 1981), and in more
popular explanations written for nonspecialists by such authors as Joseph
Champlin and Lawrence Mick.[143]

---

140. "Liturgical action is theological. This is already real theology even though it is
performed communally. . . . In the Church's *lex orandi* theology happens, and that makes
it the ontological basis for the Church's expression of herself in *lex credendi*" (ibid., 45).

141. "The community's transformation in liturgical encounter with God is understood
to be truly a *theologia prima*, and Christian theology arises from the Church-at-liturgy like
civilization arises *in* and *at* play" (ibid., 63).

142. Ibid., 68. Later on that same page, "The distinctive character of liturgical theology
stems from the fact that it is in the liturgy, under God's judgment and in God's presence, that
theologia prima is done." See also 110–11.

143. For example, Joseph M. Champlin, *The Mystery and Meaning of the Mass* (New
York: Crossroad, 1999); and Lawrence E. Mick, *Forming the Assembly to Celebrate the Mass*
(Chicago: Liturgy Training Publications, 2002).

Christian worship is supposed to be intentionally connected to Christian living, so books such as Mark Searle's *Liturgy and Social Justice* (Liturgical Press, 1980) and William Willimon's *The Service of God: Christian Work and Worship* (Abingdon Press, 1983) can be considered liturgical theology with an ethical dimension. In a similar way, Shawn Madigan's *Spirituality Rooted in Liturgy* (Pastoral Press, 1988) puts liturgy in a spiritual perspective; Ernest Falardeau's *One Bread and Cup: Source of Communion* (Michael Glazier, 1987) looks at the Eucharist's ecumenical possibilities; Anscar Chupungco's *Cultural Adaptation of the Liturgy* (Paulist Press, 1982) examines liturgy's multicultural potential; Teresa Berger's *Women's Ways of Worship* (Liturgical Press, 1999) discusses ritual from a feminist perspective; and Richard Giles' *Creating Uncommon Worship: Transforming the Liturgy of the Eucharist* (Liturgical Press, 2004) proposes creative practical possibilities for worship. Needless to say, many books on liturgy and worship published in recent decades do not neatly fall into any of the above categories, but they may still be called works of liturgical theology in the general sense.

Moreover, besides being found in books, liturgical theology regularly appears in religious newspapers, liturgy magazines, and theological journals whenever the focus is on the theological meaning of church rituals. Liturgical theology can also be found in books and articles about the sacraments when the focus is not on doctrine but on liturgical celebration, spiritual formation, and pastoral application. Popular and scholarly works about the RCIA and about the eucharistic liturgy are often written from such perspectives. It can almost be said that whatever is written about liturgy and theology, except for sacramental theology in the traditional sense and liturgical theology in the restricted sense described above, can be called, broadly speaking, liturgical theology. □

9. Approaches as Models

The existence of five markedly different approaches to the sacraments today (and there are others[144]) naturally leads to the question: Which of these is the correct one? In one sense at least the best answer is: None of them. For all of them are abstract theoretical models, and sacraments are neither abstract nor theoretical nor models. □

144. Besides the traditional scholastic approach, there have been in history various Protestant and Orthodox accounts of the sacraments. Two additional Catholic approaches, one based on process theology and one inspired by the charismatic renewal movement, were treated in the first edition of this book, *The Catholic Sacraments* (Wilmington, DE: Michael Glazier, 1983).

Sacraments are not abstractions but concrete realities. They are what Catholics actually do in churches and other places, on Sundays and other days, in the United States and other countries. Sacraments are not theories but practices. They involve real people doing real things such as speaking, reading, gesturing, praying, thinking, and feeling. Sacraments are not models but originals. Each instance of sacramental worship is unique and individual, involving different people at different times and places, and displaying a host of other details that can never be exactly repeated.

The initial question in sacramental theology, put very simply, is: What the dickens is going on here? What in the world are these people doing? And this leads to other questions: Why are they doing these things? What connection do these rituals have with Jesus, with each other, and with similar rituals that Catholics have performed in the past? And finally the fundamental question is: How is God involved here? How are these practices related to the Christian revelation of divine mysteries?

To answer these questions, theologians have to find some intelligent way of pulling the bewildering variety of information about the sacraments (scriptural data, historical records, Christian doctrines, liturgical regulations, findings of psychology and sociology, their own experiences, and so on) into some sort of logically coherent arrangement. When they succeed in doing that, the result is a theory, a theory of the sacraments, a sacramental theology. The theory is abstract because it leaves out or abstracts from the myriad details of sacramental data. And it is a model because in leaving out the details it is something like a sketch that roughly approximates the originals but loses a lot of the originals' richness. So the theoretical model is never the reality; it is always some abstract approximation of it. Moreover, the shape of the model will vary in accordance with the data that it is supposed to cover. Contemporary sacramental theologians, for instance, have more historical data to deal with than the medieval theologians did, and so their models will naturally differ from the older ones in that respect. Similarly, theologians who pay more attention to the texts of the liturgical rites than to the factual experiences of people participating in the sacraments will develop different models than those who do the opposite.

Philosophers today tell us that there are basically two types of models: picture (or representative) models and disclosure (or interpretative) models.[145] Examples of picture models are things like scale model cars or planes, archi-

---

145. See Max Black, *Models and Metaphors: Studies in Language and Philosophy* (Ithaca, NY: Cornell University Press, 1962), esp. chap. 13; Frederick Ferré, "Mapping the Logic of Models," in *New Essays on Religious Language*, ed. Dallas M. High (New York: Oxford University Press, 1969), 54–96; Ian T. Ramsey, *Models and Mystery* (London: Oxford University Press, 1964).

tects' blueprints and engineers' drawings, geographical globes and maps. Disclosure models are usually less visual and more conceptual. They are things like psychological theories of personality development, scientific explanations of natural phenomena, political models such as democracy and socialism.   ☐

In various ways we all use models all the time in our thinking. We all make generalizations from our experience, and then use those generalizations as mental models for interpreting our further experience. For example, we all have a general idea or mental image of a mother or father (role models), a saint or a scoundrel (moral models), a telephone or a computer (technological models), and so on, that we have learned and then use to understand the people and things in the world around us. We also get first impressions of the people we meet and the places we visit, and these impressions function as mental models or conceptual structures that become more detailed as we learn more from experience. We also have a general idea about what our neighborhood looks like, how our business works, and so on, that operates as a model when we need to find our way around in them. Such practical, everyday models can be clear or fuzzy, extremely simple or fairly complex.   ☐

Practical everyday models are in some ways both picture models and disclosure models, because they represent realities in our experience for us and they also help us to interpret our further experience. And because we are so familiar with these sorts of models (though of course we do not usually advert to them or realize that they are indeed models), we tend to take theoretical models in the same way. That is, we tend to take scientific, economic, political, and theological theories as pictures of reality. In fact, however, they are not. But because everyday thinking takes them to be pictures of reality, it has a hard time letting go of one model and accepting another. The resistance that people felt about giving up the Ptolemaic theory (the sun goes around the earth) in favor of the Copernican theory (the earth goes around the sun) is a historical case in point. The resistance that many Catholics felt about changes in the liturgy following the Second Vatican Council was the same sort of phenomenon: they had lived with one liturgical model for so long that they took it to be the only true picture of worship.   ☐

Since theology is theoretical, however, what it actually contains are not picture models but disclosure models. Most scientists, in both the natural and the human sciences, today regard their theories as disclosure models, and a growing number of Catholic theologians as well accept David Tracy's observation that "theological models do not purport to present exact pictures of the realities they disclose."[146] Rather, they give us general conceptual

146. David Tracy, *Blessed Rage for Order: The New Pluralism in Theology* (New York: Seabury Press, 1975), 22.

frameworks within which we can situate and try to understand particular religious realities such as the church and the sacraments. In Bernard Lonergan's words, models give us "not descriptions of reality, not hypotheses about reality, but simply interlocking sets of terms and relations" that are "useful in guiding investigations, in framing hypotheses and in writing descriptions"[147] of what the church has done in the past, or of what Catholics are doing today in their sacramental celebrations, for example.

Natural scientists (physicists, chemists, biologists, etc.) can often work within a single large conceptual structure that remains relatively stable even though they have to try out various smaller models for doing new research in particular areas. It is only infrequently that natural science experiences massive shifts in its fundamental paradigm or basic structural models.[148] Social scientists on the other hand (psychologists, sociologists, historians, philosophers, etc.) are acutely aware that in their fields the data are so complex and fluid that there is often no single model that they can all agree on and use for interpreting the data on human life. The social or human sciences, which include theology, are for this reason becoming familiar with the practice of using multiple models in their work.

It is true that for the past few centuries Catholic theology relied rather exclusively on one model for its intellectual framework, the model provided by scholastic philosophy, and indeed it seemed so solidly entrenched in our mental landscape that we took it to be a picture model that represented the essential truth about natural and supernatural realities. But as we saw in the introduction to this chapter, before the Middle Ages Catholic thinkers used other models for understanding and interpreting the Christian mysteries. In the twentieth century theologians once again began to allow for the possibility of multiple models or alternative theologies to exist side by side. Each model can shed some light on one or another of the Christian mysteries, each can suggest that we look at them from a particular point of view, and each can attempt to describe them in very general terms, but none of them can give us an exhaustive or definitive analysis of those realities. "Theologies do not—or should not—claim to provide pictures of the realities they describe—God, humanity, and world; they can be shown to disclose such realities with varying degrees of adequacy." For theologies give us

---

147. Bernard Lonergan, *Method in Theology* (New York: Herder and Herder, 1972), 284f. For other examples, see Avery Dulles, *Models of the Church* (New York: Doubleday, 1974); and also his *Models of Revelation* (New York: Doubleday, 1983).

148. See Thomas S. Kuhn, *The Structure of Scientific Revolutions* (Chicago: University of Chicago Press, 1962).

disclosure or discovery models, and so they "should be taken seriously but not literally."[149]

Such an attitude toward theological models has two important consequences. First, it helps us to overcome the model fixation that characterized Catholic theology in the past and to some extent still operates in the present. Arguing that the sacraments *are* this and *not* that (e.g., they are encounters with Christ and not causes of grace) is actually a disagreement about theological models and not about the sacraments, and the argument results from accepting one model as usable and rejecting the other as unusable (e.g., accepting the existentialist model and rejecting the scholastic model) for interpreting the sacraments. In fact, this sort of model-fixation (mistaking a single model for the reality) happens both among conservatives who insist on the traditional sacramental theories and reject the newer ones, and among the liberals who declare that some new theory is true and the old ones false. But since the models are abstract and theoretical, they are not sacramental realities but ways of interpreting and explaining our individual and social experiences of sacramental worship. They are thus not true or false in themselves but relatively adequate or inadequate for helping us to understand the sacraments as concrete church practices that we all participate in.

Second, this more flexible attitude toward theological models enables us to use different ones at different times, depending on what it is that we want to understand about the sacraments. Disclosure models are interpretative models, giving us a framework within which to situate our personal experience or ecclesiastical practice of sacramental worship, and giving us names for what we find happening within us personally and within us as a community. But disclosure models are also discovery or heuristic models, giving us hints as to what further things there are to be found in sacramental worship—but that we may not yet have experienced or that we as a parish community, for instance, may not yet have put into practice. Sacramental theologies, therefore, are not necessarily models of what *is* going on in some concrete practices. Whether something happens in or as a result of a particular ritual has to be determined by looking at it through the lens of a particular model, and verifying whether what the model focuses on can actually be found in our personal and social experience. Sacramental theologies are therefore better understood as models of what *can be* but *might not be* going on in concrete sacramental practices. And depending on one's doctrinal, liturgical, and pastoral orientation, such theologies can provide

---

149. Tracy, *Blessed Rage for Order*, 22.

models of what *should be* or *should not be* going on when Christians gather
for sacramental worship.

The existence of multiple models for sacramental theology thus moves
us to ask a wider range of questions than we did when we as Catholics accepted and used only one basic model. About any particular sacramental
ceremony and about the concrete sacramental practices of a particular group
of people we can ask questions such as the following, which are suggested
by the existential, phenomenological, transformational, liberation, and liturgical models: Do I experience and encounter Christ in our worship? Is this
liturgy expressing what we are as a community? Do our sacramental celebrations contribute to our ongoing conversion? Is my attitude one of magic or
social responsibility? Are we doing in our daily lives what we are celebrating
in ritual? These of course are not the only questions that arise out of these
five models, but they indicate the direction in which such honest questioning
and reflecting on our experience of sacramental worship can go.

Above all it is important to remember that the models can only help us
to ask the questions; they cannot answer the questions. Each model does of
course suggest the answers that make the best sense within its own particular
framework. But the framework itself cannot give us the answers; it can only
help us to locate and interpret the answers. For the answers are not to be
found in the models, which are abstract and theoretical, but in the originals,
that is, in the concrete experience of the church's sacramental practices. And
this is because it is within the experience of sacramental worship itself that
the Christian mystery, or some aspect of it, is disclosed to us.

Additional Reading

History of Theology

Congar, Yves. *A History of Theology*. New York: Doubleday, 1968.
Gonzalez, Justo L. *A History of Christian Thought*. 3 vols. Nashville, TN:
   Abingdon Press, 1970–75.
Pelikan, Jaroslav. *The Christian Tradition: A History of the Development
   of Doctrine*. 3 vols. Chicago: University of Chicago Press, 1971–78.

Scholastic Theology

Leeming, Bernard. *Principles of Sacramental Theology*. Westminster, MD:
   Newman Press, 1956.

McAuliffe, Clarence R. *Sacramental Theology: A Textbook for Advanced Students*. St. Louis, MO: B. Herder, 1958.

Roguet, A.-M. *Christ Acts through the Sacraments*. Collegeville, MN: Liturgical Press, 1954.

Contemporary Approaches

Sacramental Theologies

Cooke, Bernard. *Sacraments and Sacramentality*. Rev. ed. Mystic, CT: Twenty-Third Publications, 1994.

Gelpi, Donald L. *Charism and Sacrament: A Theology of Christian Conversion*. New York: Paulist Press, 1976.

———. *Committed Worship: A Sacramental Theology for Converting Christians*. 2 vols. Collegeville, MN: Liturgical Press, 1993.

Kilmartin, Edward J. *Christian Liturgy: Theology and Practice*. Kansas City, MO: Sheed and Ward, 1988.

Lawler, Michael G. *Symbol and Sacrament: A Contemporary Sacramental Theology*. New York: Paulist Press, 1987.

Lee, Bernard J. *The Becoming of the Church: A Process Theology of the Structures of Christian Experience*. New York: Paulist Press, 1974.

Osborne, Kenan B. *Sacramental Theology: A General Introduction*. New York: Paulist Press, 1988.

Rahner, Karl. *The Church and the Sacraments*. New York: Herder and Herder, 1963.

Roberts, William P. *Encounters with Christ: Introduction to the Sacraments*. New York: Paulist Press, 1985.

Ross, Susan A. *Extravagant Affections: A Feminist Sacramental Theology*. New York: Continuum, 1998.

Van Roo, William A. *The Christian Sacrament*. Rome: Editrice Pontifica Università Gregoriana, 1992.

Schillebeeckx, Edward. *Christ, the Sacrament of the Encounter with God*. New York: Sheed and Ward, 1963.

Segundo, Juan Luis. *The Sacraments Today*. Maryknoll, NY: Orbis Books, 1974.

Liturgical Theologies

Chan, Simon. *Liturgical Theology: The Church as Worshiping Community*. Downers Grove, IL: Inter-Varsity Press, 2006.

Fagerberg, David W. *Theologia Prima: What Is Liturgical Theology?* Chicago: Liturgy Training Publications, 2001.

Irwin, Kevin W. *Context and Text: Method in Liturgical Theology.* Collegeville, MN: Liturgical Press, 1994.

Kavanagh, Aidan. *On Liturgical Theology.* New York: Pueblo Books, 1984.

Lathrop, Gordon. *Holy Things: A Liturgical Theology.* Minneapolis: Fortress Press, 1993.

Saliers, Don E. *Worship as Theology: Foretaste of Glory Divine.* Nashville, TN: Abingdon Press, 1994.

Schmemann, Alexander. *Introduction to Liturgical Theology.* Crestwood, NY: St. Vladimir's Seminary Press, 1986.

Vogel, Dwight W., ed. *Primary Sources of Liturgical Theology: A Reader.* Collegeville, MN: Liturgical Press, 2000.

Postmodern Reflections

Boeve, Lieven, and Lambert Leijssen, eds. *Sacramental Presence in a Postmodern Context.* Leuven, Belgium: Leuven University Press, 2001.

Boeve, Lieven, and John C. Ries, eds. *The Presence of Transcendence: Thinking "Sacrament" in a Postmodern Age.* Leuven, Belgium: Peeters, 2001.

Chauvet, Louis-Marie. *The Sacraments: The Word of God at the Mercy of the Body.* Collegeville, MN: Liturgical Press, 2001.

———. *Symbol and Sacrament: A Sacramental Reinterpretation of Christian Existence.* Collegeville, MN: Liturgical Press, 1995.

Garrigan, Siobhán. *Beyond Ritual: Sacramental Theology after Habermas.* Aldershot, England: Ashgate, 2004.

Theologies of Individual Sacraments

Balasuriya, Tissa. *The Eucharist and Human Liberation.* Maryknoll, NY: Orbis Books, 1979.

Elliott, Peter. *What God Has Joined: The Sacramentality of Marriage.* New York: Alba House, 1990.

Empereur, James L. *Prophetic Anointing: God's Call to the Sick, the Elderly, and the Dying.* Wilmington, DE: Michael Glazier, 1982.

Greshake, Gisbert. *The Meaning of Christian Priesthood.* Dublin: Four Courts Press, 1988.

Hellwig, Monika. *Sign of Reconciliation and Conversion: The Sacrament of Penance for Our Times.* Wilmington, DE: Michael Glazier, 1982.

Kasper, Walter. *Theology of Christian Marriage.* New York: Seabury Press, 1980.

Lawler, Michael G. *Secular Marriage, Christian Sacrament.* Mystic, CT: Twenty-Third Publications, 1985.

Macy, Gary. *The Theologies of the Eucharist in the Early Scholastic Period: A Study of the Salvific Function of the Sacrament according to the Theologians.* New York: Clarendon Press, 1984.

Maloney, George A. *Your Sins Are Forgiven You: Rediscovering the Sacrament of Reconciliation.* New York: Alba House, 1994.

O'Connor, James T. *The Hidden Manna: A Theology of the Eucharist.* San Francisco: Ignatius Press, 1988.

O'Meara, Thomas F. *Theology of Ministry.* New York: Paulist Press, 1983.

Primavesi, Anne, and Jennifer Henderson. *Our God Has No Favourites: A Liberation Theology of the Eucharist.* Tunbridge Wells, England: Burns and Oates, 1989.

Schillebeeckx, Edward. *The Church with a Human Face: A New and Expanded Theology of Ministry.* New York: Crossroad, 1985.

——. *The Eucharist.* New York: Sheed and Ward, 1968.

Searle, Mark. *Christening: The Making of Christians.* Collegeville, MN: Liturgical Press, 1980.

Thomas, David. *Christian Marriage: A Journey Together.* Wilmington, DE: Michael Glazier, 1983.

Scientific and Theological Models

Barbour, Ian G. *Myths, Models and Paradigms: A Comparative Study in Science and Religion.* New York: Harper and Row, 1974.

Dulles, Avery R. *Models of the Church.* Expanded ed. Garden City, NY: Doubleday, 1987.

——. *Models of Revelation.* New York: Doubleday, 1983.

Irwin, Kevin W. *Models of the Eucharist.* Mahwah, NJ: Paulist Press, 2005.

Kuhn, Thomas S. *The Structure of Scientific Revolutions.* Chicago: University of Chicago Press, 1970.

O'Grady, John F. *Models of Jesus Revisited.* New York: Paulist Press, 1994.

CHAPTER 6

The Sacraments and Morality

U ntil recently, the relation between sacraments and moral behavior has not been an issue. True, the purpose of penance (now called reconciliation) has always been to help people get their moral house in order, and there have always been moral standards for participating in the Eucharist (for example, not being an unrepentant sinner). Indeed, growth in holiness for Catholics was for a long time thought of in terms of frequent confession and the devout reception of Communion. Before Vatican II, however, the other sacraments were not often regarded as having moral or ethical implications.[1]

In the wake of the Second Vatican Council, the scene began to change. Scripture scholars pointed out that sin in the Bible is more a matter of violating a relationship than one of violating a law, moral theologians pointed out that mortal sin has to be thought of as a total rejection of one's relationship with God, and Catholic psychologists pointed out that it is very difficult to reject God completely. At the same time, liturgists proposed that the Eucharist should be thought of as a meal shared by all rather than as a sacrifice offered by the priest, and scripture scholars observed that Jesus in the gospels often shares meals with sinners. Within a decade, Catholics stopped feeling as though they always had to go to confession before receiving Communion; confession lines dwindled and Communion lines lengthened. At the same time, sacramental theologians and liturgical scholars began suggesting that sincere participation in symbolic rituals brings about—

---

1. One could point out that those who were baptized were supposed to be good Christians, those who were confirmed were supposed to be soldiers of Christ, those who were married were supposed to be faithful spouses, and those who were ordained were supposed to be pious priests, but the fact is that moral failings and ethical lapses were not thought of in relation to those sacraments. For example, adultery and pedophilia were regarded as sexual offenses rather than sins against matrimony or holy orders.

or at least should bring about—changes in attitude and behavior. They were saying, in other words, that what people see and hear in their religious ceremonies should have an effect on the way they feel and behave toward others.

Some of these writers have already been mentioned. Others have written not about sacraments in general but more specifically about individual sacraments, especially the Eucharist. And in this age of ecumenism, not all of the writers have been Catholic.

1. Examining Worship and Ethics

Bernard Cooke's *Christian Sacraments and Christian Personality*,[2] written during the Second Vatican Council, was the first book in English to move sacramental theology beyond an explanation of doctrine and into a discussion of Christian behavior. But it was liberation theologians in Latin America and Asia who first began to point out that the traditional doctrine ignored what was going on in people's lives, and that focusing on doctrine obscured what was happening in the actual life of the church. Juan Luis Segundo treated the sacraments within a wide theological horizon that included a broadened understanding of humanity, the church, God, society, and culture.[3] In 1977, Rafael Avila pushed this argument further, suggesting that church rituals had in effect devolved into a type of religiosity that had been rejected by the Jewish prophets and then by Jesus himself. In order to be authentic worship, Avila argued, liturgy must always be aware of the political context in which it occurs, it must address the immorality of political and economic oppression, and it must avoid becoming a cultic objectification of doctrine.[4]

Around the same time, but on the other side of the world, Tissa Balasuriya was working in Sri Lanka, a predominantly Buddhist country whose people suffered from many of the same deprivations as the poor in Latin America. Balasuriya noted that Christianity in his country had been tainted by colonialism since its first introduction by the Portuguese in 1605. Not only was the Mass performed in a strange ancient language (Latin) but the Catholic Church had made virtually no effort to ordain native clergy or to address oppression by both the local rulers and the colonial powers. For

2. Bernard J. Cooke, *Christian Sacraments and Christian Personality* (New York: Holt, Rinehart and Winston, 1965).

3. See chap. 5, n. 53.

4. Rafael Avila, *Apuntes sobre las implicaciones socio-politicas de la Eucharistia*, published in English as *Worship and Politics* (Maryknoll, NY: Orbis Books, 1981).

centuries, eucharistic doctrine had focused narrowly on personal salvation, although during a century of Dutch rule in Sri Lanka, when Catholics were severely persecuted, the Mass became a true source of community cohesion and spiritual strength. Before Vatican II, scripture scholarship enlarged Catholics' understanding of worship in biblical times, and after the council the reform of the liturgy raised questions about the relevance of worship to people's daily lives. Balasuriya proposed that the Eucharist should in some measure celebrate people's aspirations for freedom and affirm God's approval of those aspirations.[5]

In 1976, an international eucharistic congress was held in Philadelphia, Pennsylvania, and the theme chosen by Pope Paul VI was "The Hunger of the Human Family."[6] Such congresses draw Catholics from around the world to celebrate their faith and deepen their appreciation for the Eucharist through reading about and discussing the sacrament and its implications for worship, spirituality, and Christian living. On the occasion of this particular gathering, Monika Hellwig wrote *The Eucharist and the Hunger of the World*, a small book in which she discussed the social and moral implications of a sacrament that most Christians had thought of exclusively in terms of church doctrine and personal spirituality. Although she addressed many of the concerns of liberation theologians, she did so without drawing on the type of Marxist analysis that turned the Vatican against liberation theology in the 1980s.[7] After that, social concerns continued to be raised by sacramental theologians, but without the harsh critique of the institutional church that had been somewhat characteristic of the 1970s.

Just as he had taken the initiative twenty years earlier to rethink the personal meaning of the sacraments in the light of Vatican II, Bernard Cooke in the 1980s looked more closely at the social dimensions of the sacraments. Catholic sociologist Gregory Baum, whose work was discussed in chapter 2, had earlier observed that people's "response to the world is determined by the symbols operative in their imagination."[8] But the symbols to which

---

5. Tissa Balasuriya, *The Eucharist and Human Liberation* (Maryknoll, NY: Orbis Books, 1979).

6. International eucharistic congresses have been held since 1881, sometimes annually and sometimes less frequently, primarily in Europe but also in other parts of the world. Two have been convened in the United States, the first in Chicago in 1926 and the second in Philadelphia in 1976.

7. Monika Hellwig, *The Eucharist and the Hunger of the World* (New York: Paulist Press, 1976); 2nd ed. (Kansas City, MO: Sheed and Ward, 1992).

8. Gregory Baum, *Religion and Alienation: A Theological Reading of Sociology* (New York: Paulist Press, 1975), 242.

he was alluding were primarily the symbol stories or myths in a cultural or religious tradition.

> Not only do these symbols order the perception of the world, they also link this perception to values and purposes that determine human action. These symbols define the vision of life out of which people operate and thus orient their actions in a certain direction. Symbols guide people in their encounter with the world as well as their response to it.[9]

Symbols of this sort are lenses through which people perceive reality. "They are dominant patterns in the imagination that mediate experience and create the world to which we belong."[10] Patriarchal sagas, Israelite history, gospel stories, Pauline images, and Johannine revelations are the symbolic structures through which converted Christians experience themselves, other people, and the world around them. Moreover, "in the process of assuming the revealed symbols in the imagination, people are greatly helped by visible signs and images that are part of Christian life and worship. These symbols enliven the imagination."[11] They include not only religious art and architecture but also religious poetry, music, and rituals such as the sacraments.

In a sense, Cooke picked up where Baum left off, for in his 1983 *Sacraments and Sacramentality* he discussed those dominant patterns or symbolic structures in the imagination as hermeneutics of experience, that is, as interpretive models through which we view and understand what happens to us and what happens in the world around us.[12] Moreover, "religion is meant to supply a hermeneutic of experience, as a matter of fact to be the hermeneutic that leads us to discover the ultimate meaning of being human."[13] Once we have adopted such models, they become relatively permanent and can be altered only when new experiences force us to question our customary way of looking at things. Cooke believes that the permanence and stability of the Christian hermeneutic of experience is what led medieval theologians to conceive the sacramental character (*sacramentum et res*) as an indelible seal on the soul, for the scholastics did not have modern social sciences to enable them to understand this phenomenon more adequately. Traditional scholastic theology also associated the acquisition of the Christian hermeneutic with the church's symbolic rituals, for rituals and celebrations can have a lasting impact on one's interpretation of experience.

9. Ibid.
10. Ibid., 243.
11. Ibid., 246.
12. Bernard J. Cooke, *Sacraments and Sacramentality* (Mystic, CT: Twenty-Third Publications, 1983), 27–33. Also, see above, chap. 5, sec. 6.

Celebrations should be occasions when we have the opportunity to step back for a moment and reflectively express our reaction to life. Not only do we discover more clearly the meaning of what is going on; if we are celebrating that meaning, we are accepting it as good and we are willing to confront the reality involved and respond to its demands by our decisions and actions.[14]

Like Cooke, Louis-Marie Chauvet has concentrated on demonstrating the credibility of traditional Catholic teaching by translating it into contemporary terms, while also considering aspects of liturgical worship that were neglected in traditional sacramental theology. His major work, *Symbol and Sacrament*, was written in the 1980s even though it did not appear in English until the following decade, and it borrowed concepts from European philosophy rather than from American social science to show how sacraments function in the Catholic Church. Chauvet devoted an entire chapter to the ethical dimension of the sacraments, arguing that it is a serious mistake to emphasize worship to the neglect of ethics (the error of religious formalism), and it is an equally serious mistake to emphasize ethical behavior to the neglect of worship (the error of religious activism). Although religion in the Old Testament may have stressed the importance of temple sacrifices, Jesus and the New Testament insist that being religious necessarily entails ethical behavior toward others.[15] In his later work, Chauvet made the connections between scriptures, sacraments, and ethics by presenting these three as constituting the structure of Christian identity within the church.[16]

Meanwhile, Protestants too were exploring the relationship between worship and ethics. Although some Protestant theologians had long insisted on the social message of the New Testament,[17] none before the late twentieth

13. Ibid., 34–35.

14. Ibid., 38.

15. See Louis-Marie Chauvet, *Symbol and Sacrament: A Sacramental Reinterpretation of Christian Existence* (Collegeville, MN: Liturgical Press, 1995), chap. 7, "The Relation between Sacrament and Ethics."

16. See Louis-Marie Chauvet, *The Sacraments: The Word of God at the Mercy of the Body* (Collegeville, MN: Liturgical Press, 2001), 20–31. It should be noted that Chauvet's method does not entail observing and analyzing sacraments as performed; rather, he accepts what the church says about the meaning and purpose of its liturgical rites and explains their effectiveness without resorting to metaphysics. In this approach, sacraments always have the effects that church doctrine says they have, whether or not these effects can be observed and verified in the lives of church members.

17. See Walter Rauschenbusch, *A Theology for the Social Gospel* (New York: Macmillan, 1917); Charles Howard Hopkins, *The Rise of the Social Gospel in American Protestantism, 1865–1915* (New Haven, CT: Yale University Press, 1940); Ronald C. White Jr. and Charles Howard Hopkins, *The Social Gospel: Religion and Reform in Changing America* (Philadelphia: Temple University Press, 1975).

century focused on sacraments and moral behavior. This may be because most Protestant churches have only two sacraments (baptism and Communion) and because nonliturgical churches do not have fixed texts for worship. But ecumenical dialogue after Vatican II brought Protestants into contact with Catholic social teaching, and Catholics at that time were beginning to write about the implications of ritual for Christian living.

Don E. Saliers, a Methodist with close ties to the Catholic liturgical renewal in the 1970s, was one of the first to write regularly about the interconnectedness of worship, morality, and spirituality, having published over a dozen articles in that area.[18] One of the first books on this topic, however, was written by an Episcopalian, Timothy F. Sedgwick, who focused on the paschal mystery as central to both Christian living and Christian worship.[19] In the 1990s, Methodists and Episcopalians (or Anglicans, as they are known outside the United States) continued to dominate the Protestant discussion of Sunday worship and moral practice, reflecting the Methodists' historical concern for personal conversion and social reform, and reflecting the strong liturgical tradition in the Church of England.[20]

In recent decades, Catholic and Protestant authors have juxtaposed liturgy and morality in a number of ways and a variety of contexts. Australian scripture scholar Francis Moloney reexamined the New Testament origins of the Eucharist and concluded that, since Jesus shared meals with sinners and gave his life for the salvation of all, it is unjust to exclude people from receiving Communion because their marital status does not square with the requirements of canon law.[21] Irish American theologian Megan McKenna reflected on all seven sacraments and drew out moral lessons for serving others, telling the truth, sharing with the poor, choosing nonviolence, fostering compassion, nurturing friendship, and valuing obedience.[22] Former missionary William Cavanaugh painfully explored the ambiguous relationship between the Pinochet dictatorship and the Catholic Church in Chile,

18. See the bibliography of Saliers' work in E. Byron Anderson and Bruce T. Morrell, eds., *Liturgy and the Moral Self: Humanity at Full Stretch before God* (Collegeville, MN: Liturgical Press, 1998), 225–30.

19. Timothy F. Sedgwick, *Sacramental Ethics: Paschal Identity and the Christian Life* (Philadelphia: Fortress Press, 1987).

20. See Harmon L. Smith, *Where Two or Three Are Gathered: Liturgy and the Moral Life* (Cleveland, OH: Pilgrim Press, 1995); also Duncan B. Forrester, J. Ian H. McDonald, and Gian Tellini, *Encounter with God: An Introduction to Christian Worship and Practice* (Edinburgh: T&T Clark, 1983 and 1996).

21. See Francis J. Moloney, *A Body Broken for a Broken People: Eucharist in the New Testament* (Australia: Harper Collins, 1990 and 1997).

22. See Megan McKenna, *Rites of Justice: The Sacraments and Liturgy as Ethical Imperatives* (Maryknoll, NY: Orbis Books, 1997).

ultimately concluding that torture and Eucharist are diametrically opposed rituals, so Christians can never morally support a government that practices or even condones the physical abuse of prisoners.[23] Social activist Joseph Grassi and moral theologian Patrick McCormick both reflected on the biblical image of the kingdom of God, drawing out implications of the Eucharist for world hunger and for feeding the poor at home.[24] Kendra Hotz and Matthew Mathews, both Presbyterian theologians, examined how Sunday worship influences moral behavior through the restructuring of religious affections.[25] And returning to the interpretation of liturgy as enunciated by Sedgwick almost twenty years earlier, Catholics Dennis Billy and James Keating extolled the paschal mystery as a way of living that is made present and is celebrated in the Eucharist.[26]

It would be impossible to develop all of these ideas in this chapter, so we shall concentrate on only two of them: the paschal mystery as a model for personal morality, and the kingdom of God as a paradigm for social justice.

2. The Paschal Mystery and Personal Morality

The Catholic Church teaches that there is a close connection between the sacraments and what is known theologically as the paschal mystery. At the Second Vatican Council, the bishops wrote:

> [B]y Baptism men and women are implanted in the paschal mystery of Christ; they die with him, are buried with him, and rise with him. (SC 6)

> [T]he church has never failed to come together to celebrate the paschal mystery. (SC 6)

> [T]he church celebrates the paschal mystery every eighth day. (SC 106)[27]

23. See William T. Cavanaugh, *Torture and Eucharist: Theology, Politics, and the Body of Christ* (Malden, MA: Blackwell Publishers, 1998).

24. See Joseph A. Grassi, *Broken Bread and Broken Bodies: The Lord's Supper and World Hunger* (Maryknoll, NY: Orbis Books, 2004); Patrick T. McCormick, *A Banqueter's Guide to the All-Night Soup Kitchen of the Kingdom of God* (Collegeville, MN: Liturgical Press, 2004).

25. See Kendra G. Hotz and Matthew T. Mathews, *Shaping the Christian Life: Worship and the Religious Affections* (Louisville, KY: Westminster John Knox Press, 2006).

26. See Dennis J. Billy and James Keating, *The Way of Mystery: The Eucharist and Moral Living* (New York: Paulist Press, 2006).

27. Austin Flannery, ed., *Vatican Council II: The Basic Sixteen Documents* (Northport, NY: Costello Publishing Co., 1996).

And the Catechism of the Catholic Church calls the seven sacraments "the sacraments of the paschal mystery."[28]

More often than not, however, the paschal mystery is conceived in nonexperiential terms, that is, the mystery is presented as something that Catholics have to believe in even though they have no personal experience of it. Often referred to as Christ's paschal mystery, it is described as something that Jesus did a long time ago but that has had an effect on humanity ever since, especially on Christians. Exactly how Christ's death and resurrection produced this effect is usually not explained, although a number of theories have been suggested through the centuries.[29] What was said earlier in chapter 3, sections 3e and 4e, about sacred realities and mysteries, however, suggests that it is possible to discuss the paschal mystery in a way that is experiential as well as theological.

☐ *

The word "paschal" comes from the Greek *pascha*, which in turn is derived from the Hebrew *pesach*, meaning to pass by or pass over in some way. In the book of Exodus, God passes over the houses of the Israelites, whose doorposts have been smeared with lamb's blood, and brings death to the firstborn in the houses of the Egyptians, which had no special sign on them.[30] Both the biblical event and the annual commemoration of it were referred to as *Pesach*, or Passover, by the Jews, and the lamb that was killed for the annual *seder*, or Passover supper, was referred to as the paschal lamb.[31] The early followers of Jesus saw a symbolic connection between the slaying of the paschal lamb and the crucifixion, which took place near the feast of Passover. The First Letter to the Corinthians speaks of Christ the paschal lamb that has been sacrificed, and the First Letter of Peter says that the blood of Christ, a spotless lamb, was the ransom paid to free people from an empty tradition.[32] In the Gospel according to John, Jesus is called the lamb of God "who takes away the sin of the world," and the book of Revelation symbolically depicts Christ as a sacrificial lamb.[33] Taking this image literally, Christian

---

*This symbol in the margin indicates an interactive question that can be found at http://www.TheSacraments.org.

---

28. *Catechism of the Catholic Church* (Vatican City: Libreria Editrice Vaticana, 1994), 1182.

29. For a summary of the ransom, satisfaction, exemplar, and liberation theories, see Billy and Keating, *The Way of Mystery*, 10–11.

30. See Exod 11–12, esp. 12:1-34.

31. See Mark 14:12; Luke 22:7.

32. See 1 Cor 5:7; 1 Pet 1:18f.

33. See John 1:29, 36; Rev 5:6–8:1.

thinkers have proposed a variety of theories to explain these texts, but none of the theories was either fully satisfactory or universally accepted.[34]

The New Testament passages are clearly metaphorical, strongly suggesting that they should not be taken literally. Moreover, since they were written by four different authors in four different contexts, it is not obvious that they are all talking about the same thing. The author of First Corinthians is arguing that Christians should pass over from their old way of life to a new way of life. The author of First Peter is arguing that Jesus paid a price so that people could dispense with empty rituals and live more fully. The author of John's gospel says that Jesus takes away the sin of the world, and it is clear from the rest of that gospel that the world's sin is a lack of love, that is, people not caring about one another. And the author of Revelation depicts Christ as a slain lamb whose blood gives salvation; but since blood in the ancient world very often symbolized life rather than death, the meaning is quite possibly that salvation comes from the life of Christ, that is, the Christian way of life, or living the kind of life that Jesus taught and died for.[35] The interpretation that most likely lies behind all four passages is that the Jesus way of life, sometimes called simply the Way in the first century, brings salvation or redemption from sin. It is a way of passing over from spiritual emptiness to the fullness of life, from apathy to vitality, from moral confusion to ethical certitude, from feeling lost to being found, from missing the target to hitting the bull's-eye, from falling short to exceeding one's expectations.

All three synoptic gospels open with a call to conversion, a cry for repentance, an invitation to turn from one way of living to another.[36] That in itself is something of a passing over from one way of being in the world to another, so it could rightly be called a paschal movement. Living through a change in attitude and lifestyle would be something that is experienced and partly, though not fully, understood, so it could also be called a mystery. But the mystery into which Jesus invited people, and the mystery that is most properly called paschal, is the mystery of self-giving love or *agápē*.

34. Expositions of the major theories of redemption or atonement can be found in Peter Schmeichen, *Saving Power: Theories of Atonement and Forms of the Church* (Grand Rapids, MI: William B. Eerdmans, 2005); R. Larry Shelton, *Cross and Covenant: Interpreting the Atonement for 21st Century Mission* (Tyrone, GA: Paternoster, 2006), esp. 155–70; James Beilby and Paul R. Eddy, eds., *The Nature of the Atonement: Four Views* (Downers Grove, IL: Inter-Varsity Press, 2006).

35. Because blood means life, robes washed in the blood of the Lamb are white, not red, in Rev 7:15.

36. Both Mark and Matthew associate John the Baptist's call for repentance and the beginning of Jesus' public ministry with that cry; see Mark 1:4, 15; also Matt 3:2; 4:17. Luke characterizes Jesus' message as one of repentance (*metanoia*), but he calls the first preaching of Jesus a proclamation of good news; see Luke 3:3; 4:18.

Of the many words for love in ancient Greek,[37] the language in which the New Testament was written, the word used nine times out of ten is *agápē*, usually thought of as self-giving love, self-sacrificing love, or unconditional love. But the word "love" in English is primarily a feeling word, a word that names a feeling, whereas *agápē* in Greek is primarily an action word, a word that denotes an activity or kind of behavior. So *agápē* is better translated as care or caring, and Jesus' message of love is better understood as one of caring about and caring for others.[38] Jesus' command to love one's neighbor as oneself means caring for other people the way one takes care of oneself.[39] Jesus' instruction to his followers, "Love one another as I have loved you" (John 13:34; 15:12), is an exhortation to take care of each other just as he had cared for them. And in this light, "There is no greater love than laying down one's life for one's friends" (John 15:12) makes perfect sense, for it is talking about doing something, not feeling something. Moreover, caring about and taking care of others is essentially an act of self-giving, self-surrender, or self-sacrifice. It is a matter of serving others and ministering to their needs rather than serving oneself and looking out for number one. It is a matter, to use the gospel metaphor, of dying so that others might live.

If kept up constantly, such altruistic behavior can be exhausting, leading to what is called burnout among teachers, ministers, nurses, social workers, and others in the helping professions. But the New Testament does not envision a situation in which individuals do this by themselves; rather, it envisions a community in which members of the community take care of one another so that those caring about the needs of others would have their own needs met by people caring about them. As late as the early third century, when Christians were still a small minority in the Roman Empire, pagans were reported to be impressed by how the followers of Jesus took care of each other.[40] In a caring community, the burdens get lighter, not heavier.

37. See C. S. Lewis, *The Four Loves* (New York: Harcourt Brace, 1960); Anders Nygren, *Agape and Eros* (Chicago: University of Chicago Press, 1982); Stephen Garrard Post, *A Theory of Agape: On the Meaning of Christian Love* (Lewisburg, PA: Bucknell University Press, 1990).

38. See Morton T. Kelsey, *Caring: How Can We Love One Another?* (New York: Paulist Press, 1981).

39. See Mark 12:30; Matt 22:39; and Luke 10:27. Indeed, since caring for others often entails serving them, the first of the two great commandments can be understood as serving God (that is, obeying God and doing what God wants) with one's whole heart, mind, and strength.

40. Around the year 200, Tertullian wrote, "But it is mainly the deeds of such a noble love that led many [pagans] to label us, saying, 'See how they love one another!' " (*Apology*, chap. 39).

Most Jews at the time of Jesus did not believe in life after death, so when the New Testament talks about salvation it is unlikely that it means going to heaven. In fact, *soteria* (the Greek word that is usually translated as salvation) does not appear in Matthew and Mark at all, but only in Luke, the gospel writer who is traditionally pictured as a physician, as well as in Acts of the Apostles, which was written by him.[41] In these places, *soteria* can easily be translated as well-being in the sense of being well in the here and now.

Converting from a life of self-seeking to a life of self-giving, while it appears to be hazardous at the beginning, turns out to be unexpectedly rewarding. It is actually a healthy way of living, and the Latin root of the word "salvation" is *salus*, meaning health. It can also be a very rewarding and satisfying lifestyle, as those in religious orders and monasteries can attest. But one does not need to be a monk or a nun to experience the benefits of choosing a life of service. Teachers and social workers, paramedics and firefighters, people who do volunteer work and people who work for non-profit organizations often find themselves being rewarded in ways that money cannot buy. They find that being dedicated to helping others is life-giving and energizing. One could say that dying to self is deeply revitalizing: death leads to resurrection. Experiencing that passage from self-effacement to self-fulfillment is one way to experience the paschal mystery.

There is a natural cycle of death and rebirth: daylight dies in the evening and is reborn in the morning; seeds die, giving birth to plants; one generation passes and another comes into the world; vegetation dies in the fall and comes back in the spring. The Anglo-Saxon goddess of this life cycle was Eostre, whose name and spring festival gave us our word for the feast of Christ's resurrection. That natural phenomenon of periodic rebirth is the reason for the appearance of bunnies, eggs, and chicks in the secular symbolism of Easter on greeting cards, chocolates, and other consumer goods. But the Christian feast of Easter does not celebrate this natural cycle, which is something that happens whether we want it to or not. It is something to celebrate, and indeed it is celebrated with new clothes, strolling through a park or zoo, and other outings. The life cycle may be a mystery, which is why it is celebrated in nature religions, but it is not the paschal mystery.

It is common among Catholic writers to say that the paschal mystery of Christ is found in his death and resurrection (and some also mention his ascension into heaven), but a broader and more experiential understanding of the mystery being presented here suggests that Jesus entered fully and

41. See Luke 1:69-71; 2:30; 3:6; 19:9; Acts 4:12; 13:26; 13:47; 28:28.

deliberately into the paschal mystery at the very outset of his public ministry. When Jesus finished praying and fasting in the desert, he started a new life of proclaiming the good news that the way to a rich and rewarding life is neither through a mechanical following of moral law nor through the formalities of ritual but through caring about and caring for others, which, according to Jesus, sums up the teaching of the *torah* and the prophets.[42] Once he embarked on this mission, he lived the paschal mystery by becoming an itinerant preacher rather than a respectable carpenter, by healing people's physical and spiritual hurts, by not giving up in the face of opposition, and in the end by going to Jerusalem rather than running away from danger. His predictable execution and unexpected resurrection symbolized what he had been living all his adult life; that is, the events of his last days on earth were an icon of what his life had been all about. ☐

Understandably, when Jesus' first followers figured this out (Luke uses the symbolic figure of forty days to represent this time of listening to the Lord after the resurrection[43]), they had something to celebrate, for Jesus' resurrection was also their rebirth—or rather, their birth as a community, as a church, or in the words of St. Paul, as the body of Christ now living the paschal mystery with one another and sharing this good news with others. They celebrated it in the breaking of bread, as eucharistic meals were first called; they celebrated it on the first day of the week, which was the day of the resurrection; and they celebrated it once a year on the Sunday closest to the Jewish feast of Passover to commemorate Jesus' passing over from death to life. In both the weekly meal and the annual feast, they gathered to give thanks (*eucharistein*) for the mystery that Jesus had revealed to them, that dying to self was the way to really come alive. ☐

When Christians today celebrate the paschal mystery, therefore, it is their own mystery that they are celebrating—or at least ought to be, for too often they believe they are celebrating something that happened long ago and far away. Indeed, church documents easily lend themselves to this interpretation in many cases. For example:

> This work of human redemption and perfect glorification of God . . . Christ the Lord completed principally in the paschal mystery of his blessed passion, resurrection from the dead, and glorious ascension, whereby "dying, he destroyed our death and rising, restored our life." (SC 5)

> The Church celebrates in the liturgy above all the Paschal mystery by which Christ accomplished the work of our salvation. (CCC 1067)

42. See Matt 7:12; 22:36-40.
43. See Acts 1:3.

In the liturgy of the Church, it is principally his own Paschal mystery that Christ signifies and makes present. (CCC 1085)

In each of these quotations, the reference is to something that happened to Jesus, through which he accomplished the salvation of others.

Catholic writers easily slip into this objectification of the paschal mystery, projecting it onto Christ alone even though it is said to have an effect on others. In *The Way of Mystery*, for example, Dennis Billy and James Keating state at the beginning of their treatment,

> Christ's paschal mystery heals humanity of its deep inner wound so that it can share in the divine fellowship. It does so by doing for humanity what humanity is unable to do for itself.
>
> Through Jesus, humanity has become divinized. This process of divinization extends to the human universal and is concretized in each individual through a divine adoption. Through Jesus, each human being has the opportunity of becoming an adopted son or daughter of God and, because of this adoption, can overcome the weakness of the human condition.[44]

If Catholic doctrine says that the paschal mystery has a redemptive effect on humanity, and especially on the baptized, Catholic theology has the task of explaining how this happens. How could something that happened to one person at a certain place and time have an effect on all people for all time? Recognizing this problem, Billy and Keating summarize various theories that have been proposed in Christian history, most notably the ransom theory, the satisfaction theory, the exemplar theory, and the liberation theory.[45] The authors suggest that each theory has its own strengths, but nonetheless, "no one theory is capable of exhausting the depths of the mystery."[46] They do broaden their approach to include Christ's life as well as his death and resurrection, and they do connect it with the process of sanctification or growth in holiness, but they never clearly state that the paschal mystery is something that we can experience.

At the same time, however, much that they say about the paschal mystery can be understood in experiential terms.

> Jesus laid down his life for us; we in turn lay down our lives for others through a life dedicated to ministry and service. In doing so we allow Christ to live out his paschal mystery anew: we become sharers in his

---

44. Billy and Keating, *The Way of Mystery*, 8, 9.
45. Ibid., 10–14.
46. Ibid., 14.

passion, death and resurrection; we also participate in the mystery of Christ's redemptive action.

Christ's paschal mystery touches every dimension of human existence. . . . [It] addresses the social dimension of experience. . . . It promises to transform every aspect of our personal makeup.[47]

Since Billy and Keating speak of the paschal mystery as something that we experience when we live selflessly and altruistically instead of being self-centered and self-seeking, what they say about Christ's paschal mystery can also be said more generally about the paschal mystery. In other words, just as Jesus experienced the paschal mystery, so also can we, when we live as he did, for the sake of others, rather than for ourselves.   □

By the same token, the quotations at the beginning of this section, from Vatican II and the Catechism, can also be understood experientially, for baptism plunges us into a community that has chosen a paschal way of life, this way of life is celebrated by Christians in their Sunday Eucharist, and it is symbolized in some way by the other six sacraments as well.   □

The eucharistic liturgy is a complex and malleable ritual that celebrates many things (divine mercy, God's glory, salvation history, the local and universal church, the Last Supper, and spiritual communion—to name some that are mentioned in the rite itself), and it is used to celebrate many more things (the life of Christ, the lives of the saints, parish and diocesan events, anniversaries, funerals, and so on). But it is also a celebration of the paschal mystery insofar as that mystery is being deliberately lived by the worshiping community in their personal and public lives, and insofar as they make the connection between what Jesus did and what they are doing. Baptism of course is an initiation into the paschal life, and confirmation is an affirmation of that way of life. Penance, or reconciliation, facilitates turning away from self-seeking attitudes and behavior, and returning to habits of caring about and caring for others. Marriage celebrates the living of the paschal mystery in sexual intimacy and family relationships, and ordination celebrates living that same mystery in service to the church. Anointing of the sick reaffirms that resurrection is a reality to be hoped for, and that both suffering and death can lead to God.   □

Understood from this perspective, the paschal morality that flows from living the paschal mystery is not the morality of the Ten Commandments but the morality of the Eight Beatitudes. It is the morality of being happy with less instead of always wanting more, of being gentle rather than aggressive,

47. Ibid., 21, 26–28.

of being compassionate rather than cold-hearted, of being fair-minded rather than prejudiced, of being merciful rather than vengeful, of having pure rather than mixed motives, of making peace rather than seeking victory, of risking persecution rather than playing it safe.[48]

In his book *Sacramental Ethics*, Timothy Sedgwick argues that Christian faith is not so much a matter of belief as a matter of trusting that the paschal way of life is the way God wants us to live. Thus the Christian life is both a gift (grace) and a struggle. It is a gift inasmuch as we receive it from being immersed (baptized) in a local community and ecclesiastical tradition, and from the example of parents and others who have modeled caring and altruistic behavior for us. It is a struggle inasmuch as the relationship to ourselves, other people, our world, and God is always in flux, always in development, "and the choices we make either separate us from or drive us deeper into the paschal mystery."[49]

3. The Kingdom of God and Social Justice

There are over a hundred references to the kingdom of God in the New Testament and about three-quarters of these are found in the gospels. Evidently, this was a recurring theme and an important image in Jesus' preaching. In Matthew and Mark, Jesus begins his public ministry by proclaiming the coming of the kingdom,[50] although to avoid mentioning the divine name out of consideration for his Jewish audience, Matthew substitutes the word "heaven" for the word "God."[51]

Like the paschal mystery, the kingdom of God is a metaphor whose meaning is not entirely clear. By the end of the first century, the kingdom had become an image of what this world will look like after the second coming of Christ: "The kingdom of this world has become the kingdom of our Lord and of his Christ, and he shall reign for ever and ever" (Rev 11:15).[52] Other books of the New Testament written late in the first century appear to speak of the kingdom as a place in the hereafter. Second Peter 1:11 speaks of "the eternal kingdom of our Lord and Savior Jesus Christ,"

---

48. See Matt 5:3-10.
49. Sedgwick, *Sacramental Ethics*, 46. See esp. chap. 3, "Worship and Paschal Identity."
50. See Matt 3:2; Mark 1:15.
51. Even today, devout Jews will often write "G-d" rather than "God." Out of reverence, the Hebrew name of God, YHWH, is never spoken by Jews, who substitute the word *Adonai* (Lord) whenever they read a biblical text, with the result that scholars are not completely sure how "YHWH" should be pronounced.
52. See also Rev 12:10.

and James 2:5 promises that those who are rich in faith will inherit the kingdom. Persuaded by this imagery, most Christians by the Middle Ages equated the kingdom of God with heaven, a place of eternal reward that could be entered only after death, and some theologians argued that the Catholic Church was the kingdom of God on earth since the church's sacraments offered all that was needed for salvation.[53]

The earliest books of the New Testament are the authentic letters of the apostle Paul, which were written before any of the four canonical gospels. Although Paul on occasion speaks of the end times when Christ will hand over his kingdom to the Father (1 Cor 15:24), he more frequently speaks of the kingdom as something in the present, as in Romans 14:17: "The kingdom of God is not about eating and drinking but about right living, peace and joy in the spirit of holiness," and in 1 Corinthians 4:20: "The kingdom of God is not a matter of words but one of strength." It must be admitted, however, that Paul also uses the phrase, "inherit the kingdom," to mean being with Christ after he returns, which Paul seems to have expected to happen during his lifetime, at least at the beginning of his ministry.[54] Perhaps one could say that, in Paul's mind, unless one were living in the kingdom of God before the second coming, one could not live in it when Christ returned in glory.

Scripture scholars sometimes speak of God's kingdom as being both in the present and in the future, reflecting the ambiguity that is found in the New Testament texts themselves.[55] In an effort to clear up some of this ambiguity, the Greek phrase, *to basileia tou theou*, is sometimes translated as "the reign of God" or "the rule of God," indicating that when the *basileia* is found in the present, it is not in any geographic location but wherever God reigns, that is, wherever God's will is being obeyed.[56] Indeed, in all but one place in Acts of the Apostles, references to the *basileia* are to God's ruling in people's hearts.[57] Nevertheless, this ambiguity can be traced back to Jesus' own use of the metaphor, for sometimes the image refers to the

---

53. Much of this theological speculation can be traced to Augustine's *City of God*, written in the early fifth century. This notion can still occasionally be found in church documents such as the Dogmatic Constitution on the Church, 3.

54. See 1 Cor 6:9f; 15:24; Gal 5:21; 1 Thess 2:12; 2 Thess 1:5.

55. On this point, see "The Kingdom of God" in Raymond E. Brown, Joseph A. Fitzmyer, and Roland E. Murphy, eds., *The Jerome Biblical Commentary* (Englewood Cliffs, NJ: Prentice-Hall, 1968), 782ff., esp. nos. 97–98; also "Kingdom of God" in John L. McKenzie, *Dictionary of the Bible* (Milwaukee, WI: Bruce Publishing Co., 1965), 479–82.

56. Feminist scholars and others interested in inclusive language also prefer avoiding the term "kingdom" because of its masculine overtones.

57. See Acts 8:12; 14:22; 19:8; 20:25; 28:23; 28:31.

political kingdom that Jews at the time expected the messiah to establish, sometimes it refers to a spiritual state of being or a moral way of living, and sometimes its reference is uncertain.

That the metaphor of living in the kingdom of God means living under the reign of God or behaving according to God's rules for living is clearest in the following texts.

Matthew 5:10; 5:20; 6:33	Living under God's rule means doing what is right.
Matthew 6:10; 7:21	Living in the kingdom of God means doing God's will.
Matthew 13:44-46	Living under God's reign is of great value.
Matthew 18:1-4; 19:14	Living in the kingdom means being childlike.
Mark 4:26-32	God's reign is like a seed planted in individuals and in society.
Mark 10:14-15	Innocent children live the way God wants people to live.
Mark 10:23-24	It is hard for the wealthy to live the way God wants people to live.
Luke 6:20	If you are poor, you are living the way God wants you to live.
Luke 4:43; 8:1; 9:2; 9:60	Jesus preaches the good news of God's way of living.
Luke 9:11; 10:9; 11:20	Under God's rule, those who are sick are healed and evil spirits are cast out.
Luke 11:20; 13:29	In God's kingdom, the hungry are fed.
Luke 17:20-21	God's reign is not something visible but it is something within.
Luke 18:29-30	Working to establish God's reign is rewarding.
John 3:3-5	Coming under God's reign requires a spiritual rebirth.

Thus we come back to the beginning of Jesus' ministry and his announcement of the good news that God's reign is available to those who repent of their old ways and convert to God's way of living.[58] Mark's re-

58. See Matt 3:2; Mark 1:15.

counting of the incident about the greatest commandment shows that living in God's kingdom means caring about God and caring for others. For in his version of the story, the official who puts the question to Jesus agrees that loving God and neighbor is more important than religious rituals, to which Jesus replies, "You are not far from the kingdom of God" (Mark 12:34).[59] Living in the kingdom therefore means living according to the two great commandments, proclaiming the kingdom of God means telling others that this is both possible and desirable, and the good news of the kingdom is that living this way is richly rewarding. But this does not mean that getting into the kingdom is easy, "For the gate is small and the path narrow that leads to life, and there are few who find it" (Matt 7:14). Nor is it easy to establish God's kingdom on earth, for God's rule is always "under attack, and the violent try to undo it by force" (Matt 11:12). ☐

In the Constitution on the Church (*Lumen Gentium*), the Second Vatican Council invoked the image of the kingdom in speaking about the work of Christ and in speaking about its own work as well, acknowledging that the kingdom of God is visible in the person and ministry of Christ, and formulating its own mission as the spreading of God's kingdom among all the peoples of the earth (LG 5). Moreover, according to the council, it is not just clergy and religious who engage in this mission because it is "the special vocation of the laity to seek the kingdom of God by engaging in temporal affairs and directing them according to God's will," that is, according to the way God wants people to live in peace and harmony with one another (LG 31). For if God reigns in people's hearts and they live according to the rules of justice and love revealed in the scriptures, the result will be "the kingdom of truth and life, the kingdom of holiness and grace, the kingdom of justice, love and peace" (LG 36).[60] Jesus commanded his followers, "Seek God's reign and justice above all," and in the vision of the council, whoever cares enough to help others by working for justice is doing precisely that.[61] ☐

But what do sacraments have to do with justice? Liberation theologians in the 1970s were quick to point out restricting religion to church rituals could actually hinder the coming of God's kingdom by leading people to believe that all they had to do was go to church in order to be good Catholics. Focusing exclusively on the sacraments could actually blind people to the deeper dimensions of their Christian faith and cause them to ignore the needs of people around them. Reading the scriptures with new eyes, Juan

59. See Mark 12:28-34.
60. See also GS 39.
61. Matt 6:33; see GS 72.

Luis Segundo and others saw in the words of the Old Testament prophets a condemnation of their own church's religious formalism:

> I hate, I despise your festivals,
>   and I take no delight in your solemn assemblies.
> Even though you offer me your burnt offerings
>   and grain offerings, I will not accept them.
> Take away from me the noise of your songs;
>   I will not listen to the melody of your harps.
> But let justice roll down like waters,
>   and righteousness like an ever-flowing stream.
>   (Amos 5:21-24)

Liberation theologians argued that in Latin America the sacraments had become instruments of oppression and domestication, and they hoped that instead they could become instruments of consciousness raising and social liberation. This did not happen broadly in the church, but Catholic theologians became more conscious of the social implications of the sacraments and they became more aware of the need for symbolic honesty, that is, for a worshiping community to be true to what its rituals say about it. The development of this dimension of sacramental theology was summarized in the first section of this chapter.

It remains that we look at each of the sacraments in relation to the kingdom of God, that is to say, in relation to caring for others in a society that is just and fair. In doing this, we will look first at social justice issues in the history of the sacrament, then at social justice issues that are raised by the symbolism of the sacrament, and finally at social justice issues that are connected with participation in the sacrament.

a. Baptism

Of all the sacramental rituals, baptism appears to be the oldest. We know from reading the New Testament that ritual immersion in water was practiced by the cousin of Jesus known as John the Baptist even before Jesus began his own ministry.[62] Both John and Jesus preached repentance—*metanoia* in Greek, which means conversion of mind, heart, and behavior—because "the kingdom of God is at hand" (Matt 3:2; 4:17). They were proclaiming that it is possible to get into God's way of living by changing one's way of looking at oneself, feeling about others, and acting in the world. As we have already seen, the way to live under God's reign is to be motivated by *agápē*,

---

62. See Matt 3:1-12; Mark 1:1-8; Luke 3:1-18; John 1:19-28.

caring about and doing what God wants by caring about and caring for others. ☐

By all indications, the early Christian community was a fellowship of people who tried to take care of one another the way Jesus had shown them. They tried to be filled with his spirit, the spirit of God, rather than with the spirit of selfishness and sinfulness that may have characterized their lives in the past. As the apostle Paul described it, together they were Christ in the world, the social body of Christ animated by the spirit of Christ.[63] They stood out in marked contrast to the society around them, whose unjust economic system left most people in poverty; whose unjust social system pitted peasants against merchants, Jews against Gentiles, and Pharisees against Sadducees; and whose unjust political system was ruled by a puppet king loyal to the Roman emperor. In a sense, the followers of Jesus were an island of social justice surrounded by a sea of social injustice. ☐

The way onto this island, moreover, was through water. Jews at the time practiced what was known as proselyte baptism for converts to their religion, a ritual of immersion in water that symbolized the converts' oneness with the Israelites who had to pass through the Jordan River in order to enter the Promised Land. Whether in imitation of John's baptism for the washing away of sins or of Jewish baptism for entering a community of believers, the early followers of Jesus adopted this practice to symbolize and facilitate people's moving from unhealthy to healthy living, or as they would have phrased it, moving from sinfulness to salvation. As time went on, the ritual symbolism became more elaborate, and by the second century people who were baptized in private homes were asked to remove all clothing and jewelry before entering the water, and they were dressed in a new white garment when they came out of it, symbolizing that they were stripping away what they used to be and adopting a new purity of mind and heart like that of Christ.[64] Today's baptismal rite still includes the white garment as well as other symbols, such as a lighted candle signifying that the lifestyle of the baptized should be a beacon of light and hope for others.[65] And of

63. See Rom 7:4; 8:9-11; 12:4-5; 1 Cor 12:12-27. Also Eph 4:1-13, which was probably not written by Paul himself but someone who adopted and expanded Paul's theological ideas.

64. On the history of baptism, see Joseph Martos, *Doors to the Sacred: A Historical Introduction to Sacraments in the Catholic Church* (Liguori, MO: Liguori/Triumph, 2001), chap. 6; also, Lorna Brockett, *The Theology of Baptism* (Notre Dame, IN: Fides Publishers, 1971). Look also at Rom 13:14 and Col 3:9-10, which possibly inspired this development in the ritual.

65. See the Rite of Christian Initiation of Adults in *The Rites of the Catholic Church*, vol.1 (Collegeville, MN: Liturgical Press, 1990), 229–30; also Rite of Baptism for Children, 99–100.

course the central symbolism of immersion itself is an action that both symbolizes and facilitates one's immersion in the Christian community and in a life of self-giving.

Since the restoration of the Rite of Christian Initiation of Adults, what used to be called the Christian vocation is now often referred to as the baptismal call, emphasizing that the life to which all are called as followers of Christ is presented in the symbols of the baptismal rite: the water, the candle, the white garment, the baptismal promises, and so forth. Ritual honesty on the part of baptismal candidates demands that they have indeed been through a conversion process, so that they do in fact intend to live according to God's rules in the spirit of Jesus. Ritual honesty on the part of the baptizing community requires that it be a true body of Christ animated by the spirit of Jesus, caring for one another and working to further God's kingdom of justice and compassion on earth.

There are adults, however, who want to join the church but who are prevented from doing so, not because they are unwilling to follow the gospel imperative to love God and others but because ecclesiastical regulations stand in their way. People who were married outside the Catholic Church are not allowed to join the church unless their prior marriage conforms to canon law, and so if they had ever been divorced, they have to subject themselves to an annulment process that may take a year and whose outcome is by no means certain. Not only this, but people who were never divorced but who married someone that had been divorced are likewise barred from full initiation into the church because, in the legalistic mentality of canon law, they would be "living in sin" with a divorced person whose prior marriage had not been annulled; in other words, they would be technically living with a bigamist. Such legalistic reasoning about technicalities brings to mind Jesus' condemnation of the Pharisees:

> Woe to you lawyers who lay unbearable burdens on people's shoulders and do not move a finger to lift them! (Luke 11:46)[66]

Social justice and care for catechumens call on the church's leadership to rethink its marriage policies and ease the legal burden on divorced people who want to become Catholics.

Expanding our horizons, we can think about baptism in relation to evangelization. From the sixteenth to the nineteenth century, Catholic missionaries braved danger and hardship, even suffering and death to convert native

66. Compare Matt 23:4.

peoples in North and South America, Africa, and Asia to Christianity, with the result that Christianity is the largest religion and Catholicism is the largest church in the world today. Those missionaries were motivated by the belief that they were saving people's souls by baptizing them, and according to one account, St. Francis Xavier in India baptized 10,000 people in just a few months. For religious orders that engaged in missionary work, bringing baptism to people was a matter of social justice, for the pagan masses needed to be converted if they were to have any hope of entering heaven, and it would have been unjust to withhold the sacraments from them.

In recent decades, however, Catholics have moved away from this magical understanding of baptism and, as a result, Catholic missionary efforts have dwindled sharply. Vatican II's Declaration on the Relationship of the Church to Non-Christian Religions (*Nostra Aetate*) implied that people could be saved (that is, they could get into heaven) without necessarily converting to Christianity, and so the impulse to save souls is not as strong today as it used to be. But if baptism is thought of as immersion into a caring community and into Jesus' way of life (rather than as converting to a new religion to obtain salvation after death), then clearly millions of people around the world are still in desperate need of baptism, and social justice demands that Christians should do all in their power to spread the kingdom of God on earth. Many people perceive this need and either join or contribute to humanitarian organizations that work with the poor and oppressed. Many of these organizations are religious in orientation and some are even Catholic, such as Caritas International, Catholic Charities, and Catholic Relief Services. But Catholics on the whole, and Catholic church leaders in particular, have not yet realized that the sacrament of baptism, understood as dying to self and rising with Christ in the kingdom of God, is key to the salvation of the world from poverty and oppression.   □

b. Confirmation

Confirmation is closely related to baptism both historically and theologically. Historically, the bishop's blessing in the initiation process was detached from the other ritual actions when Christian communities got too large for the bishop to be present at all baptisms. Beginning in the fourth century, newcomers into the church were baptized by priests, and later these baptisms were confirmed by the local bishop. Theologians in the Middle Ages reflected on the words and gestures in this separated rite and developed an explanation for it, a theology of confirmation. Since the words accompanying the bishop's action made reference to the Holy Spirit, the theology of confirmation invariably tried to show how the rite was connected to receiving the Spirit.[67]

Although the emergence of confirmation as a separate sacrament was definitely a matter of pastoral concern, it could not really be viewed as a matter of social justice except insofar as each bishop now owed it to the newly baptized to confirm their membership in the church and give them his blessing. Sadly, the history of the sacraments shows that bishops were too often remiss in meeting this obligation. Nevertheless, the traditional theology of the sacrament could easily be related to the kingdom of God because the recipients of the bishop's blessing were said to be strengthened by the Holy Spirit for spreading and defending the faith.

Today the symbolism of the sacrament lends itself to a connection with social justice because the words of the rite ask that confirmation candidates receive "the spirit of wisdom and understanding, / the spirit of right judgment and courage, / the spirit of knowledge and reverence,"[68] which gifts are needed if they are to "give witness to Christ / by lives built on faith and love."[69] Moreover, the ritual actions of laying on hands and anointing with chrism both symbolize the Holy Spirit being poured down on the candidates, and if the Holy Spirit is the spirit of self-giving love, then the rite is symbolically saying that those who are confirmed ought to be filled with compassion and practice self-sacrifice toward others.

As with baptism, however, the current practice of confirmation raises social justice concerns with regard to those who are invited to participate in the sacrament. Depending on the operative theology in a given diocese, the ages of those who are confirmed can range from seven to eighteen years, that is, from before First Communion to senior year in high school. Although religious educators undoubtedly do their best to explain the rationale for each diocese's confirmation policy, it is hard to see how such a wide variety of practices can be explained with much intellectual coherence. It would seem that the U.S. bishops owe American Catholics a unified and plausible theology of confirmation.

It can be argued, moreover, that in those places where teenagers are confirmed, there is little or no active support for those youngsters. The theology behind the confirmation of adolescents suggests that the ceremony is an occasion for them to consciously affirm the baptismal promises that were made for them in infancy, and that this is an opportunity for them to

67. On the history of confirmation, see Martos, *Doors to the Sacred*, chap. 7; also, Austin P. Milner, *The Theology of Confirmation* (Notre Dame, IN: Fides Publishers, 1971).

68. Rite of Confirmation, 25.

69. Ibid., 30.

assume their rightful roles as adult members of the church. But the fact is that most parishes are not equipped to invite young people into lay ministry, nor to support such an expanded ministry spiritually and financially. As a result, instead of confirmation being the beginning of an adult faith life, it is often the end of participation in church activities. In justice, dioceses and parishes need to do more to enable the confirmed to live up to their baptismal promises and heed their baptismal call to ministry.   ☐

c. Reconciliation

Looking at the history of this sacrament, it is clear that it arose out of a pastoral concern for social justice. In the first decades of Christianity, the only way into the community of believers was through the baptismal process, and there was no provision for welcoming back those who had fallen away and wanted to return. In the second century this began to change, and by the third century there was a fully functioning process of public reconciliation for those who repented of having publicly left the church. Late in the fourth century, this system of canonical penance (as it was sometimes called, because it was governed by church rules or canons) became increasingly dysfunctional for a variety of reasons, and it fell into disuse. In the fifth and sixth centuries, monks in missionary lands saw a need to assure repentant sinners of God's forgiveness, and so they took the monastic practice of privately confessing one's shortcomings to a spiritual guide and adapted it for use outside the monastery. For some centuries it did not matter whether the confessor was a priest or not (many monks were lay brothers), but by the twelfth century private confession had become a clerical practice and confession to a layperson gradually disappeared. It can be said, therefore, that at the beginning of the Christian era and at the beginning of the Middle Ages, pastors felt it was not fair to exclude people from the life of the church, and so they devised sacramental means to bring them back into full communion with the body of Christ.[70]   ☐

If any sacrament today is about justice, it is certainly the sacrament of reconciliation. We often think of justice as being rewarded for doing good and punished for doing bad, and it is true that the theology of penance in the past often dwelt on punishment for sins and doing penances to make up for sins that had been committed. (The words "penance," "repentant," "penalty," "penitential," and "punishment" are all related to a common Latin

---

70. On the history of sacramental reconciliation, see Martos, *Doors to the Sacred*, chap. 9; also, Ladislas Orsy, *The Evolving Church and the Sacrament of Penance* (Denville, NJ: Dimension Books, 1978).

root, *poen.*) Although the concept of punitive or retributive justice is a valid one, the Bible is more often concerned with restorative justice or restoring broken relationships. Thus Old Testament law often insisted on returning stolen goods or otherwise making reparation to someone who had been sinned against, and in the New Testament Jesus tells his followers to make amends with those they offended and to reach out to those who have offended them.[71] The change in the English name of the sacrament after Vatican II, from penance to reconciliation, reflects this biblical mentality.

The symbolism of the sacrament tells us that God is willing to forgive any sin if we repent of that sin and return to the path of right living. The theology of reconciliation affirms that people are not what they did; rather all are children of God even though they sometimes cause harm to themselves and others. Jesus himself notoriously hung out with prostitutes, extortionists (a.k.a. tax collectors), and other people of ill repute (generally referred to in the gospels as sinners).[72] Catholics who take the sacrament of reconciliation seriously should be the last to condemn people as prostitutes or pimps, thieves or murderers, addicts or pushers, abortionists or child abusers, dismissing them as unworthy of love and attention. Faith in God and in the teachings of Jesus, hope for the salvation of others, and self-giving love or caring for others—these three guiding principles (traditionally referred to as the virtues of faith, hope, and charity) suggest that Christians should reach out to sinners rather than ignore, belittle, and punish them.

Moreover, if the church is truly a reconciling community, dioceses and parishes should be doing more to bring about reconciliation in society. Some Protestant churches offer family counseling and domestic mediation services to foster reconciliation between husbands and wives and between parents and children. Others have a special mission to work with addicts or gangs or others who are engaged in self-destructive and antisocial behavior. Every Catholic diocese has an office of Catholic Charities, but many parishes could also be engaged in reaching out to and helping the homeless, the unemployed, the poor, and the neglected in society, showing them how God loves them, and creating community between the fortunate and the unfortunate in the parish. Taking the value of reconciliation seriously, the church should also be at the forefront of prison reform, transforming the penal code and the criminal justice system from one that emphasizes retribution to one that is based on restorative justice.

71. See, for example, Matt 5:23-24; 18:15-17.
72. See Matt 9:10-13; 11:19; Mark 2:15-17; Luke 5:29-31; 7:34; 15:1-2.

There is even room for greater justice in the practice of this sacrament. During the decade following Vatican II, some bishops used the third form of the restored rite, which allows for general confession and absolution in extraordinary circumstances, to convey God's love and forgiveness to large groups of people who had little access to private confession (mainly in Latin America and mission lands with insufficient numbers of priests) or to people who had become alienated from the institutional church (mainly in North America and Europe). Although this imaginative use of the rite met with pastoral success and popular approval, church authorities in Rome eventually intervened and defined extraordinary circumstances more narrowly, restricting the third form of the rite to emergency situations such as an impending disaster. This legalistic concern for the formalities of the ritual (such as the personal confession of individual sins) protects what is called the integrity of the rite, but at the same time it removes a sacrament of reconciliation from people for whom it could be a genuine sign of God's care for them. As it stands, large numbers of people are deprived of the benefits of the sacrament, which on the face of it is a condition of social injustice. The situation could be remedied by loosening the restrictions on the third form of the rite, or alternatively, by creatively restoring the ministry of this sacrament to laypeople, as was the practice in the early Middle Ages.   □

d. Anointing of the Sick

This sacrament arose out of a pastoral concern that could also be called a social concern and a matter of distributive justice. During the first eight centuries of Christianity there was no liturgical ritual for ministering to those suffering from physical ailments, but in many places people with a reputation for holiness practiced what might today be called a healing ministry, praying over and touching people who were sick or in pain, and asking God to grant them relief and recovery. In a world without modern medicine, spiritual practices such as these, along with folk remedies, offered the only way to deal with illness and suffering. And in a world without modern transportation, those with healing powers could not always get to those who were in need of healing, so they would bless something (water, oil, a piece of cloth, a cross of wood) that would be carried to the sick person in the hope of conveying the power of the healer to those who needed to receive it. This was a magical practice, to be sure, but it was effective enough that the practice continued for generations.[73]   □

---

73. The practice was magical in the sense discussed in chap. 3, sec. 4d, above. Medical research has found that the placebo effect (the belief in the curative power of a substance or

The distribution of healing symbols in the church was restricted in the ninth century when some well-intentioned bishops in France added anointing of the sick to the duties of priests, and once anointing was perceived as a clerical duty, anointing by laypeople was discouraged and eventually forbidden. Because recovery did not always follow anointing, the prayers of the rite slowly evolved from petitions for healing to requests for God's mercy and preparation for death, and the name of the sacrament became *extrema unctio* or last anointing. Historical research prior to the Second Vatican Council brought to light this restrictive development, so the world's Catholic bishops directed that the sacrament be restored to its original purpose and that its name be changed to anointing of the sick. Very prudently, the practice of the sacrament was located within the pastoral care of the sick, and different forms of the rite allowed it to be performed in group as well as in individual settings, and in church as well as in health-care settings.[74]

The symbolism of the sacrament is seen more clearly in the action of praying for and anointing the sick rather than in the words of the rite, for the visual image of the healthy attending to the aged and infirm often has a greater impact than the prayers being said. As the old adage has it, actions speak louder than words. The sacramental ceremony is an icon of Christlike care and concern for the needy, especially when it involves caregivers as well as clergy in the liturgical performance.

Today's health-care industry originated centuries ago in the monastic practice of offering hospitality to travelers and those in need of physical or spiritual care. In fact, the words "hospital" and "hotel" are both derived from the Latin *hospitalitas*. Christian care for the sick led to the establishment of religious orders dedicated to nursing and to the founding of Catholic hospitals that offered high quality care at little or no cost to the poor. In recent decades, however, most Catholic hospitals have gotten so big and expensive that they have become virtually indistinguishable from public hospitals, and their value as symbols of Christian caring is being lost. At the same time, the health-care needs of the rural poor and urban poor are

---

action that has no medicinal value) is effective about 30 percent of the time, so it is quite plausible that a third of those who sought healing from Christian practitioners experienced some relief from their ailment. This rate of success would have been sufficient to keep the practice alive for centuries. Even today the placebo effect is not fully understood, and it plausibly has a spiritual dimension that cannot be accessed by physical research. See, for example, Richard L. Kradin, *The Placebo Response and the Power of Unconscious Healing* (New York: Routledge, 2008).

74. On the history of anointing, see Martos, *Doors to the Sacred*, chap. 10; also, James L. Empereur, *Prophetic Anointing: God's Call to the Sick, the Elderly, and the Dying* (Wilmington, DE: Michael Glazier, 1982).

being neglected, and millions of people without health insurance have nowhere to turn for their most basic health needs. Especially in the developing world, children and adults die every day from illnesses that are preventable by adequate sanitation and from diseases that are curable with elementary medical attention. Perhaps the time has come for Catholics to return to the roots of monastic hospitality and envision a new mission of service to the sick, not in expensive hospitals, but in rural and urban clinics that extend Christ's compassion to the sick and the needy.   □

The shortage of priests in recent decades is exacerbating the problem that was first created in the ninth century, when the ministry of anointing was assigned to the clergy. Today there are simply not enough priests to bring the sacrament to all who could benefit from it. The need is being met informally by hospital chaplains who devise their own rituals for bringing spiritual comfort to the sick, and also by some courageous bishops who devise simple rites to be used by deacons and lay ministers, but in justice there ought to be an institutional response from the church to address the problem of the sacrament's unavailability around the world.   □

e. Marriage

Although official Catholic documents since the Council of Trent (1563) say that Christ raised marriage to the dignity of a sacrament,[75] this must be understood theologically as an action of the risen Christ in the church. It is a matter of historical record that the institutional church did not get involved in marital matters before the early Middle Ages, very often because of justice concerns and the protection of women. In those days it was possible for a couple to exchange marriage vows without witnesses and without a public record, and sometimes women who entered such clandestine marriages were later abandoned by their husbands and left without any legal recourse. Even women who were publicly married were vulnerable if their husband wanted to divorce them, or if they were widowed, or if they could not recover their dowry. For these and a variety of other social reasons, the church began insisting that all marriages be witnessed by a priest, entered in parish records, and protected by canon law. By the twelfth century, a religious church ceremony had displaced the family wedding ceremony that had earlier been customary.[76]   □

---

75. See GS 48; Canon 1055; CCC 1601.

76. On the history of marriage as a sacrament, see Martos, *Doors to the Sacred*, chap. 11; also, Edward Schillebeeckx, *Marriage: Human Reality and Sacred Mystery* (New York: Sheed and Ward, 1965).

Today's wedding rite offers several options for the wording of the marriage vows, but all of them speak of fidelity and service to one another—faithful love in the sense of caring for and taking care of each other's needs—which is a pledge to live in the kingdom of God by following the divine rule of charity in a family setting. Pope John Paul II spoke of the Catholic family as a domestic church, implying that the family should be both a place of prayer and a place where Christians are empowered to reach out to others and help spread God's reign to their local community.[77] But couples cannot easily be good news to their neighborhood or town unless they receive the support they need to build and maintain their own relationship, to develop and practice good parenting skills, and to receive community support when they go through periods of emotional and financial crisis. Although our industrial society assumes that what goes on in a home is private, churches that offer family support services (child care, marital counseling, parent support groups, emergency financial assistance, and so on) not only strengthen marriages and families but they are a visible sign of self-giving love that is supposed to characterize relationships among Christians. The ideal of indissolubility is much more attainable in communities that work hard to ensure that marriages do not fall apart. If marriages and families are to be saved from the stresses of contemporary society, they need real help from the people around them, including their church community.

But the primary justice issue related to marriage is in the area of annulments. Although divorce was generally regarded as sinful during the first centuries of Christianity, it is a social fact that was dealt with pastorally rather than juridically. Today, Orthodox churches maintain that early church tradition, acknowledging divorces when they occur, and blessing the marriages of divorced persons, while recognizing that the second marriage does not have the same sacramentality as the first marriage. The Catholic Church, on the other hand, developed a theology of marital indissolubility in the twelfth century that reflected the social stability of the Middle Ages but that causes more problems than it solves in today's changing society. In order for divorced Catholics to remarry in the church, they must first obtain an annulment of their first marriage, and they must go through a lengthy juridical process in order to get it. Technically, an annulment is a declaration by a church tribunal that a first marriage which seemed to be valid was not really sacramental, thus legally enabling a divorced Catholic to enter into a second and, it is hoped, sacramental marriage.

---

77. See John Paul II, Apostolic Exhortation on the Family (*Familiaris consortio*; 1981), 21 and *passim*.

To many divorced Catholics, the annulment requirement seems like an unfair intrusion into their private lives by an organization that had previously shown little concern for their marriage, and it seems to place unjust demands on them and their former spouse at a time when they are trying to get on with their lives. In addition, many are reluctant to have a marriage declared completely null and void when in their own heart they feel it was a good marriage at the beginning. As a result, only about ten percent of divorced Catholics in the United States obtain an annulment before remarrying,[78] and this raises the question of social justice at the institutional level. For is it right for a church to maintain a theology of marriage that in effect forces people out if they want to remarry? And is it honest for pastors to welcome remarried couples into a parish, knowing full well that many of them have not gone through the annulment process? There seems to be a double standard here, raising strict legal requirements for those who want to remarry and ignoring the requirements for those who are already remarried. ☐

Understandably, the Catholic Church does not want to let go of a theology that says that marriage is indissoluble, but questions have been raised by Catholic theologians themselves about the appropriateness of retaining a medieval theology in a modern world. And Catholic canonists sometimes wonder whether all the time, effort, and money that is put into maintaining the marriage tribunals that examine and decide marriage cases might be better spent on the pastoral care of marriages and families.[79] In fairness, these questions should at least be discussed at the institutional level instead of being dismissed as matters that are closed to discussion. ☐

f. Ordination

Like marriage, ordination originated out of pastoral concerns that had a social justice dimension. The book of Acts relates how the apostles saw needs in the early community that they themselves could not meet, so they

---

78. See George M. Anderson, "Marriage Annulments: An Interview with Ladislas Orsy," *America* 177, no. 9 (October 4, 1997). For more recent but less precise figures, see Mark M. Grey, Paul M. Perl, and Tricia C. Burke, *Marriage in the Catholic Church: A Survey of U.S. Catholics* (Washington, DC: Center for Applied Research in the Apostolate, 2007), 92.

79. Most of the books calling for a reexamination of the theology of marriage and the process of annulment were written during the decade after Vatican II, before these questions were considered off limits. See, for example, Victor Pospishil, *Divorce and Remarriage: Towards a New Catholic Teaching* (New York: Herder and Herder, 1967); Lawrence G. Wrenn, ed., *Divorce and Remarriage in the Catholic Church* (New York: Newman Press, 1973); Barry Brunsman, *New Hope for Divorced Catholics: A Concerned Pastor Offers Alternatives to Annulment* (San Francisco: Harper and Row, 1985).

appointed others to minister to those needs.[80] Very quickly, Christians developed ways of training and appointing ministers, and this system evolved over the centuries to meet changing social needs and cultural conditions. During some periods of history, a good deal of ministry was done by laypeople, and during other times ministry was almost exclusively the province of the clergy. Among other things, the ordination ceremony certified that those who engaged in ministry did so with the approval of ecclesiastical authorities. Ordination, it could be said, was a way to preserve social order and see that the needs of the faithful were being met.

That the early church was successful in meeting people's needs and spreading the kingdom of God can be seen in the way Christianity expanded during the first three centuries when being a Christian was technically illegal in the Roman Empire. While it is common to think that thousands of people converted to Christianity upon being told that God loves them and Jesus died for their sins, it is historically more likely that people were attracted to the church by the way the followers of Jesus cared about and took care of one another in a community that was focused more on right living than on correct doctrine. One could say that the early Christians preached the good news by being good news to others, and that they practiced social justice by creating a more just society among themselves than was found in the world around them.[81]

As local churches grew, it was natural that people took on various community tasks according to their gifts or charisms, and in the course of time the church developed an organizational structure that imitated the social structure of the Roman world, which was both patriarchal and hierarchical. Different ministries were assigned to different groups or orders of ministers, and individuals entered into these orders through a ceremony that was appropriately called ordination. Although women performed many ministries during the early decades of Christianity, they were slowly excluded from important leadership roles as the church increasingly mirrored the larger society around it. On the one hand, there is no conclusive evidence that women were ever ordained to perform liturgical functions, but on the other hand it is clear that the exclusion of women from leadership was something of an injustice.[82]

---

80. See Acts 6:1-6.

81. For a sociological look at early Christianity, see Rodney Stark, *The Rise of Christianity: A Sociologist Reconsiders History* (Princeton, NJ: Princeton University Press, 1996); and *Cities of God: The Real Story of How Christianity Became an Urban Movement and Conquered Rome* (San Francisco: HarperSanFrancisco, 2006).

82. On the history of ordination and ministry, see Martos, *Doors to the Sacred*, chap. 12; also, Bernard Cooke, *Ministry to Word and Sacraments: History and Theology* (Philadelphia:

In past centuries, the rite of ordination focused on the duties and powers of the ordained, but the ordination rite since Vatican II puts more emphasis on ministry and service. By definition, a life of service to others is a life dedicated to living the paschal mystery, so both ordination and the ministerial life to which it leads are symbolic of the way all Christians are supposed to live. While it is true that the public image of the priest has been somewhat tarnished by pedophilia scandals, it is also true that, for most Catholics, priests are living exemplars of what ministry—and by extension, the Christian vocation of caring for others—is all about. ☐

As already indicated, something so central to Christianity as ministry is not immune to social justice concerns, for women continue to be excluded from ordained ministry in the Catholic Church. The church's leadership offers theological justifications for an all-male clergy, but not all Catholics find these convincing, especially since they seem to justify a system that is on its face unfair to women. ☐

The exclusion of married men from the priesthood is another justice issue related to ordination today. Even conservative Catholics admit that clerical celibacy is a matter of church law and not a matter of theological doctrine, for during the early centuries of Christianity priests and bishops were usually married men. Celibacy was imposed on the clergy only in the Middle Ages, and then for reasons that have little historical relevance today. The rule of celibacy is even more difficult to justify because it is often relaxed for married Protestant clergy who want to become priests in the Catholic Church, but it is never relaxed for married Catholics who want to become priests in their own church. Since the Second Vatican Council, married men have been allowed to be ordained as deacons in the Catholic Church, but in most places the permanent diaconate is an unpaid or part-time position that can be filled only by individuals with other sources of income, so the diaconate is not an order that is available to all married Catholic men. ☐

A third requirement for ordination that seems unjust to some is the education requirement. Today's priests must do four years of graduate work before being ordained, and in some parts of the Catholic world this requirement prevents many otherwise qualified Catholics from seeking ordination. For most of Christian history, there were no such things as seminaries, and

Fortress Press, 1976); and Kenan B. Osborne, *Priesthood: A History of Ordained Ministry in the Roman Catholic Church* (New York: Paulist Press, 1988). On women in ministry, see Elisabeth Meier Tetlow, *Women and Ministry in the New Testament* (New York: Paulist Press, 1980); and Ben Witherington, *Women in the Earliest Churches* (New York: Cambridge University Press, 1988).

men received what might be called on-the-job training to be priests, much the same as apprentices in other professions. Seminaries were established in the sixteenth century to combat what was perceived as clerical ignorance and immorality, and they emphasized Catholic doctrine in a church threatened by the emergence of Protestantism. In subsequent centuries, however, the strict education requirement prevented mission churches in Latin America, Africa, and Asia from cultivating a native clergy, and to this day churches in those lands suffer from a shortage of priests. Arguably, then, this is an injustice to those who aspire to the priesthood in developing countries, and it is an even greater injustice to those who want but do not receive the services of a priest because of the stringent education requirement.

g. Eucharist

Of all the sacraments that are written about in relation to social justice, Eucharist is the one most frequently mentioned. The biblical scholarship that provided the theological foundation for many of the documents of Vatican II also broadened the church's understanding of the origins of the Eucharist, moving it from a narrow focus on the Last Supper to a wider appreciation of meals in the ministry of Jesus.[83] As already noted, liberation theologians were the first to connect the good news of the kingdom with good news for the poor and oppressed, and thereafter writers in scripture, theology, and spirituality continued to expand the meaning of Eucharist to include an ever-widening range of social implications.

Judging by the number of times that meals are mentioned in the four gospels, eating with others was a significant aspect of Jesus' ministry. In various settings, Jesus is both accused of and shown eating with women and men of ill repute, which he justified by saying, "It is not the healthy but the sick who need a physician" (Matt 9:12).[84] Scripture scholar John Dominic Crossan has made much of what he calls Jesus' "open commensality," that is, Jesus' habit of eating with anyone and everyone, thereby demonstrating his own and God's care for all types of people, whether they be rich or poor, liberal or conservative, moral or immoral.[85] If living in God's

---

83. See, for example, Eugene LaVerdiere, *Dining in the Kingdom of God: The Origins of the Eucharist according to Luke* (Chicago: Liturgy Training Publications, 1994).

84. See also Mark 2:17 and Luke 5:31; also the many references to Jesus eating with sinners in n. 72 above.

85. See, among other works, John Dominic Crossan, *The Historical Jesus: The Life of a Mediterranean Jewish Peasant* (San Francisco: HarperSanFrancisco, 1991); and his shorter *Jesus: A Revolutionary Biography* (San Francisco: HarperSanFrancisco, 1994).

kingdom means doing what God wants, then Jesus' table fellowship shows that God wants everyone to be treated equally and fairly, which means practicing social justice. □

All four gospels tell the story about thousands of people being fed after listening to Jesus' preaching.[86] Some scripture commentators suggest that this physical food parallels and symbolizes the spiritual nourishment that the crowd received from Jesus' words, but it is also possible that the miraculous feeding and the abundance of food illustrates what happens when people live in God's kingdom: everyone has more than enough to eat, and by extension, everyone has all their needs met. So whether the historical event behind the story is a miraculous multiplication of food or a miraculous sharing of food, the point of the story is the same. This point is also made in the gospels' banquet parables, in which the kingdom of God is likened to a great feast in which all are welcome except those who refuse to do what God wants.[87] So it is not wealth or status or religiosity or reputation that gives one a seat at the table, but obeying God by caring for others and practicing social justice. □

Seen in this light, Jesus' last supper with his disciples was not only a celebration of the Israelites' escape from slavery but also a celebration of freedom from the slavery of self-centeredness, otherwise known as sin. That last meal celebrated Jesus' passing over to a life of self-giving when he began his ministry, his passing over from a life-giving ministry to his imminent arrest and death, and his passing over from living in a single body to living in the bodies of all who would receive his spirit. And when his followers continued the practice of sharing what they called the Lord's supper, they were celebrating not only Jesus' passover but also their own passover from an old life to a new one, living and dining in the kingdom of God. Thus, when Paul upbraided the Christians in Corinth, telling them that their community meal was not really the Lord's supper, it was not because the Corinthians were not saying the right words or not using the right type of bread, but because they were not caring about and taking care of one another.[88] □

The central symbolism of the Eucharist is therefore the blessing of and sharing of food that Catholics call the body and blood of Christ. This food is made at the altar in the sense that at the beginning of the liturgy it is

86. In fact, Matthew and Mark each contain two feeding stories. See Matt 14:14-21 and 15:32-38; Mark 6:35-44 and 8:1-9; Luke 9:12-17; John 6:1-13.

87. See Matt 22:1-14; Luke 14:16-24.

88. See 1 Cor 11:17-21. For commentary and interpretation, see Kenan B. Osborne, *Community, Eucharist, and Spirituality* (Liguori, MO: Liguori Publications, 2007), 1–18.

ordinary bread and wine, but at a certain point it becomes a sacrament through which believers can experience the presence of Christ. The food does not become the body and blood of Christ for nonbelievers because they can look at it but they cannot see what can only be seen with the eyes of faith. For this reason, nonbelievers may sometimes take Communion but they cannot experience communion, which is also what happens when Catholics receive Communion without the proper spiritual disposition. By the same token, Catholics who are properly disposed and spiritually receptive can experience Christ not only in the sacramental elements but also in the scripture readings and in the people around them.[89]

Sharing the eucharistic food is symbolic in three ways. It is first of all a sign of what Christians should be doing, namely, sharing with others the way Jesus gave of himself and the way God fills our lives with gifts and blessings. The Greek word behind the name of this sacrament means thanksgiving, and so in the liturgy we are invited to give thanks for all that we have received from God, both directly and indirectly through the mediation of Christ and the church. Second, the Eucharist is also a sign of what Christians are doing, at least when they actually do what they are supposed to be doing as followers of Christ, namely, sharing with others and ministering to them, giving of themselves the way Jesus did. For it is only insofar as we engage in such activity that we die to ourselves and rise to new life, experiencing the paschal mystery whether faintly or intensely. And, third, in keeping with the theme of thanksgiving, the Eucharist is a symbolic way to give thanks to God for revealing this mystery to us and allowing us to experience the joy that comes from living it.

If we live the conversion of heart and mind to which baptism invites us, if we have been strengthened by the spirit of Jesus as confirmation celebrates, if we get up after falling as penance encourages us to do, if we care for the weak as the anointing of the sick suggests that we should, if we care for those who are close to us as marriage is supposed to be, and if we minister to the needs of those beyond our family and friends as ordination symbolizes, then indeed we have much to celebrate and much to be thankful for when we gather for Eucharist. For what a celebration celebrates is primarily what is experienced as real in the present, remembered from

89. According to Vatican II's Constitution on the Sacred Liturgy (SC 7), Christ is present in the Mass and the sacraments, in the person of the priest, in the scriptures, and in the liturgical assembly, as well as in the eucharistic elements. The real presence of Christ in the Eucharist may be understood to mean a personal presence in the sense of an experienced (or at least experienceable) presence, which is real but nonetheless unavailable to those who are not able to perceive it.

the past, and anticipated in a future that is an extension of what has already happened in our lives. Only secondarily is it a celebration of what we might be, should be, and may later be experiencing. In other words, at Mass we celebrate living in the kingdom of God to the extent that we are consciously living under God's reign and doing what God wants, which is caring about and caring for others. □

This being said, it is clear that we should be concerned about social justice not only in our city and state and country and world but also in our church. What then are some social justice issues related to our eucharistic celebration?

If one visits a wide variety of parishes on a Sunday morning, one observes a wide range of liturgical quality, with "full and active participation" (SC 14)[90] often limited to those around the altar and those in the choir, if there is one. Catholics at worship are, for the most part, silent observers, and the majority of Catholic children stop going to church as soon as they can no longer be forced to go. The Eucharist is supposed to be the "source and summit of the christian life" (LG 11),[91] yet few diocesan and parish resources are put into ensuring that those words have some basis in the lived reality of liturgical worship. In justice to the people in the pew, the church's leadership ought to stop taking Mass attendance for granted and start supplying liturgists and musicians who can make the Eucharist a truly sacramental experience. □

Part of the Catholic problem is that the Eucharist is a genre of worship that is both complex and historical. We stand at some times, sit at others, and kneel at still others. Why? Sometimes we sing and sometimes we are silent. Why? There is a penitential rite at the beginning and a communion rite at the end. Why isn't it the other way around? None of this is explained to the people in the pew, with the result that most Catholics attend Mass mechanically and somewhat unconsciously. Many of them understand the rules of sports better than they do the rules of liturgical worship. In most Protestant churches, there is little that needs to be explained: hymns are sung, the Bible is read, a sermon is preached, prayers are offered, a collection is taken up, and the service concludes with another hymn. But there are elements of the Catholic liturgy that are biblical, others that are medieval, and still others that are modern. There are elements that originated in the Middle East, elements that are European, and elements that are culturally local. Yet very little is explained, and so most Catholics do not understand

---

90. See also CCC 1373.
91. See also CCC 1324.

the significance of many of the words, actions, and symbols to which they are exposed in the liturgy. Even things that were once very familiar, such as liturgical colors and the liturgical calendar, are no longer understood by many Catholics. Yet our church leadership does not see the injustice of ☐ depriving the faithful of their Catholic heritage.

But the faithful are also in danger of losing the Eucharist itself, for due to the shortage of priests, many parishes can no longer have Mass every weekend. This is not to disparage alternative forms of worship, which can sometimes be as spiritually satisfying as the traditional liturgy, but there is a point of justice to be raised when the church's leadership proclaims the supreme importance of the Eucharist and then allows it to lose its place in Catholic life because institutional rules do not permit the ordination of liturgical leaders who are qualified in every way except for their gender or marital status. Importing foreign priests to preside at Mass raises justice issues as well, not only because the language barrier often makes them poor preachers but also because very often they are taken from countries that ☐ need priests to stay home and minister to their own people.

The greatest injustice, however, does not have anything to do with what happens (or fails to happen) during the liturgy. Instead, it has everything to do with what happens—or rather, what fails to happen—in the time surrounding and preceding eucharistic worship. As we have seen, the meaning of a symbol is not found in the symbol but in what is experienced before exposure to the symbol. Moreover, what is meant by a symbol—its referent—is not a concept or idea (the notion that the color red symbolizes the blood of martyrs or the lighted candle symbolizes the light of Christ, for example) but a spiritual reality that has already been experienced and is to some extent reexperienced in the presence of the symbol. To say it another way, a celebration does not celebrate itself, but it celebrates spiritual realities or experienced mysteries that are remembered from the past, alive in the present, and anticipated in the future. Therefore, if what the Eucharist celebrates is not being lived by people, or if church leaders do not explain the connection between liturgy and life, then either there is nothing to celebrate at Mass or people do not realize what it is that they are supposed ☐ to be celebrating.

The sacraments, and the Eucharist especially, are celebrations of the paschal mystery, not only of that mystery as lived by Jesus for the salvation of others but also—and even primarily—as it is lived by those of us who call ourselves his followers, working for the well-being of others in our family, our neighborhood, our country, and our world. We live under God's reign to the extent that we actually care about and actively care for others, putting their needs ahead of our own wants, and to that extent we are help-ing to establish the kingdom of God on earth. We do this by making sacrifices for our family; by volunteering in parishes, schools, and community orga-nizations; by working to address hunger and poverty, homelessness and poor housing, inadequate health care and bad education; by supporting government policies that protect human rights, enlarge civil rights, and safeguard the natural environment; by informing ourselves about economic and political injustice in the world, and supporting efforts to right those wrongs. In the end, we can say that when a Catholic community such as a parish is actively committed to social justice and consistently encourages its members to respond to their baptismal call by living the paschal mystery in service to others, then it truly has much to celebrate and it is very aware of what it is celebrating when it gathers to thank God for revealing the secret of joyful living.

Additional Reading

Personal Morality

Billy, Dennis J., and James Keating. *The Way of Mystery: The Eucharist and Moral Living*. New York: Paulist Press, 2006.

Downey, Michael. *Clothed in Christ: Sacraments and Christian Living*. New York: Crossroad, 1987.

Duffy, Regis A. *Real Presence: Worship, Sacraments, and Commitment*. San Francisco: Harper and Row, 1982.

Hamilton, David S. M. *Through the Waters: Baptism and the Christian Life*. Edinburgh: T&T Clark, 1989.

Mick, Lawrence E. *To Live as We Worship*. Collegeville, MN: Liturgical Press, 1984.

Sedgwick, Timothy F. *Sacramental Ethics: Paschal Identity and the Chris-tian Life*. Philadelphia: Fortress Press, 1987.

Smith, Harmon L. *Where Two or Three Are Gathered: Liturgy and the Moral Life*. Cleveland, OH: Pilgrim Press, 1995.

Willimon, William H. *The Service of God: Christian Work and Worship*. Nashville, TN: Abingdon Press, 1983.

Social Justice

Avila, Rafael. *Worship and Politics*. Maryknoll, NY: Orbis Books, 1981.

Cavanaugh, William T. *Torture and Eucharist: Theology, Politics, and the Body of Christ.* Malden, MA: Blackwell Publishers, 1998.

Empereur, James L., and Christopher G. Kiesling. *The Liturgy That Does Justice.* Collegeville, MN: Liturgical Press, 1990.

Grassi, Joseph A. *Broken Bread and Broken Bodies: The Lord's Supper and World Hunger.* Maryknoll, NY: Orbis Books, 2004.

Hellwig, Monika. *The Eucharist and the Hunger of the World.* 2nd ed. Kansas City, MO: Sheed and Ward, 1992.

Labberton, Mark. *The Dangerous Act of Worship: Living God's Call to Justice.* Downers Grove, IL: Inter-Varsity Press, 2007.

McCormick, Patrick T. *A Banqueter's Guide to the All-Night Soup Kitchen of the Kingdom of God.* Collegeville, MN: Liturgical Press, 2004.

McKenna, Megan. *Rites of Justice: The Sacraments and Liturgy as Ethical Imperatives.* Maryknoll, NY: Orbis Books, 1997.

Searle, Mark, ed. *Liturgy and Social Justice.* Collegeville, MN: Liturgical Press, 1980.

Wannenwetsch, Bernd. *Political Worship: Ethics for Christian Citizens.* Oxford, England: Oxford University Press, 2004.

White, James F. *Sacraments as God's Self Giving: Sacramental Practice and Faith.* Nashville, TN: Abingdon, 1983.

CHAPTER 7

The Sacraments and Spirituality

T he relation between church rituals and spirituality has not been widely discussed. Before Vatican II, if you looked for Catholic books on spirituality, you would have found none related to all seven sacraments and only a few related to the Mass and the Blessed Sacrament. Books about the priesthood and spirituality discussed the priestly vocation, but not priestly ordination. Books about monastic spirituality or the spirituality of those in religious orders said virtually nothing about the ceremonies through which they entered those orders. And there were few books about lay spirituality or the spirituality of the laity.

This situation began to change with the promulgation of two major conciliar documents—The Constitution on the Sacred Liturgy (*Sacrosanctum Concilium*, 1963) and The Pastoral Constitution on the Church in the Modern World (*Gaudium et Spes*, 1965). Three shorter documents—The Decree on the Apostolate of the Laity (*Apostolicam Actuositatem*, 1965), The Decree on Renewal of Religious Life (*Perfectae Caritatis*, 1965), and The Decree on the Ministry and Life of Priests (*Presbyterorum Ordinis*, 1965)—reflected and also promoted changes in the spirituality of laypeople, religious orders, and ordained clergy in the cultural ferment of the sixties. Catholics at the time called it the spirit of Vatican II.

In tune with that spirit, Yves Congar had published *Lay People in the Church* in 1957,[1] reminding the faithful of their vocation to be Christ in the world and working out the implications of their status as a priestly people. Religious books appeared on previously unheard-of topics such as the spirituality of work and the spirituality of play, while secular books on personal development and self-fulfillment expanded the notion of spirituality even

---

1. Yves Congar, *Lay People in the Church: A Study for a Theology of the Laity* (Westminster, MD: Newman Press, 1957).

further.[2] The reinstatement of the permanent diaconate in 1967 as well as changes in the self-perception of priests led to an expanded theology and spirituality of ministry, including lay ministry. After the promulgation of the Rite of Christian Initiation of Adults in 1972, which restored the catechumenal process to adult baptism, theologians and liturgists began speaking of the baptismal call of all Christians to discipleship and ministry. Henceforth, spirituality would no longer be thought of as the exclusive province of religious professionals.

Knowledge of the psychological and social, ritual and historical, theological and moral dimensions of liturgical ceremonies makes us aware that the sacraments have been and still are shaped by individual, institutional, cultural, and even ideological forces. But the opposite is also true, that is, sacraments have a shaping force of their own.

In the past, they have exerted such a force on the individual, communal, and institutional life of Catholics and Catholicism. And the same is true today. Sacraments have a transforming effect on those who believe in what they symbolize. They help us to realize more fully who we are, and they call us to actualize what we are not yet. And in doing this, they touch every aspect of our life, from its most intimate dimensions to its most global proportions.

To fully understand the implications of the sacraments, we need to look at them in a number of contexts, in a series of ever-widening theological horizons.

1. Personal Spirituality

Every person has a spirit. The question is, whose spirit is it?

This is not a question of uniqueness. Every individual has his or her own unique spirit—or soul, as the ancients used to call it. Rather, it is a question of type, or sort.

We sometimes ask, what type of person is he? What sort of person is she?

Again, we sometimes say: His spirits are high. Her spirits are low. I'm □ * in good spirits today.

* This symbol in the margin indicates an interactive question that can be found at http://www.TheSacraments.org.

2. For example, Joe Holland, *Creative Communion: Toward a Spirituality of Work* (New York: Paulist Press, 1989); Gregory F. Augustine Pierce, ed., *Of Human Hands: A Reader in the Spirituality of Work* (Minneapolis: Fortress Press, 1991); Johan Huizinga, *Homo Ludens: A Study of the Play-Element in Culture* (Boston, MA: Beacon Press, 1955); Hugh Prather, *A Book of Games: A Course in Spiritual Play* (Garden City, NY: Doubleday, 1981).

Sometimes we also say that a person is spiritual, or even that a place is spiritual. Here, when we say "spirit" we usually mean a religious spirit, a holy spirit, even a Christian spirit.

It is possible, then, to speak of spirit in terms of type, in terms of the sort of spirit that we have, or are.

Christians are supposed to have a spirit that is different from those who have never heard the gospel. They are supposed to have, and to live in, the spirit of Jesus.

New Testament authors occasionally personified the spirit of Jesus, calling it the Holy Spirit. And trinitarian theology spoke of three "persons" (the original Greek word is *prosōpa*, meaning masks or faces) in God, one of them being the Holy Spirit.

But that trinitarian theology derived, in part, from the fact that many people who saw Jesus in his lifetime perceived in him a spirit that was more than human. It was a divine spirit, God's spirit, or, again, the Holy Spirit.

And how did they know it was the Holy Spirit? Since they were Jewish and still waiting for the messiah, they weren't yet Christians, and so they hadn't learned it in religion classes or Sunday school.

They must have perceived that Jesus was more than just an ordinary person from the things that he did and said. He touched people's bodies and he touched their hearts, and they were healed physically and spiritually. He spoke to them (and his actions also spoke) and their minds were changed, and so were their lives.

At least some of them were. They were who the gospels call the disciples, *mathētēs*, of Jesus. But the Greek *mathētēs* means something more like the word "student" in English. And so we can say that the first followers of Jesus were his students, that is, those who were willing to learn from him.

What they learned from him were not just ideas, concepts. What they learned was the true way to live. In the fourth gospel, Jesus says, "I am the way, the truth, and the life" (John 14:6). An early name for Christianity was "the Way" (Acts 9:2).

Ancient Hebrew had various ways of talking about receiving something spiritual from another person or from God. Just as the Israelites used the word "breath" (*ruah*) metaphorically to talk about spirit, so also they used another word, another concrete image, to speak about another reality that was just as real but for which they had no abstract word. The reality was that of being spiritually transformed, of being inwardly renewed. To the Israelites it was as though God's spirit was being "poured out" on that person.

Moreover, they imaged the pouring as being done with olive oil, for oil was a precious commodity to a desert people who lived in a dry land, and so they spoke metaphorically of receiving God's spirit as "being anointed," and they spoke of someone who had received that spirit as an "anointed one" (*mashiah*).

The early Jewish followers of Jesus, recognizing that the spirit of God was in him, therefore spoke of him as being anointed and called him "messiah." The equivalent Greek word is *christos* (similar to the word "chrism"), and so the New Testament speaks of *Iesous ho Christos*, Jesus the Anointed One, Jesus the Christ.

The point here, however, is not etymology; it is not the meaning or usage of words. The point is that Jesus showed that he was filled with the spirit of God, and that that is why he was called anointed, or messiah, or Christ.

Even later (though not much), followers of the Way who were living in Antioch were called *Christianoi* or Christians (Acts 11:26). In that name-calling there was an implicit recognition that to learn from Jesus meant to share in his spirit, that is, to be anointed with the same spirit with which he had been anointed.

In a number of passages, the New Testament speaks of "receiving the spirit" or "receiving the Holy Spirit" (Acts 2:38; 8:14; 19:1-6; 1 Cor 6:19). It also speaks metaphorically of "being filled with the spirit" or "being anointed by the Holy Spirit" (Acts 2:4; 4:23-31; 6:5-6; 10:44-47; Eph 1:13) when, for example, the first followers of Jesus laid their hands on others who wanted to become his followers. Many of these passages say, in effect, that the apostles laid their hands on people and they received the Holy Spirit.

A logical question we can ask is: how did the writers of those passages (or before them, the witnesses to those events) know that those people had received the Holy Spirit? There was as yet no theology of baptism or confirmation from which they could draw their ideas.

So the logical answer to that question is: They knew that people had received the spirit of God because these people behaved differently than the way they used to. They exhibited a different spirit in their lives. They lived by the power of some spirit other than the ordinary human one. The way the New Testament writers spoke of it, these people were filled with the spirit of Jesus. They were anointed with the Holy Spirit.

We Catholics today have a sacrament called confirmation. It is a liturgical anointing with oil, and the words of the rite speak of receiving the Holy Spirit. The name itself dates from the early Middle Ages. The Orthodox churches have a parallel sacrament, but it is called chrismation. Both the Eastern ritual and the name (which is closer to the word "Christ") are more ancient. But like the Western ritual, chrismation is understood to be an anointing with the Holy Spirit. ☐

Likewise, all Christians (Catholics, Orthodox, and Protestants) have a sacrament called baptism. Now, the Greek word *bapto* in Jesus' time was an ordinary word with an ordinary meaning. It meant to dip or to dunk, or perhaps a little less colloquially, to immerse. When the early Christians spoke about "being baptized in water," therefore, it may have sounded more to their ears like "being dunked in water." Which is what the ritual was, literally. Today, however, it might sound odd to our ears to speak of the sacrament of dunking instead of the sacrament of baptism. ☐

But the New Testament also speaks about "baptism in the Holy Spirit" (Matt 3:11; John 1:33; Acts 1:5; 11:16). Pentecostal Christians and charismatic Catholics also speak about being baptized in the Holy Spirit. In this case, however, it is the word "baptism" that sounds strange to our ears, for we now associate baptism with an ecclesiastical ritual. If we return to the primitive meaning of *baptizo* (a word derived from *bapto*), however, the meaning of the phrase is clear. "Being baptized in the Spirit" means the same as "being immersed in the Spirit." The image is simply the reverse of the anointing image. The one speaks of being covered all over by the Spirit (and the ancient rite of anointing was a liberal smearing with oil over the whole body); the other speaks of being inserted completely into the Spirit (and the ancient rite of baptism was a thorough immersion in water or drenching with water). ☐

Those who used the two metaphors of anointing and immersion were trying to stretch the ordinary meaning of those words (for that is what anyone does when one resorts to metaphor) to describe something extraordinary. What was extraordinary was something for which there were no ordinary words. It was the extraordinary transformation of a person's spirit that St. Paul referred to in yet another metaphor: putting on Christ (Gal 3:27; Eph 4:24). ☐

Thus baptism and confirmation both point to a profound spiritual reality that today we call by the simple word "conversion." Ancient Greek did have a word for it: *metanoia*. It meant a change in one's mentality. But conversion is more than a change in thinking. As Donald Gelpi points out, it is also a change in one's feelings or attitudes, and it is also a change in one's way of acting or behaving. Conversion is a thorough change. It involves the whole person. This is what is more fully implied by the metaphors of total immersion and complete anointing. ☐

Besides being a profound (that is, deeply penetrating) reality, therefore, conversion is also a complex reality. It encompasses a transformation of one's entire personality, of one's whole spirit, which shows up as a change in one's thinking, feeling, and behaving. For, as Rahner reminds us, we symbolize what we are in everything that we do—and thinking and feeling are as much "doings" as physical actions are.

Conversion is also a complex reality because it never ends until we are dead. It may start at some memorable point in time (for example, the moment we said yes to God or when we turned our life over to Christ), but this is not the end of it. We are always finding sections of our personality that we have been unconsciously keeping to ourselves, refusing to allow them to be washed by the Spirit. And if we are growing, we are not always sure whether those new areas of our life will be extensions of our converted or our unconverted self. And sometimes, even those spots that were once anointed mysteriously dry up.

But conversion is also complex because it is of many kinds. One may be converted to a life of crime as well as to a life of charity. One may be converted aesthetically or ethically without being converted religiously. One may be religious without necessarily being Christian, and one may have experienced a Christian conversion without having become a Catholic.

Being a Catholic is therefore more than being ethically converted to doing what is morally good rather than what is pleasant or advantageous. It is more than being religiously converted to God as the ultimate good and the source of life's basic meaning. It is even more than being converted to Christianity, to accepting Christ as the Word of God spoken in human history. It means accepting Christ as he is mediated through a historic tradition of some twenty centuries and a sequence of cultures. It means both coming to know about Christ and coming to know him through a church that calls itself Catholic because historically and culturally it *is* catholic.

Historically and through a variety of cultures, Christian conversion has been mediated to people who call themselves Catholics not only through word but also through action, not only through the scriptures but also through the sacraments. This is why the sacraments are said to be part of the Catholic tradition, for *traditio* in Latin means to hand down or to hand over. In other words, conversion to Christ, becoming immersed in him and being anointed by his spirit, has been passed down to us or mediated to us through those special church rituals that we call the sacraments.

But the sacraments are signs; they are symbols of what we are, when we are indeed converted to Christ in a Catholic way; and they are symbols of what we ought to be, when in fact we are not yet converted or not yet as fully converted as we want to be.

The question then becomes: If I call myself a Christian and a Catholic, are these signs symbols of me? Do they symbolize what I have become, and what I am becoming, and what I want to become? Are they authentic symbolizations or externalizations of my present spirit, or are they false symbols of me?

Whether I was baptized as an infant or as an adult, does the fact that I *was* baptized symbolize that I am today immersed in Christ?

Whether I was confirmed as a matter of course or as a result of a personal decision, does the fact that I *was* confirmed symbolize that today I live as one anointed with the Holy Spirit?

In a similar way I can ask, if I have been married in the church or ordained as one of its ministers, does the fact that I *was* thus married or ordained symbolize my present way of being a Christian, either giving myself to another or giving myself in service to others? □

Theoretically, sacraments effect what they signify. In theory, they cause to happen in our lives what it is that they symbolize. But this does not always happen. Even the scholastic theology of the sacraments recognized this, which is why it spoke of the inner disposition that was needed for the fruitful reception of a sacrament. Today's theology also recognizes this, which is why it speaks of conversion and of authenticity in sacramental worship. Scholastic theology also spoke of the reviviscence of a sacrament, which was its own way of talking about what happens in us when, some time after a sacramental action, its meaning hits home, or comes alive for us, and affects our life in a way that it didn't before. □

Ideally, however, sacraments ought to effect what they signify. That is, they should be true symbols of what we already are, and should cause us to become that more fully, since that is what we want to become. The first time that children risk diving off a board, they become, if you will, divers. In some simple, secular way, they have become "converted" from cautious jumpers to more confident individuals. And with every dive that they take after that first one, they both actualize what they have become and become more of what they want to be, what they have decided to become. □

So it is with our repeatable sacraments, Eucharist and reconciliation and, when it is appropriate, anointing of the sick. Eucharist is a true symbol of ourselves only when we come to it in thanksgiving, when we are already grateful for what we have, when we already see it all as gift and not as right, not as something we have earned. □

But the Eucharist is also a sacrament composed of many symbols, not the least of which is sacrifice. It has the power to ritually represent the self-giving that we do every day—but only when that is what we are doing every day. When the words of the liturgy speak of "our sacrifice" they refer to us.

It is in the daily giving of ourselves to God, through meeting the needs of others, that we participate in or become part of Christ's sacrifice. Our worship at Mass can symbolize this, but only if it is already something that we have begun to make real in our life.

We sometimes speak of participation in the liturgy, but authentic participation is not just bodily presence or physical action in the midst of a ritual. It means partaking of its symbolism, letting it represent what we are already a part of, and letting its meaning become part of us, because it signifies what we want to become more fully.

It is the same way with penance or liturgical reconciliation. It is a true symbol for us to the extent that it gathers together the forgiving that we are already doing in our life. If we are already participating in the mystery of reconciliation, of forgiving and allowing ourselves to be forgiven, then taking part in a liturgy of reconciliation can express that authentically and (like the child practicing a new skill) it can give us the inner power we need to become more authentically forgiving people.

For sacraments are signs of mysteries. (As a matter of fact, the Latin word *sacramentum* was sometimes even used as a translation of the Greek word *mysterion*.) But the mysteries are not "out there," removed from us. When we encounter them, when we consciously confront them, they are undeniably larger than we are. But they are also so close that we are experientially touching them or being touched by them. Whether the mystery is that of Christ's presence, or the Father's graciousness, or the Spirit's healing of hearts and relationships, or whatever—whenever it is truly encountered it is experienced as already there, an encompassing reality into which we are somehow inserted. In this sense only is it "out there." But if it is not also "in here," if it is not already becoming part of us and if we are not already becoming part of it, then a sacrament signifies nothing that is real as far as we ourselves are concerned.

The repetition of some sacraments ought to have a cumulative effect in our life. Like the children who practice their skills through repetition, repeating the symbols of what we are to some extent but not fully enables us to live into the mystery that they symbolize. Like children who are so exuberant about what they have learned that they do it over and over again, repeating a symbol of what we have become can also be a celebration of the mystery that is becoming a real part of our life. But like children who are sometimes content with what they have learned and are not interested in developing their skills, repeating the symbols can become lifeless, a dull redoing of a duty. For sometimes, like children who give in to pressure from their peers, we repeat our sacraments not because they truly express us or because they truly present us with what we desire, but because the church tells us to do them. ☐

Dull repetition, however, is not the attitude of a learner, a student, a disciple. In and through our sacraments (though of course these are not the only ways) we ought to be expressing the conversion of our inner spirit to that of Christ's spirit. They should be a means through which that conversion is continued in our life, through which our discipleship is made more complete. They should be moments of liminality in which we allow ourselves to let go of the spirits of self-seeking and self-sufficiency, of bitterness and competition, of division and alienation, and in which we enter into dialogue with the Lord who reveals to us a different spirit, a spirit of trusting dependence on God, of befriending cooperation with others, of integrating unity with both. ☐

To be truly effective in our lives, our sacraments should symbolize what we are already living: our daily dying to whatever it is that robs us and others of the fullness of life, and our daily rising to a newer, more abundant life; our awareness of the miraculous wonder that is life itself; our acknowledgment of everything—absolutely everything—as gift, for there is nothing that we have entirely earned (though we may have worked hard for some of it); our participation in the mysteries of transcendent reconciliation, of psychical and physical healing, of the transformation of our inner and outer life, of our experienced unity with God and our empowerment by a divine spirit that is not ours but that is becoming ours as we become immersed in it. ☐

If this happens, and to the extent that it happens, we become truly disciples of Jesus, for we are learning his way of living and being; we are becoming anointed with the same spirit that anointed him and made him Christ for us. And to that extent we also become Christ for others, signs of what God can do in a person's life, and therefore human sacraments of salvation in the world.

2. Communal Spirituality

Some parishes are dead, lifeless; others have spirit. The difference is tangible. You can feel the difference when you talk with the parishioners. You can sense it even by reading the Sunday bulletin. You can notice it at Mass, by the way people say the responses or sing the hymns, and by the way they hang around and talk to each other—or rush off silently to their cars—afterward. ☐

But spirit in a community is not just on or off, present or absent. There are different types of spirits. Get to know a parish better and you begin to recognize a pervading spirit in the place. Sometimes it is haughty and proud; sometimes it is weak and timid; sometimes it is a spirit of wealth and self-sufficiency; sometimes it is a spirit of destitution and desperation; sometimes it shows itself as a concern for children and their education; sometimes it shows itself as an awareness of global politics and economic issues.

In a large parish with a number of weekend liturgies, the spirit of the Saturday evening crowd is different from that of the early Sunday morning few, and both are different from the spirit of the groups that regularly attend the other Masses. Sometimes there are specialized communities within the parish: the Catholic school parents and kids, the public school parents and kids; the elderly and the old faithfuls, the young marrieds and the new arrivals; the teenagers, the college students, the working singles; the Knights of Columbus and the Altar and Rosary Society; the Knights of Peter Claver and the Ladies Auxiliary; and don't forget the bingo crowd.

Still, having discerned these different spirits, the question we must always ask is: Whose spirit is it? Is it the spirit of Jesus? Is it a welcoming, affirming, strengthening, forgiving, healing, unifying spirit? Is it a sanctifying spirit, a holy spirit? Or is it some other spirit?

We catch a glimpse of the spirit of the early Christian community in the idyllic picture painted by St. Luke:

> The whole group of believers was united in heart and soul. No one claimed what they had as their own possession, but everything they had was held in common. . . . None of the group was ever in want, for those who owned land or houses would sell them and bring the proceeds to the apostles. The money was then distributed to those who needed it. (Acts 4:32, 34f.)

> They remained faithful to the teaching of the apostles, to the community, to the breaking of the bread and to prayer. Many were awestruck by the many signs and wonders worked through the apostles. . . . They went together to the temple every day but met in their houses for the breaking of bread. They shared their food gladly and generously, praising God and respected by everyone. Day by day the Lord added to their number those who were being saved. (Acts 2:42f., 46f.)

Indeed it was an idyllic picture. Modern exegetes piece together a more realistic picture from other direct and indirect evidence found in the New Testament, such as the scolding that the apostle Paul gives the Corinthians in his first letter to them, or such as the warnings that Jesus addresses to his disciples in the gospels.

Nevertheless, ideals have a reality of their own, and they are not to be treated lightly. Ideals (of whatever sort they might be) set standards that we try to live up to, and they give us norms against which we measure ourselves. They give us images that govern our thinking, feeling, and acting. When presented in story form—such as the Bible or any book within it, or such as the life of Christ or any of Jesus' parables—they give us pictures within which we can situate and interpret our own life story.

None of us, however, live entirely within the Jesus story; all of us fail to fully live up to our Christian ideals. Sometimes the failure is deliberate; more often it is unintentional. But it is nonetheless real, so we notice the difference between our real ideals and our real lives. We call that gap, that falling short, sin. The Greek word for sin in the New Testament means, literally, missing the mark.

When we fail to live up to our ideals, we tend to do one of two things. Either we change our lives or we change our ideals. When our ideals are private standards that we have set for ourselves, it is easy to lower or even switch our standards. But when our ideals are those that we hold in common with others, doing that is not so easy. Often the only realistic way to remove ourselves from the group's norms is to remove ourselves from the group. When the group is large enough, however, another alternative is to escape into anonymity, to hide our shortcomings, and hope that no one will notice.

For the community that calls itself Christian, the norms are set by the New Testament and in particular by the words and example of Christ. Since the early days of the apostolic community, these norms have been kept alive through preaching and teaching, exhortation and example; and it was this community, despite its human shortcomings, that preserved the story and the message of Jesus for decades before they were written down and canonized as scriptural. Ever since then, scriptural norms have been primary in the Christian church.

For the community that also calls itself Catholic, moreover, Christian ideas and ideals have also been kept alive from the beginning in the church's sacramental worship. As was noted earlier, what we pray is what we believe: *lex orandi, lex credendi.* As a matter of historical fact, much of what is found in the gospels was preserved within the early community by being told and retold at times of common prayer. And some of the church's official sacraments had informal roots in Christian practice before they were given ecclesiastical form. Marriage and the anointing of the sick are the two clearest examples of this, but a case could also be made for ordination and reconciliation.[3]

---

3. See Joseph Martos, *Doors to the Sacred: A Historical Introduction to Sacraments in the Catholic Church* (Liguori, MO: Liguori/Triumph, 2001), chaps. 9–12.

What we as Christians find in the Bible, therefore, is first of all a kerygmatic and prophetic revelation of who we are and what we are called to be. It is kerygmatic (from the Greek *kerygma*, meaning proclamation) because it is a public announcement, made for all to hear. The facts and the ideals that it discloses are not private standards that individuals may take or leave, but realities and values that have a transcendent truth and validity. It is prophetic (from the Greek *prophēteuein*, meaning to speak on behalf of) because it is God's word spoken in the midst of the community. It reveals what God wants us to hear, not about there and then, but about here and now.

Similarly, what we as Catholics find in the sacraments is the same kerygmatic and prophetic revelation. This is obviously true of our eucharistic worship, which is founded on the gospel command of Christ to do this in his memory, and in which we hear God's scriptural word prophetically proclaimed in our midst. Most of the other sacramental rites also contain scripture readings, but we should not overlook the fact that the sacramental actions themselves have a message for us. Those actions in some way speak louder than words, especially when we are not passive observers but active participants in the rituals, for they immediately affect our behavior; and through repetition over weeks and years and generations, they influence our perduring attitudes and inclinations. The sacraments thus prophetically proclaim God's living word, for in them the divine reality and its norms are lived out in human gestures, and through them we come to perceive the mystery of which they are a revelation.

Now, of course, there is a sense in which all of this is a bunch of baloney. A lot of times we read the Bible or hear it read in church, and we get nothing out of it. Just as often we go to Mass or attend a wedding or a baptism and the same thing happens—at least as far as any prophetic proclamations are concerned. We are like the people in the gospels who look but do not see, who hear but do not understand. So it would be more accurate to say that the scriptures and the sacraments *ought to be* kerygmatic prophecies for us, instead of suggesting that this is what they always are for us.[4]

When the sacraments do speak to us, however, we find ourselves addressed simultaneously in two different manners: we are addressed as individuals and as members of a group. As individuals we hear ourselves called to discipleship in one or more of the many ways that were discussed in the previous section. And as members of a group we hear ourselves called to community in one or more parallel ways.

---

4. See Matt 13:13; Mark 8:18; Luke 8:11.

First and foremost, then, our sacramental actions call us (if we are sensitive to what they are symbolically saying to us) simply to be a community. The very fact that we are gathered together around common symbols in which we all profess belief unites us in some rudimentary yet fundamental ways. The fact that we repeat words and gestures in unison (often speaking in the first person plural: "We give thanks," "Our Father," etc.) both consciously and subconsciously suggests that we should be living up to what we are calling ourselves, namely, a "we" group, a community. And the fact that we repeat these symbolic rituals together tells us without saying it outright that we should accept the others in the group into the rhythm of our lives, and that not to do so is somehow dishonest.   □

Second, our sacramental actions call us to enter into the mysteries that they symbolize. When we attend baptisms we hear ourselves called to be an accepting and believing community. At confirmations we find ourselves asked to be a supportive and strengthening community. At penance services we recall that we should be a forgiving and reconciling community. At weddings we are reminded that we should be faithful and loving in a particular way to our spouse and family. At ordinations we are reminded of our collective call to discipleship and service within and beyond the church. When we participate in an anointing of the sick we hear ourselves being asked to be a healing and hopeful community. And when we attend the eucharistic liturgy, through its rich and complex symbolism we are called to be a community in many ways, but especially in a way that unites itself with the dying and rising of Christ.   □

Moreover, the prophetic call of the sacraments comes to us both overtly and covertly. Overtly we are sometimes asked in the sacramental rites to publicly assent to what the sacraments symbolize, and we often pray for the grace to be what we are supposed to be as Christians. But more subtly, the rituals proceed on the assumption that those who are attending them are already what they are supposed to be; that is, the rites are written in a way that presumes that those who join in them are already a faithful, loving, hopeful, serving, healing, and reconciling people. And so we find ourselves facing an existential gap between what we are presumed to be if we call ourselves a church and what we know we actually are. But if we allow ourselves to be pulled into that gap, we suddenly find ourselves attracted to and stretching toward the other side, the side of what we are not yet but ought to be. And it is in that liminal moment that we hear most clearly God's prophetic call to self-transcendence.   □

Unfortunately, however, community, like conversion, is not simple but complex. There are, of course, the complexities of every concrete situation:

the people involved and their individual personalities, their particular gifts and hopes, shortcomings and fears, their moral and intellectual and emotional maturity or lack of it. But in addition to these there is the complexity of community itself. For community can exist on many different levels, and so the call to be a Christian community is an invitation to a multileveled unity embracing common experiences, common ideas, and common values. People can be united in common experience. Even total strangers thrown together by a natural disaster can find themselves receptive of and cooperative with each other. The bond that holds a family together, or gives a small town its identity, or provides the motivation for class reunions is largely an experiential bond. By sharing—or having shared—a common experience, people are united in a community of feelings and images through which they perceive themselves as having something basic in common.

People can also be united in common ideas. Again, even total strangers can find themselves open and at ease with one another once they discover that they share common beliefs and assumptions. They find that they can communicate at the idea level even if their personal backgrounds are different, and even if their plans for utilizing those ideas are different. A lot of shop talk is based on this sort of intellectual commonality, as are classroom discussions and professional meetings or conventions. A common basis in understanding makes it possible for people to understand others and to make themselves understood by others.

Finally, people can be united in common decisions and in the actions that flow from those decisions. Even total strangers at a political demonstration, for example, can find themselves united in a common purpose. When they start a conversation with each other they may find that their backgrounds and motivations for coming are quite different, though they still agree on a common goal or course of action. A common decision—even the open-ended decision that something has to be done—can join people in a community of action and social interaction.

Now all too often, it seems, Catholics are strong on community at the middle level and weak on community at the other two levels. We tend to feel (or at least we act as if it were true) that we have a community if we all believe the same things. We call people Catholics when they believe what Catholics are supposed to believe, and we call them other names (Protestants, Buddhists, atheists, cafeteria Catholics, and so on) if they believe something else. Very often the preaching that we hear at Mass and the teaching that we hear in school are focused on what we should or should not believe. And even in our sacramental worship the emphasis is often on what we believe about God, about ourselves, and about what is happening in and through the ritual.

But this emphasis on belief just as often robs our sacramental symbols of their truth and effectiveness. At the very least it denies much of the existential truth about ourselves and depletes much of the sacraments' potential effectiveness. For how can our symbols speak the truth about our lives unless we are actually living it? And how can they truly express what we intend to do unless we actually do it? ☐

If we ask these sorts of questions with reference to our personal spirituality we easily see their validity. For example, if I go to Communion and I neither experience the presence of Christ nor intend to unite myself with his redemptive suffering, isn't my ritual gesture somewhat empty and ineffective? Or if I go to confession neither having asked forgiveness nor intending to be reconciled with others, isn't my symbolic action somewhat meaningless and futile? ☐

In the same way, then, we can ask those same kinds of questions about ourselves as a community. For sacraments, as symbolic rituals, are not just kerygmatic and prophetic statements of what we are called to be. First and foremost they are meant to be symbolic expressions of what we truly are. This is why, when we are not living up to the ideal that they hold forth for us, they have a certain prophetic power. We implicitly recognize that they ought to be symbolic of what we are, even when we are not yet what they symbolize. ☐

But what we are is not just our ideas. It is not just what we are thinking. An awful lot of what we are comes from our environment through our experience; we absorb it into ourselves, as it were, and so what was in our past becomes an element in our present selves. We become united as a social group, therefore, only when we have common experiences—especially experiences of each other—as the foundation of our common growth. We form an experiential community, in other words, to the extent that we are united on the level of experience. ☐

Likewise, what we are is not just our thoughts but also our actions. As Karl Rahner suggests, from a phenomenological viewpoint our actions are living symbols of our inner selves. Our decisions spring from our innermost beliefs and convictions (whether or not these correspond to the things that we *say* we believe in), and our actions flow from our decisions. And so we become a community that is joined together on the level of principles and values only to the extent that we share common decisions and common courses of action. They may be essentially the same decisions that we could and would make singly, but unless we make them and carry them out together they do not join us to each other in community. ☐

Now it is clear, both from the words of our liturgical rites, and from the nature of religious ritual itself, that our sacraments call us to be a multileveled community, even as they call us individually to complete conversion and not just a change in ideas. It is only when we interact with each other on all three of these levels that we truly become a community at worship (as opposed to an audience of spectators) and that we can honestly call ourselves a community (as opposed to giving ourselves a euphemistic label).

This means that in order to be a community at worship we must first of all be a community. And in order to be a community at Christian worship we must first of all be a Christian community. In other words, the things that we have in common must be things that are specifically Christian. And at least some of the things that make us specifically Christian are precisely those things that the Catholic sacraments are intended to signify.

The sacraments in traditional theology were considered to be signs of the Christian mysteries. Because of the emphasis on the intellectual component of our faith, the mysteries were often taken to be beliefs such as the incarnation, the Trinity, and so on. But these in fact are not the mysteries that the sacraments signify and are supposed to celebrate. Rather, what the sacraments directly signify are those mysteries as they are found in the life of the church. This is why Rahner and others can speak of sacraments as expressions of the church's nature. But it is only when that nature is alive in a given group of human beings that the sacraments can outwardly express what those persons inwardly are as a Christian community, as a church.

Another traditional way of speaking about the sacraments was to say that they derive their effectiveness from participating in the realities that they signify. This was sometimes taken to mean that the Mass derives its efficacy from Christ's sacrifice, or that penance puts us in contact with God's forgiveness, and so on. But these vague explanations fail to identify what ancient and medieval thinkers were referring to when they talked about participation in spiritual realities. In their way of thinking, an action participated in a spiritual reality if that larger and more general reality was found in the specific and individual action. Thus they might say, for example, that a ruler's decision participated in divine justice if the decision was actually a just one.

Concretely, what those theological statements mean is that the realities that the sacraments signify should be existentially present in the worshiping community, and if they are in fact present then the sacraments are effective in more than just a kerygmatic and prophetic sense. Pope Paul VI in his encyclical on the Eucharist called it the *mysterium fidei*, the mystery of faith. The same could be said of all the other sacraments as well, for in every truly sacramental celebration two elements must be present: the mystery and faith. It is not the faith, however, that makes the mystery present;

that would be mere fideism or autosuggestion. Rather it is in faith that we recognize the presence of the mystery, acknowledge its reality, and name it in some fashion. And this implies that the mystery must already be both present and experienced as present. □

Again, traditional theology spoke of the sacraments as causing their effects *ex opere operato*, through the performance of the sacred ritual itself. Our tendency as Catholics has been to interpret this medieval formula in rather mechanical terms that suggest that the sacraments work automatically, without any human contribution. But this interpretation does not adequately express the insight of the medieval theologians who first gave us that phrase. What they perceived was that when sacraments are effective, their effectiveness does not depend on who the minister is (or how holy he is) but on what the church does (that is, the purpose of the ritual). For at bottom the sacraments are not the work of a minister (*opus operantis*) but the work of the church, of the Christian community. □

If we recast that medieval insight in more modern terms, the *ex opere operato* concept is quite plausible. By ordaining a man a priest, for instance, a Christian community empowers him to be a sacramental minister for them. He thus receives through this ritual a "priestly character" that thereafter distinguishes him from nonordained Christians: he has a significance that laypeople do not have and that Catholics can recognize even when he is not dressed like a priest. Ideally, when children are baptized they enter a community that communicates its own spirit to them, a spirit of faith, hope, and love that empowers them to be saved from sin, that is, to become like Christ. They thus receive through that ritual a "baptismal character" that thereafter distinguishes them from unbaptized persons, or persons who are not immersed in the community. But this does not happen automatically. If baptized children are not raised in a supportive community that forms their character, they are no different from unbaptized children, even though canon law may still regard them as Catholics. □

What the scholastic theologians called the *sacramentum et res* or sacramental reality is what today might be called social empowerment—individuals' ability to be or do something because they have been given that power by others as a result of having passed through a ritual. This is true whether a kid gets to choose other players for a team by winning a round of rock-paper-scissors, or whether an adult gets to represent clients in court as a result of passing a bar exam. The empowerment results from passing through a ritual, and it lasts as long as everyone believes in it and plays their role. In a stable and stratified society, such as was found in the Middle Ages, such roles could last a lifetime; in today's fluid and mobile society, it is possible for people not to enter the game or to stop playing it. Thus children who are baptized and confirmed may never become Catholic adults, and adults who enter marriage or the priesthood may not remain there for a lifetime.

In addition to social empowerment, however, there are other spiritual realities that become available through sacramental rituals, at least in the sense that we become more aware of them or they are felt more intensely. When we think of the sacraments formally and abstractly, we tend to believe that it is the sign that makes the spiritual reality present, but when we look at the sacraments concretely and existentially, we see that it is the presence of the reality that makes the sign sacramental. It is when those mysterious realities are present in the community—realities that in human terms we can designate as acceptance, forgiveness, love, healing, trust, support, hope, and so on—that they can be truthfully and effectively symbolized in sacramental ritual. And it is when those realities are present in an uncommonly noticeable degree that we as Christians find ourselves compelled to say that they are not our doing but God's, that they are not natural but supernatural mysteries. Yet actually, their presence to any degree is a gift of God, and in that sense a grace, which may be recognized and named as such by those who have faith.

Moreover, the specifically Christian mysteries are those that are revealed to us through the life, death, and resurrection of Jesus: having a living relationship to God as Father, perceiving God's word spoken in our midst, being empowered by the spirit of Christ in our hearts, surrendering everything we thought was important and thus discovering what is truly valuable, living under the liberating reign of God rather than under the enslaving rule of sin, and so on. These are the very same mysteries that are disclosed to us through the sacraments, and whose very disclosure reinforces them in our lives. This becomes more evident once we remember that the sacraments, like the scriptures, often speak of these mysteries not in such general but in theologically specific terms: love of enemies (reconciliation), the call to discipleship (ordination), receiving the Spirit (confirmation), and so on.

The basic question that we must ask ourselves as a community celebrating the Christian mysteries is, therefore: Are those mysteries present among us simply as common beliefs, or also as common experiences and as communally lived-out values? With reference to the seven ecclesiastical sacraments our questioning can become more specific.

Baptism is a sacrament of initiation, bringing incorporation into the church and separation from the sinfulness that contaminates the world, and bestowing the basic gifts of faith, hope, and love. As a parish community we can ask ourselves: To what extent are we a recognizable community into which the ritual action marks a real initiation? Do we truly incorporate that infant or adult into our common life? Will those who are baptized be any more free from sin than if they had not been baptized? How do they receive faith, hope, and love from the other members of the community? ☐

Confirmation is a celebration of a fuller reception of the same Spirit that was once received through baptism. But as a parish do we really give those who are confirmed any more of our spirit than we did before? What do we do to strengthen their faith, to raise their hopes, to deepen their ability to love? Are we spiritually empowering them to be more mature Christians, to participate more fully in the death and resurrection of Christ? How are we enabling them to become disciples of Jesus, learners of his way of living, witnesses to each other, servants within and beyond the community? ☐

Eucharist is a sacramental celebration of our unity with Christ and with each other, of our openness to and reception of God's word, of our identification with the death and resurrection of Jesus. As a parish we can ask: Is there really a unity here to be celebrated? To what extent are we openly receiving God's word on other days besides Sunday, by reading the scriptures and studying them together, by sharing with each other what God speaks to us in our own hearts, by seeing God's word uttered in the living example of the community? How do we willingly die with confident hope of resurrection, individually and communally sacrificing our time and money, our self-interest and ambition, so that others may live, and in doing so discover that we ourselves are born to new life? ☐

Penance is a ritual symbolization of God's forgiveness and our reconciliation with one another. Is that forgiveness also present and alive in our parish? Are we a reconciled and reconciling community, taking the initiative to forgive others and asking their forgiveness? What are we doing to make it possible for adults and even children (not to mention parents and teenagers) to become reconciled with one another, to learn to live in the spirit of forgiveness? ☐

Anointing is a sacramental sign of spiritual and physical healing. Do we as a parish community bring that healing to one another at other times as well? Are we alert and responsive to the hurt of neglected and abused children, to the anxieties of adolescents, to the problems and frustrations of families, to the loneliness of the bedridden and the aged? Are we meeting the needs of those who are sick or poor or handicapped or unemployed or imprisoned? ☐

Marriage is a ceremony that symbolizes the intimate relation between Christ and the church, and that initiates two persons into that same sort of self-giving relationship. Can we honestly ask engaged couples to take as

the model for their future life together the present relationship between our parish and our Lord? Are we a living witness to what a married life of fidelity, intimacy, and service ought to be? What are we as a larger community doing to prepare young people and empower families to be smaller but no
☐   less real Christian communities?

Ordination is a sacramental calling and initiation to ministry in the church. Are we as a parish a ministering community? Are we individually and collectively engaged in ministering to the spiritual and physical, personal and social, religious and Christian needs of our parish and the people in it? Do we encourage and praise service within the community so that some,
☐   at least, are enabled to choose ministry as their life's work?

These are but some of the specific questions that we as members of Christian communities must ask ourselves if our sacraments are to be truly symbolic and truly effective. If our sacraments are truly symbolic, they have to participate in the realities that they symbolize, that is, they have to be a living extension, an outgrowth of Christian mysteries that are already being experienced and believed in and acted out in our midst. And if they are indeed truly symbolic in this way, then they will be truly effective; for as symbolic actions they will intensify our appreciation and understanding of the mysteries that they represent, as repeated actions they will constantly recall us to an awareness and response to those mysteries, and as communal actions they will unite us in a common involvement with and commitment
☐   to their life-giving effects on us.

If our sacramental celebrations are genuinely symbolic, in other words, they will be truly sacramental and truly celebrations. They will be truly sacramental for they will not only express the mysteries that they signify but they will also draw us into them, transforming us in the process. They will be not only expressing community at all three levels but also creating community at all those levels. They will be, to use St. Paul's phrase, build-
☐   ing up the body of the Lord in strength and unity.

When this happens, there will be less danger that the sacraments will be seen as some sort of magic, except in that wonderfully childlike sense in which everything is marvelous and sparkles with mystery. There will also be little danger that the sacraments will be thought of as automatically effective, except in that authentically existential sense in which inner vitality is spontaneously life-giving. And there will be less temptation to be careless in our sacramental celebrations, except in that healthy and mature sense in which concern for what is central frees us from worrying about what is
☐   peripheral.

For when our sacraments are truly expressive of our spirit, and when our spirit is the Holy Spirit of our Lord, they are at one and the same time effects and causes of our being a Christian community.

3. Ecclesial Spirituality

In his modern classic, *The Spirit of Catholicism*, Karl Adam endeavored to define what made the Roman Church catholic and to explain how it was different from other Christian churches.[5] Both in the title and in the book he called attention to the fact that being a Catholic means possessing and being possessed by a distinctive religious spirit.

If you talk about religion with other Christians, you soon discover that there is a certain flavor or style to being a Catholic that is different from that of being a Protestant, no matter what the denomination. If you read confessional theologians or listen to the sermons of Protestant ministers, you often sense an attitude and mentality that underlies an other than Catholic way of being Christian. And if you attend Protestant services or Orthodox liturgies, you discover that there is a spirit about them that is somewhat familiar yet somehow dissimilar from the spirit of Catholicism.   □

In ecumenical circles, the Catholic Church is referred to as a liturgical church. In this way it is similar to the high Anglican and Eastern Orthodox churches, which also put a great deal of emphasis on traditional rituals of public worship. The nonliturgical churches for the most part build their church services around the scriptures, give less attention to rituals such as the sacraments, and are generally less concerned with ecclesiastical traditions. One aspect of the spirit of Catholicism, then, is its continuing insistence that traditional church rituals (in particular the sacraments) express, maintain, and foster what it is as a Christian institution.   □

Speaking very broadly, any church—indeed any religion—is sacramental. Karl Rahner uses the phenomenological analysis of symbolism to show that the church is necessarily sacramental inasmuch as it expresses itself in symbolic forms; that is, it externalizes its inner nature in words and actions that make that nature something real and concrete in the world and at the same time make it visible or tangible to people. This is true of any church or any religion, for it is clear that this general phenomenological description fits any social institution whatsoever: by doing what it does, it expresses what it is. And because social as well as individual actions are unavoidably

---

5. Karl Adam, *The Spirit of Catholicism* (New York: Macmillan, 1930).

symbolic, it is possible to perceive the inner spirit of a church through the public actions that manifest that spirit.

One can plausibly argue, as Catholic theologians do, that the sacraments are the expressions of the church par excellence. Sociologists might object that this perspective is too narrow since it leaves many social, economic, political, historical, and organizational factors out of consideration. Protestant theologians also might object that such an approach does not give sufficient attention to preaching the word, to individual and social witness to Christ, or to other nonliturgical dimensions of their churches. But Catholicism as a liturgical church has traditionally maintained and continues to assert that it is first and foremost a community of believers who encounter God in and through that system of rituals known as the sacraments. Granting, then, that other things could be said about the nature of the church from other perspectives, it is certainly legitimate for Catholics to examine their sacraments for some insight into the essence of Christianity as it is found in their own ecclesiastical tradition.

What, then, is the spirit of Catholicism as it is embodied and symbolized in its liturgical rituals?

Beginning from the wider perspective of the church's entire sacramental system, or the church's liturgical life in general, we can say that the spirit of Catholicism is an incarnational one, which in turn implies that it stretches vertically in a transcendental direction and horizontally in a historical direction.

We are an incarnational church. We accept the Pauline description of ourselves as the body of Christ, the continuing incarnation of Christ in the world. In the church as an institution, in our various ecclesiastical institutions, and specifically in our liturgical rituals the spirit of Christ is embodied and made visible. St. Augustine in the fourth century defined sacraments as signs of sacred realities, but Catholic theologians in our own century have called our attention to the fact that the church itself is fundamentally a sacrament, for it is a visible sign of the reality of God. As such it is a sacrament that underlies and grounds all the other sacraments, which are liturgical manifestations of the church's basically sacramental nature. Through its rituals it reveals what it is, what the message of Jesus is, and what Christians are called to be.

Being an incarnational church, we are in our sacraments a worshiping church. We accept the Second Vatican Council's description of ourselves as the people of God, a community of persons who are receptive and responsive to the self-revelation of the transcendent Person. St. Thomas Aquinas in the thirteenth century argued that sacraments are necessary because human beings need signs for communication: we communicate to others and receive their communications to us only through the medium of signs.[6] If, therefore, we are to receive God's communication to us, it must come through signs. Almost spontaneously we think of this in terms of visible signs, words, and especially the words of scripture. But St. Thomas' argument causes us to pause and reflect on the fact that through those peculiar signs called sacraments, what God is communicating to us is not ideas but divine life. Apart from the eucharistic liturgy they do not contain very much in the way of verbal communication, and the basic traditional teaching about the sacraments is that they are instruments of God's grace. In our sacramental rituals we become receptive to that almost ineffable energy that we sometimes name sanctifying grace or even the Holy Spirit itself. Having opened ourselves up to that transcendent vitality, we respond by allowing it to permeate our attitudes and affectivity, by letting it convert our intentions and govern our actions, and in so doing we become what we call ourselves: God's people. Not that we deny that those who are not in the church can also receive and respond to God's self-revelation in other ways; but as a church we stand for the fact that sacramental worship is a primary focus of transcendental communication.   □

Moreover, as an incarnational church we are also a historical church. We accept the Israelite insight that time is not cyclical but directional, and we embrace as our own the whole of history from the creation of the world to its ending in the Parousia. More specifically we trace the history of ours and the world's salvation from before the time of Jesus, through the apostolic and patristic periods, through the Dark Ages and the medieval period, through the Renaissance and modern times, through the present and into the future. Our church history alone spans twenty centuries, and it is a history not only of theological speculation and ecclesiastical politics but also of liturgical worship. We see ourselves as the church founded by Christ, in the line of the apostles, bringing Christian baptism to the ends of the earth, celebrating the Eucharist in diverse ways down through history, reconciling the repentant, comforting the sick and the dying, sanctifying family life, and ministering to the Christian community not just as individuals but as an institution, as a church. The history of Catholicism as an incarnational church, in other words, is from a sacramental perspective the historical mediation of divine life into human lives. It has been an imperfect mediation, to be sure, blemished as it has sometimes been with dogmatism and

---

6. See Thomas Aquinas, *Summa Theologiae* III, q. 61, a. 1; also *Summa Contra Gentiles* IV, chap. 56.

fanaticism, provincialism and superstition, venality and even criminality. We can be chagrined and even ashamed at what has sometimes passed for Christian worship. But the Catholic spirit is not to deny the past but to acknowledge it, the bad with the good, to attempt to discern the one from the other, and to affirm that sacramental worship is and will continue to be a primary means of transcendental communication.

Narrowing our perspective now, we can briefly examine the seven ecclesiastical rituals historically designated as sacraments to see what they reveal about the spirit of Catholic Christianity.

The one sacrament that touches on all the others both historically and theologically is holy orders. The sacrament is so named because it covers various orders or levels of ministry in the church, and historically the administration or celebration of all the other sacraments has been connected with those in ministerial orders. Theologically the sacrament of orders is related to the others through the notion of mediation, the idea that the divine life is communicated into human lives through the sacramentality of human actions. Traditionally we have trained and ordained specific individuals to minister to Christians through sacramental rituals, but the theological implications of this practice are much broader than the fact that we are a church with ministers called priests; it implies that we are a priestly church. As an institution we stand committed to the principle that ministry is a mediation of transcendent reality, to the concept of service as a Christian vocation, and to the practice of empowering individuals to perform the service of sacramental mediation in the church.

A sacrament that touches the lives of all Catholics in one way or another is marriage. Academically one can debate whether the sacrament is the wedding ritual or the union of two persons in wedded life, but ecclesiologically this makes little difference since the meaning of Christian marriage in both instances is the same. Having endowed marriage with a church ceremony since the twelfth century, we Catholics have institutionally ratified what was said in the Epistle to the Ephesians, namely, that the ideal marital relationship is one of unending fidelity and self-sacrificing love. Such a relationship is truly Christian for it symbolizes the relationship between Christ and the church: self-donation and loving obedience to God's will. As an institution that symbolizes what it stands for in its rituals, therefore, we take that relationship as a paradigm of communal love, primarily for the natural family but by extension in the spiritual family, which is the church.

A sacramental means of maintaining and regaining that sort of relationship whenever it is lost is the sacrament of reconciliation, officially known as penance. The name derives from the Latin word *paenitentia*, which is often translated as penitence but which is closer in meaning to the Greek word *metanoia* in its sense of conversion. Quite obviously, conversion—or more accurately here, reconversion—to loving God and caring for others can take place outside a liturgical context. But by retaining a sacrament of reconciliation within our liturgical tradition we say in deed as well as in words that we are and are committed to being a forgiving community, a reconciling church. ☐

Sacramentally too we express our belief that we are and are committed to being a healing community in the anointing of the sick. Very early in our history this anointing was done by ordinary Christians for themselves and others; later as a liturgical ritual its administration was reserved to the clergy; still later its reception was restricted to those who were so sick that they were at the point of dying, and so its name for a few centuries was extreme unction, the last anointing. Throughout all these variations, however, anointing as a sacramental ritual has expressed our ecclesial faith in the power of God to touch and transform people's lives, not just spiritually, but even physically. And it has said that we are to be channels of God's healing power not just singly as individuals but also collectively as a church. ☐

Another sacrament of strengthening, though in a somewhat different sense, is confirmation. This particular ritual of anointing dates back to the ancient rite of Christian initiation. Although the name of the sacrament comes to us from the early Middle Ages (when it was separated from baptism and hence needed a separate name), in the patristic period it signified, through the action of the bishop, a spiritual empowerment that came with full membership in a ministering, loving, forgiving, and healing community. Even later, when the sacrament was given a more individualistic interpretation, it still represented a strengthening of the spirit that is available through active adult membership in the church. ☐

As the basic sacrament of Christian initiation, baptism has an inescapably ecclesial meaning. As with confirmation its meaning was for a long time privatized so that it was looked at as a means of individual salvation, but even then it was baptism *into the church* that was seen as making salvation available. Initiation into the church means incorporation in the body of Christ and hence into his death and resurrection, symbolized in the ancient rite by actual immersion into and reemergence from the baptismal waters. This sacrament therefore symbolized the fact that what we as Christians call salvation comes initially and continually through participation in Christ's redemptive suffering and rebirth, and that this mystery is at the very heart of our reality as a church. ☐

The sacrament that epitomizes the Catholic Church's liturgical life is the Eucharist. Through its association with Christ's death and resurrection, it signifies the same redemptive mystery as baptism. Through its bringing Christians into experiential contact with that mystery, it is a source of strength and healing. Through its call for conversion and reconciliation, it is a sacrament of mutual forgiveness. Through its symbolic sharing of Christ's body and blood, it is an expression and cause of unity within the church. And through its call to self-sacrifice and its mediation of the divine power that makes self-sacrificing love possible, it is an exercise in both ministerial and communal priesthood. It is, in brief, the sacrament that summarizes the sacramentality of the church. Every eucharistic celebration proclaims, symbolically, that we are the body of Christ, participants in his redemptive mystery, a converted and loving community, a source of healing and forgiveness, an agent of reconciliation in the world, obedient and faithful to the Father, dedicated to the service of others. In reading and reflecting on God's word we proclaim that we are a listening and responding church; in the offering of gifts we announce that we are a self-sacrificing church; in the eucharistic prayer we present ourselves as a dependent and thankful church; in the □   partaking of Communion we symbolize that we are a sharing church.

Nevertheless, we can still ask, once the euphoria of such theological rhapsodizing has worn off: Is that what we are, really? Haven't we as a church often been the opposite of what our sacraments say we are? Can't we sometimes sense the hypocritical triumphalism that our critics accuse us of? Is it possible that more than occasionally our sacraments are false signs, symbolic lies, behind which we institutionally hide from the truth? And isn't the truth that we have often been, still are in many ways, and will undoubtedly persist in being a sinful, unforgiving, and unredeemed assem-
□   blage of individuals?

Gregory Baum in *Religion and Alienation*, cited in chapter 2, argues that all too often the image of the church as a social organization (that is, the organizational structure of the church and the pattern of its institutional activities) does not correspond to the image of the church found in its symbolic expressions (that is, in its liturgy and sacraments). And Juan Luis Segundo, whose *The Sacraments Today* was discussed in chapter 5, charges that this lack of correspondence is not merely incongruous but subversive:
□   it undermines the sacraments and draws away their redemptive power.

And yet, despite criticisms from both outside and inside the church, we continue to insist that the sacraments are important and even necessary. Not even Baum or Segundo, for example, suggest that as a church we should do away with them. Why is this? It is, I believe, because the unique spirit of Catholicism is found within the sacramental system itself. The sacraments make our church what it is. Despite all their shortcomings and despite all our failures, they make us a church, and they make us the particular incarnation of Christ that we are. They give us, in short, our Catholic identity.   □

For the sacraments are ecclesial symbols. They give us a common set of symbols with which we can identify as a church, over and above the scriptures and creeds with which all Christians can identify. They are the same seven sacraments for Catholics the world over, and they stretch back in time in one form or another across nearly twenty centuries of our institutional history. They have been the ritual vehicles for the continuous transmission of our common heritage. Even when we individually or collectively fail to live up to them, they signify what Catholicism claims to be and what we as Catholics believe we are.   □

They are, in this sense, prophetic symbols. Like the prophets of old they sometimes bring us the bad news that we are not what God wants us to be. By presenting us with images of what we ought to be as Christians and as a church, they pronounce God's judgment on the way we actually behave. But prophecy can also be the telling of good news, and the good news announced by the sacraments is that God makes it possible for us to be a faithful, reconciling, strengthening, and serving community.   □

Thus the sacraments are also kerygmatic symbols. Not only do they announce in a general fashion the good news that salvation is possible, but they also apply that message to critical junctures in our individual and collective lives: birth, growth, unity, choice, estrangement, weakness, death. They give us in ritual and song, scripture and pastoral commentary the word that we need to hear at that precise moment if we are to be what we claim to be, and what we sacramentally say we are.   □

For the sacraments are redemptive symbols. If we allow ourselves to listen to what God is telling us through them, if we open ourselves to the energizing grace that the Spirit communicates through them, they make salvation available and operative in the church. When we consciously and deliberately enter into the mysteries that they present through symbolic representation, our minds and our hearts and our actions are transformed, sometimes in subtle and sometimes in dramatic ways.   □

Sacraments are therefore eschatological symbols. They bring about in sacred space and time a realization of the final times, when sin will be washed away, when divisions will be healed, when anger will be melted, when sorrow will be turned to joy, when death will have no sting. They give us hope for the future by making it present here and now.   □

But the sacraments do this because they are liturgical symbols. They are symbols that invite us into an attitude of prayer and worship, and through which we pass into that very same attitude. Moreover, we do this not singly but together, not as individuals but as a church, which is why they form and transform not only our personal spirit but also our ecclesial spirit.

The sacraments are therefore the symbols that make us Catholic and that make us a church. Were we to eliminate them we might still be a church, for there are nonliturgical churches and there are other churches without all seven of the Catholic sacraments. But these are not catholic churches; they do not have our historical or global universality. Perhaps it would be more accurate to say, then, not that the sacraments make us a church, but that it is the sacraments that make us the Catholic Church, and that give Catholicism its particular spirit.

Furthermore, the sacraments are the symbols that make us individually Catholics. We can be Christians without these sacraments, for there are Christians who seem to do all right without them. Still, there seem to be few generic Christians in the world, that is, people who are neither Catholic nor Protestant nor Orthodox nor members of some other group that call themselves a Christian church, but who are still identifiably Christian. To become a Christian in any deep sense seems to necessitate that we identify with some Christian church and allow that church's spirit to shape our own.

Being a Catholic, therefore, means more than just being a Christian. It means being a Christian in a certain way, sharing in a certain ecclesial spirit. It means encountering the message of Jesus as it has been handed down through history within a definite community. And it means responding to God's grace in and through the symbolic rituals of that church's tradition, the sacraments.

4. Global Spirituality

As Catholics we make much of our lengthy tradition and our worldwide presence: they are indicators of our catholicity. It is something to be proud of, but it also gives us a responsibility. For the church is not in the world to be a monument to the past; it is there to be a leaven for the future. It is not there to be admired by people but to transform society.

Not very long ago the world was a very large place. Distant lands had unpronounceable names and foreign cities seemed strange and exotic. The people of those faraway cultures were at least odd and sometimes even inscrutable.

It has become commonplace to say that the world has shrunk, but it is truer to say that we have stretched. Our eyes and ears reach around the planet through communications media. Our feet have been given wings by jet transportation. Our voice can travel anywhere through the telephone. Our ideas can reach around the globe through the world wide web.   ☐

What has embraced the world in our lifetime is the Western technological spirit. And it has not only touched the Far East and the southern hemisphere; it has transformed them. It has made them less strange. It has made them more like us. It has made them our neighbors.   ☐

Jesus was once asked, "Who is my neighbor?" In replying with the parable of the Good Samaritan, he said in essence that anyone who is close enough to know about is your neighbor. But today we know about people who are affected by racism in our cities, poverty in our countryside, economic oppression in Latin America, political suppression in China, starvation in Africa, antagonism in the Middle East, destitution in India; the list goes on.   ☐

Whether we like it or not, therefore, ours is a global spirit, for it encircles the world and it makes us conscious of people all over the planet. It is not necessarily our Christian or Catholic spirit, but it is mainly our Western, scientific, technological, political, and economic spirit. Thus the question is posed, for those of us who call ourselves Catholics: Should it also be a Christian spirit? That is to say, if the personal spirit of each of us has assumed global proportions, should it also be permeated by the spirit of God as revealed in the person of Jesus?   ☐

To give a flat no to that question would be schizophrenic, if we want to maintain that we are both Christian and modern. Like it or not, we are citizens of the world. Television and radio, newspapers and magazines, cell phones and computers have expanded our consciousness so that it now reaches around the planet. Yet our natural tendency is to withdraw into ourselves. We would prefer to think that we can live our personal lives and let the world go its own way. For Christians, this is also our perennial temptation. We would like to limit religion and make it a private affair, or at most a province of the church. At one time in history, when our world and our awareness of it were both much smaller, that might have been possible, but the only way to do that today is to compartmentalize religion, to divorce it from what we know about so much of life. And that would be schizophrenic. At least for most of us.   ☐

But not for all of us. There are some whose world is inescapably small: the very young, the disabled, the illiterate, the impoverished. It is hard for them to see beyond their own needs, and so they really do not close their eyes to the needs of the global community. But this is not true of the rest of us. We see the slums in our cities and the shacks on our rural areas. We read about worldwide food shortages, peak oil, depleted aquifers, and global warming. We are reminded about the spread of HIV and AIDS, of drug-resistant tuberculosis, and of alcoholism and other addictions. We hear about the unemployed, the uneducated, the uninsured, the homeless, the incarcerated, and the malnourished. And yet our spirit does not want to embrace them.

☐   All too often our supposedly catholic spirit is in fact very provincial. Our Christian spirituality is a personal spirituality, a communal spirituality, and an ecclesial spirituality. And it stops there. But just as being a Christian individual implies membership in a Christian community, and just as being an individual parish implies participation in an ecclesial tradition, so also being Catholic has implications that reach beyond the church and into the world at large.

☐   Theologians today call the church a sacrament. Indeed it is that. But that is also what it ought to be. A sacrament is a sign that mediates salvation; it is an instrument of grace. The church, then, is and ought to be a medium of salvation. To some extent it is, but to some extent it is not and it ought to be. And to that extent it is not a sacrament. Likewise our parishes and other liturgical centers are supposed to be sacramental communities. And in parallel fashion we too are each called to be sacramental persons. And yet so often we are not. Why?

☐   Part of the answer lies in the nature of sacramental religion itself. The psychology of sacramental experience is that it takes us out of the secular world and into the realm of the sacred. It tends to be a private experience, and in its most intense moments it is intensely personal. The sociology of religious ritual shows that it tends to become ritualism. Often-repeated ceremonies quickly become mechanical, forms of prayer and worship wither into empty formulas, and concern for their performance devolves into legalism. The history of religion during the classical phase in which Christianity began was characterized by a concern for salvation, for overcoming the estrangement between human beings and God. Yet despite theological nods in the direction of universal salvation, and despite occasional outbursts of missionary zeal, classical Christianity spoke mainly about individual redemption and about salvation within the church. Not only did the Catholic sacraments reflect this mentality, but sacramental theology inevitably did so as well. The result is that even when theologians spoke about the social dimensions of the sacraments they hardly ever looked beyond the limits of the institutional church.

☐   Another part of the answer, however, lies in the fact that global consciousness is an entirely new phenomenon. Phenomenologically speaking, the world that most people lived in until the twentieth century was quite small:

it reached only to the edges of their town, their region or, at most, their country. Maps in the Middle Ages, for example, did not cover much territory, and even at the beginning of modern times they still showed large tracts of unexplored areas. Even historical consciousness, the stretching of the imagination back in time and forward into the future, and the awareness that the past was really different from the present, is a relatively recent expansion of the human mind. Until the nineteenth century most people, including scientists, thought that the world was about six thousand years old, based on the computation of time periods in the Bible. So it would be anachronistic and somewhat unfair to expect earlier generations of Christians to have developed a global spirituality. Theirs was simply not a global spirit. ☐

The challenge of developing such a spirituality is therefore ours. Fundamentally it is a task of allowing the dynamism of spiritual development to stretch beyond the confines of personal holiness and institutional sanctity, and to reshape first in our imagination and then in reality the world in which we live. The task is thus a dialectical one, for it is a matter of simultaneously acknowledging the gospel message of salvation and confronting the global dimensions of a suffering humanity. Neither side of the dialectic can be denied, both must be affirmed, and each must be allowed to transform the other. For if there is a true dialogue between Christianity and the world (and theology in an incarnational church is committed to such a dialogue), ultimately neither one will remain the same. ☐

Needless to say, the task of developing theology in a global spirit has already begun. Looking at it from a Catholic viewpoint, we can say that it began with the social encyclicals of popes Leo XIII and Pius XI, the Knights of Labor and the Catholic Worker movement, and similar developments that attempted to apply gospel principles to inequities in modern economic systems. In the middle of the twentieth century, when biblical scholars were released from the burden of having to use scriptural quotations to prove Catholic dogmas, they were freed to find in the Bible social implications that had long been ignored. In the 1960s moral theology broke out of its long confinement to canon law and began to address questions of peace and justice in the light of the gospel. In the 1970s liberation theologians in Latin America, Africa, and Asia began to resist the restrictions of academic theologizing in order to translate Christianity into non-European terms. In the 1980s concern for the nuclear arms race between the United States and the USSR led many to rethink the just war theory and to rediscover the Christian roots of pacifism. In the 1990s the metastasis of the prison system and the return of the death penalty led Catholics to expand their pro-life ethic beyond the opposition to abortion. In the first decade of the twenty-first century, the rise of militant Islam led to more intensive interfaith dialogue, the use of torture and indefinite detention led to a more intense emphasis on human rights, the explosion of illegal immigration led to a rethinking of economic justice, and the disastrous effects of global warming led to recasting environmental concerns in terms of stewardship of God's creation.

This bursting of the religious imagination beyond the boundaries of traditional teachings impels the sacramental theologian to reexamine the classical Christian rituals and to reevaluate them within a wider horizon. The issue is not one of negating what has been and still remains true on an individual, communal, and ecclesial level, but of affirming that the meaning of the sacraments transcends all those levels of understanding.

The task, then, of sacramental theology on a global level is to work out the implications of the traditional Christian rituals for Catholics who are truly catholic in a contemporary sense. That is to say, the task is to initiate reflection on the central meaning of each of the sacraments and to ask: If we are to be faithful to that meaning, knowing what we do now about the world in which we live, how are we to live? Or to ask the same question in a different way: If our sacramental rituals are to be authentic signs of what we are—and we are, willingly or not, citizens of the world and members of a global community—then what must we become? Or to put the question in dialectical terms: What are the discrepancies between our symbolic self-expressions and our actual selves, and how must each be changed if these discrepancies are to be overcome?

What then do the Catholic sacraments say we are? How do we fall short of that (bearing in mind that the New Testament word for sin, *hamartia*, means to fall short) when we look at ourselves within a global perspective? And what do the sacraments themselves suggest that we must do or become in order to overcome this shortfall, that is, to authentically participate in the salvation of the world?

First of all, as already indicated, contemporary theology has expanded the meaning of the notion of sacramentality to include not only our ecclesiastical rituals but also ourselves, our communities, and the church itself. But calling ourselves sacraments is only pious rhetoric if nobody else knows it but us, or if we ourselves do not realize it until we hear it in a homily or read it in a book. Moreover, being a sacrament is not something that we should have to accept totally on faith; we should have some solid evidence for suspecting that it is true! That such concrete sacramentality is in fact a real possibility is evident from the way individuals, groups, and movements past and present have been perceived as doing God's work, being signs of hope and instruments of salvation. And so the way to translate that possibility into actuality is also clear: simply do those things, individually, in groups, and through ecclesiastical institutions, that alleviate human suffering, that overcome self-alienation and mutual estrangement, and that promote human self-transcendence and fulfillment. For sacraments participate in the realities that they signify. And so to bring such sacraments into existence, one needs only to be instrumental in bringing such realities into existence. ☐

Second, then, baptism is the sacrament of initiation into the church, and it signifies immersion with Christ in death as well as rising with him transfigured. As we are reminded every Easter when we are asked to renew our baptismal promises, baptism is a sign that we have heard the good news, that we have renounced our allegiance to sin, and that we have accepted the way of Jesus as our own way of life. In the early days of Christianity, baptismal candidates were literally stripped naked, went down into and rose out of the baptismal pool, and were reclothed in white robes. It was a symbolic way of divesting oneself of the things of this world, of dissolving one's entanglement with sin, and of being reborn into a new life. ☐

Viewed from a global perspective, baptism is arguably the sacrament of gospel poverty, Christian renunciation, and a transformed affirmation of life. In a world where 80 percent of the people are poor, it can and should be a sign that we have renounced our attachment to whatever keeps people in poverty, and that we are engaged in activities that affirm our solidarity with their struggle for a fuller life. Individually baptism makes sense if I am continually contributing time and money to those who are in need, giving not out of my surplus but out of what I would need to maintain a standard of living that is grossly disproportional to theirs. In the local community baptism takes on a global dimension when it invites new members to live beneath their means and give to the poor, and when it makes it possible for them to do so in a way that is life-affirming for both the giver and the receiver. And baptism is an honest sacrament of the universal church when as an institution it relinquishes its attention to wealth and through its institutions it identifies itself with the poor, the hungry, the naked, and the homeless. For baptism is above all a sign of having died to one way of life and of having been reborn into another. ☐

Third, confirmation as the completion of baptism is its complement. It signifies the fullness of life that comes from drawing one's vitality from the spirit of God, which is the spirit of Jesus, which is the Holy Spirit. It is the energy that can fill our hearts once we have emptied ourselves of our own self-concern. But in the sacramental ritual, that spirit symbolically comes to us through the action of the bishop, who in turn is acting on behalf of the community. Thus the new life that baptism symbolically promises and begins is an empowerment toward self-transcendence that comes not in isolation from others but from our openness to being strengthened by them. And conversely, as bearers of that life we communicate it to others through our concern and commitment to them, that is, through touching them.

As a sacrament of God's spirit in the world, therefore, confirmation is a sign of our faith in the communicability of that spirit to others. Ours is largely a world of despair, in which the impoverished have no hope of human betterment and in which the wealthy have no hope of escaping ecological disaster. In either case there is no future, and where there is no future, there is no hope. Hope is possible only if there is energy available to change the present course of events. As an individual, therefore, I can affirm the symbolic truth of my confirmation if I am working to change the world's situation, thus reversing the downward spiral of despair in those to whom the energy for change is passed. As parishes, we do the same when we make social concerns a part of our community commitment not only in words but also in deeds, beginning with the poor in our own neighborhood and reaching outward to the hungry of the world. And as a church, Catholicism acts out what it symbolizes in confirmation when it commits its spiritual energies to social justice, environmental stewardship, and world peace. For confirmation is, among other things, a sign that the power needed to change the world and redeem the future is available here and now.

Fourth, penance is the sacrament of reconciliation in the church, and it stands as a perpetual sign of our failure to fully live the gospel. It therefore symbolizes our continuous need to overcome our estrangement from each other and from our deepest self, and in doing so to lessen our separation from God. More important, however, it signifies that such reconciliation is indeed possible if we would but accept it from God and work toward it with others. Nevertheless, since the Middle Ages penance has suffered from a privatism that suggested that forgiveness by God was all that was needed, and from a legalism that suggested that conformity to law was all that was asked. In early Christianity, however, when penance was called for it was a public enactment of repentance and forgiveness, and what was aimed at was not legalistic conformity but social reintegration.

Today, then, our more total awareness of alienation in the world makes penance a reminder that we are still too spiritually separated from our global neighbors, and that we in fact are a cause of much of their misery. The world's wealth is not well distributed, partly the result of our own overconsumption. The world is not at peace, partly the result of our own country's economic and ideological priorities. The world's poor suffer indignity and injustice, partly the result of our indifference to their plight, partly the result of corporate profit seeking, and partly the result of U.S. support for oppressive governments. The sacramental call for reconciliation therefore makes me aware of my personal guilt for the suffering of the world to which I would rather close my eyes, but at the same time it reminds me that international peace and cooperation are possible if I work toward them. Communal penance services are likewise sacraments of global reconciliation if, on the one hand, they awaken our sense of social sinfulness and, on the other hand, offer real possibilities for doing more than beating our breasts about what we have failed to do. And reconciliation at the ecclesial level reaches global dimensions when the church is instrumental in mediating conflicts and reducing tensions between hostile groups in the world. All too often, it seems, the church has been actively or passively a party to war, but this does not mean that it cannot or should not be a sacrament of peace; it means only that it has not heeded the global implications of its own ecclesiastical rite. ☐

Fifth, however, the church's commitment to what is symbolized by the anointing of the sick is much more evident both in history and in the present. Hospitals began in the Middle Ages as extensions of the monastic rule of hospitality; even in patristic times clerics were caring for orphans and widows, and the New Testament itself mentions collections for the poor and other ministries to the needy. For the past ten centuries or so, the ecclesiastical rite that came to be called extreme unction was directed toward spiritual care for the dying rather than toward physical care for the sick, but even here the sacrament was a sign of God's concern for the helpless in their hour of need. As an anointing, this sacrament, like confirmation, is a symbolic strengthening, but its focus is on the strength that individuals need to cope with their debilities rather than on the strength needed to go forth and help others. ☐

Viewed in terms of the world's suffering, the anointing of the sick points to those millions who will never be rescued from sickness and starvation in time to escape their premature death. Our natural inclination is to forget about them and let them die, but Christ's words and the church's tradition tell us that even the least are worthy of our attention. I personally live the meaning of this sacrament, therefore, when I keep the helpless in my heart, resisting the temptation to dismiss them as deserving of their lot, arguing with myself and others that we owe them care and aid for no other reason than that they are suffering. Likewise, our parish healing services take on global significance when they are done in a community that, besides extending itself to comfort its own members, is working to touch the physically and emotionally wounded of the world beyond its parish boundaries. And the church too is a sacrament of global healing and caring insofar as it continues to be an institution through which people can help the helpless, not in the name of progress but simply in the name of love.

Sixth, marriage is the sacrament of fidelity and devotion between Christian men and women living in a lasting relationship. The Christian tradition since the days of St. Paul has taken as the model of that relationship the commitment of Christ to the church and of the church to its Lord. Thus Christian marriage has always been understood to be a relationship of love "in the Lord," not based on sexual attraction or the benefits to be gained for oneself, but based on mutual self-giving and the good that it bears for one's spouse, children, and even the family that extends beyond that nucleus. In fact, the nuclear family as we know it today is a fairly recent invention of Western society, a product of the industrial revolution. In agricultural societies still, the extended family of in-laws and cousins and other relatives is the basic social group to which people owe their love and in which they find their home.

The church sometimes calls itself the family of God, and both here and in the local community the human paradigm for it is not the nuclear family but the extended family. Marriage as a Catholic sacrament therefore is not only a sign of fidelity between spouses but also a symbol of their acceptance of the larger family into which they are entering. As such it is a sign of their willingness to orient themselves to the well-being of others, not as a part-time service but as a full-time commitment. Viewed in its widest context, therefore, the sacrament of marriage implies not only a willingness to establish a lasting relationship with a new natural family but a concern for the whole human family. It implies that I broaden my perception of the family to which I belong and look on all people as my own brothers and sisters, parents and children. In the parish it means that we take an active interest in the well-being of families, the education of children, the social needs of the aged, the unemployed, the imprisoned, the handicapped, and so on. And in the institutional church it means working for social and economic structures that promote the good of natural families and family-style communities, and sponsoring organized efforts not only to foster family life but also to help people deal with the stresses and breakdowns that, in the larger picture, are inevitable in close human relationships.

Seventh, holy orders is the sacrament of Christian ministry, and although for a good deal of the church's history ministry was identified with clerical priesthood, a broader study of history and a fuller appreciation for ministry in the church today reveals that what is involved here is more than sacramental administration and other clerical functions. As an ecclesiastical ritual, ordination is a sign through which a person accepts the call of the community to lead it in prayer and worship and other aspects of church-related life. But it is also a sign through which the church as a religious society affirms that there are certain tasks that must be performed, and to which individuals must be appointed, if it is to be a church at all. ☐

If one conceives of the church narrowly so that the word is the equivalent of "clergy" or "hierarchy," then ministry in the church is necessarily limited to the formally ordained priesthood. But if one conceives of the church broadly so as to include all its members, clergy and laity alike, then both the notion of ministry and opportunities for it are likewise broadened. Within this wider perspective only a fraction of the church's ministers are ordained, for there are many who minister to the needs of the church without ever being commissioned to do so in an ecclesiastical ceremony: teachers, administrators, secretaries, pastoral workers, musicians, liturgical assistants, parish nurses, and so on. The official sacrament of orders is therefore symbolic of ministry, but it is not in any way coextensive with it. ☐

Now, ministry in either the narrow or the broad sense is ordinarily conceived of as service within the church. But what then is the ministry or service of the church itself? Its mission and therefore its service is to the world, and so the notion of ministry as applied to the whole church necessarily has a global dimension to it. As an individual Catholic, therefore, I participate in the church's ministry to the world when I respond to the needs of those outside the church. Parishes do the same when they sponsor local efforts and support more distant attempts to meet the human needs of non-Catholics, and when they encourage their members to pursue lives of service to others rather than careers of profit to themselves. The church as an organization is inescapably involved with ministry, to be sure, but that ministry takes on a global dimension when it is directed outward, to meeting the spiritual and physical needs of persons and groups not in the church, or to addressing problems in the secular society in which it finds itself. ☐

Eighth and finally there is Eucharist, which is the sacramental celebration of who we are as individual followers of Jesus, as a local Christian community, and as a worldwide church. It is, as its name implies, a celebration of thanksgiving for all that we are and all that we have received from God through Christ and through each other. It is a listening and responding to God's word, not singly but together. It is an offering in which, with Christ, we give ourselves back to God in return for all that we have been given. It is a meal in which bread and wine are blessed and shared, in commemoration of Christ's death and resurrection, and as a sign of what we ourselves are called to do. ☐

In our eucharistic worship, therefore, in union with those present, we unite ourselves with the whole church and by extension with all of humanity in an act of self-giving thanks. In accepting the bread that is broken and the cup that is shared, we identify ourselves with our Lord whose body was beaten and whose blood was shed so that others might live. Such an act permeates my global consciousness and affirms my commitment to the world, therefore, to the extent that I am already thankful not only for what I myself have received but for all the good things of both natural and human creation, and to the extent that I am already aware that so much is still not enough when so many have so little. The Eucharist is also a fitting sign of our communal dependence on God and of our self-giving to the world in the measure that together we acknowledge our dependence on other people and together we commit ourselves to sharing the world's abundance with them. And the Eucharist is an act of global worship in the church to the extent that as a worldwide organization it pours itself out in sacrifice for the salvation of all people.

The global implications of the sacraments, therefore, tell us that today we must be in the world at large what we have always acknowledged we must be as Christians: those who are willing to surrender themselves to Christ and the gospel, those who would give rather than receive, those who love their enemies and bless those who hate them, those who are prepared to commit their lives to the world's redemption, those who by their words and actions are announcing the arrival of the kingdom of God. For if there is a truly dialectical relationship between ourselves as Christians and the world in which we live, a dialogue that is mediated through the church's sacramental worship, then as indicated earlier in this section, neither we nor the world will remain the same.

But there is also another dimension to the dialectic that was suggested, namely, that through such a dialogue the sacraments themselves would be changed. What we have now in the Catholic Church is a system of seven sacramental rituals that have evolved through twenty centuries of history. But that history has run its course mainly within the confines of European Christianity. The liturgical forms of the Catholic Church are therefore at the present time not only Christian but also predominately European, even though some of them have Middle Eastern origins and elements. As if underscoring this fact, the recent revisions of the sacraments endorsed by the Second Vatican Council and promulgated by Rome were by and large reworkings of the traditional European rites, and the revisions themselves were made by liturgists trained in the Western theological tradition.

At the present time, however, Catholicism as a world religion is breaking out of the European mold in which it was formed, and it is pouring itself into the cultures of Latin America, Africa, and Asia. True, it had sent missionaries there in the past, but the colonial Catholicism that they took with them was Roman in both name and style, whereas today both missionaries and native clergy see the importance of allowing cultural diversity into the church. Is it not reasonable to expect, then, that in the course of time the church in those regions will develop sacramental forms that are quite different from ours today? After all, the church's present sacraments developed in dialogue with European culture over the course of centuries, sometimes through a series of startlingly different mutations. How many early Christians, for instance, would have recognized the grandiose patristic liturgies as the descendants of the Lord's Supper that they shared around a table in their homes? Or for that matter, how many patristic bishops would have acknowledged that the private Mass of the Middle Ages, offered silently by a single priest with no congregation, could be the lineal offspring of episcopal liturgies concelebrated with many ministers, attended by throngs of the faithful, and embellished with hymns and responses? The words of the sacraments, the sacramental gestures themselves, and even the material elements in them have all changed to a greater or lesser extent through the ages. ☐

Today we look back at the first century or two of Christianity as the "early days" of the church. But what if the world is still around two hundred centuries from now? Isn't it conceivable that historians then will call us the "early" Christians? From such a futuristic as well as global perspective, therefore, it seems futile to restrict the coming course of sacramental history to a narrow continuation of its past history. Especially if Christianity continues its dialogue with the world—this time a world of many cultures—we can expect both a transformation of the world and a transformation of the church. ☐

That transformation of the church, however, will in fact make it more catholic. Until recently, our catholicity has been spatial and temporal, but it has also been monocultural. Now, the ongoing globalization of the church will make it more multicultural or pluralistic. Of course, there is, as was stated earlier, a growing secular and technical mentality that is enveloping our planet, and this is having its own impact on the cultures that it touches. But in its dialectical transformation of the cultures of different regions, it itself is transformed in various ways, so that cultural differences remain. And a Catholic spirituality, even a Catholic sacramental spirituality, must come to terms both with the technological spirit of the age and with the cultural spirits of various peoples around the globe. The resulting Catholicism may not be as homogeneous as it has been in the past (actually, in the recent past, for during the first thousand years of Christian history there was much more cultural diversity among the churches of the Middle East, North Africa, and Europe), but it will be more universal. And it may be harder to define the Catholic spirit and to describe the Catholic sacraments when this happens, except in a way that allows for a pluralistic spirituality and that tolerates a plurality of sacramental forms.

But we should not anticipate the coming sacramental revolution with dread, nor with premature nostalgia for the good old days of Vatican II. It is the business of sacramental worship to transform us inwardly and outwardly, by awakening in us the dynamics of religious self-transcendence, and by making available the grace to be what we are called by God to be. And it is the heritage of a sacramental church to develop liturgical rites that mediate the eternal in a symbolic language that is always contemporary.

Additional Reading

Personal Spirituality

Andersen, Frank. *Making the Eucharist Matter.* Notre Dame, IN: Ave Maria Press, 1999.

Boff, Leonardo. *Sacraments of Life: Life of the Sacraments.* Washington, DC: Pastoral Press, 1987.

Bro, Bernard. *The Spirituality of the Sacraments: Doctrine and Practice for Today.* New York: Sheed and Ward, 1968.

Caldecott, Stratford. *The Seven Sacraments: Entering the Mysteries of God.* New York: Crossroad, 2006.

Chappell, Arthur Barker. *Regular Confession: An Exercise in Sacramental Spirituality.* New York: Peter Lang, 1992.

Corbon, Jean. *The Wellspring of Worship.* New York: Paulist Press, 1988.

Dobson, Theodore E. *Say But the Word: How the Lord's Supper Can Transform Your Life.* New York: Paulist Press, 1984.

Dominian, Jack. *Dynamics of Marriage: Love, Sex, and Growth from a Christian Perspective.* Mystic, CT: Twenty-Third Publications, 1993.

Durrwell, François-Xavier. *The Eucharist: Presence of Christ.* Denville, NJ: Dimension Books, 1974.

Fourez, Gérard. *Sacraments and Passages: Celebrating the Tensions of Modern Life.* Notre Dame, IN: Ave Maria Press, 1983.

Gallagher, Charles A., George A. Maloney, Mary F. Rousseau, and Paul F. Wilczak. *Embodied in Love: Sacramental Spirituality and Sexual Intimacy*. New York: Crossroad, 1983.

Häring, Bernard. *The Sacraments and Your Everyday Life*. Liguori, MO: Liguori Publications, 1976.

Hotz, Kendra G., and Matthew T. Mathews. *Shaping the Christian Life: Worship and the Religious Affections*. Louisville, KY: Westminster John Knox, 2006.

Huebsch, Bill. *Rethinking Sacraments: Holy Moments in Daily Living*. Mystic, CT: Twenty-Third Publications, 1989.

Irvine, Christopher. *The Art of God: The Making of Christians and the Meaning of Worship*. Chicago: Liturgy Training Publications, 2006.

Irwin, Kevin W. *Liturgy, Prayer and Spirituality*. New York: Paulist Press, 1984.

Jansen, G. M. A. *The Sacramental We: An Existential Approach to the Sacramental Life*. Milwaukee, WI: Bruce, 1968.

Johnson, Ben Campbell. *Pastoral Spirituality: A Focus for Ministry*. Philadelphia: Westminster Press, 1988.

Jones, Alan W. *Sacrifice and Delight: Spirituality for Ministry*. San Francisco: HarperSanFrancisco, 1992.

Keating, Thomas. *The Mystery of Christ: The Liturgy as Spiritual Experience*. Warwick, NY: Continuum, 1994.

Keifer, Ralph A. *Blessed and Broken: An Exploration of the Contemporary Experience of God in Eucharistic Celebration*. Wilmington, DE: Michael Glazier, 1982.

Kehrwald, Leif. *Marriage and the Spirituality of Intimacy*. Cincinnati, OH: St. Anthony Messenger Press, 1996.

Kelly, Tony. *The Bread of God: Nurturing a Eucharistic Imagination*. Liguori, MO: Liguori Publications, 2001.

Kelsey, Morton T., and Barbara Kelsey. *Sacrament of Sexuality: The Spirituality and Psychology of Sex*. Warwick, NY: Amity House, 1986.

Oliver, Mary Anne McPherson. *Conjugal Spirituality: The Primacy of Mutual Love in Christian Tradition*. Kansas City, MO: Sheed and Ward, 1994.

Pennington, M. Basil. *Eucharist: Wine of Faith, Bread of Life*. Liguori, MO: Liguori/Triumph, 2000.

Pennington, M. Basil, and Carl J. Arico. *Living Our Priesthood Today*. Huntington, IN: Our Sunday Visitor, 1987.

Powers, Joseph M. *Spirit and Sacrament: The Humanizing Experience*. New York: Seabury Press, 1973.

Roberts, Challon O'Hearn, and William P. Roberts. *Partners in Intimacy: Living Christian Marriage Today*. New York: Paulist Press, 1988.

Saliers, Don E. *Worship and Spirituality*. Philadelphia: Westminster Press, 1984.

Whitehead, Evelyn Eaton, and James D. Whitehead. *A Sense of Sexuality: Christian Love and Intimacy*. New York: Doubleday, 1989.

Wilson-Kastner, Patricia. *Sacred Drama: A Spirituality of Christian Liturgy*. Minneapolis: Fortress Press, 1998.

Communal Spirituality

Christensen, Michael J., ed. *Equipping the Saints: Mobilizing the Laity for Ministry*. Nashville, TN: Abingdon Press, 2000.

Collins, Patrick W. *More Than Meets the Eye: Ritual and Parish Liturgy*. New York: Paulist Press, 1983.

Forrester, Duncan B., J. Ian H. McDonald, and Gian Tellini. *Encounter with God: An Introduction to Christian Worship and Practice*. Edinburgh: T&T Clark, 1983.

Gaillardetz, Richard R. *A Daring Promise: A Spirituality of Christian Marriage*. New York: Crossroad, 2002.

Guzie, Tad W. *The Book of Sacramental Basics*. New York: Paulist Press, 1981.

Foley, Leonard. *Signs of Love*. Cincinnati, OH: St. Anthony Messenger Press, 1976.

Krause, Fred. *Liturgy in Parish Life: A Study of Worship and the Celebrating Community*. New York: Alba House, 1979.

Kraybill, Ronald S. *Repairing the Breach: Ministering in Community Conflict*. Scottdale, PA: Herald Press, 1981.

Madigan, Shawn. *Spirituality Rooted in Liturgy*. Washington, DC: Pastoral Press, 1998.

Maxwell, John. *Worship in Action: A Parish Model of Creative Liturgy and Social Concern*. Mystic, CT: Twenty-Third Publications, 1981.

MacNutt, Francis. *The Power to Heal*. Notre Dame, IN: Ave Maria Press, 1977.

Miner, Malcolm H. *Healing Is For Real*. New York: Morehouse-Barlow, 1972.

Mick, Lawrence E. *Forming the Assembly to Celebrate the Mass*. Chicago: Liturgy Training Publications, 2002.

Osborne, Kenan B. *Community, Eucharist, and Spirituality*. Liguori, MO: Liguori Publications, 2007.

Pfatteicher, Philip H. *Liturgical Spirituality*. Valley Forge, PA: Trinity Press International, 1997.

Schreiter, Robert J. *Reconciliation: Mission and Ministry in a Changing Social Order*. Maryknoll, NY: Orbis Books, 1992.

Thomas, Leo, and Jan Alkire. *Healing as a Parish Ministry: Mending Body, Mind, and Spirit*. Notre Dame, IN: Ave Maria Press, 1992.

Upton, Julia. *A Time for Embracing: Reclaiming Reconciliation*. Collegeville, MN: Liturgical Press, 1999.

Wilson, Earl and Sandra, Paul and Virginia Friesen, and Larry and Nancy Paulson. *Restoring the Fallen: A Team Approach to Caring, Confronting and Reconciling*. Downers Grove, IL: Inter-Varsity Press, 1997.

Ecclesial Spirituality

Champlin, Joseph M. *Healing in the Catholic Church: Mending Wounded Hearts and Bodies*. Huntington, IN: Our Sunday Visitor, 1985.

Collins, Mary, and David N. Power, eds. *The Pastoral Care of the Sick*. Philadelphia: Trinity Press International, 1991.

DiOrio, Ralph A. *Called to Heal: Releasing the Transforming Power of God*. New York: Doubleday, 1982.

Dulles, Avery. *The Priestly Office: A Theological Reflection*. New York: Paulist Press, 1997.

Evely, Louis. *The Church and the Sacraments*. Denville, NJ: Dimension Books, 1971.

García de Háro, Ramon. *Marriage and Family in the Documents of the Magisterium: A Course in the Theology of Marriage*. San Francisco: Ignatius Press, 1993.

Gy, Pierre-Marie. *The Reception of Vatican II Liturgical Reforms in the Life of the Church*. Milwaukee, WI: Marquette University Press, 2003.

Hahn, Scott. *Swear to God: The Promise and Power of the Sacraments*. New York: Doubleday, 2004.

Hogan, Richard M., and John M. LeVoir. *Covenant of Love: Pope John Paul II on Sexuality, Marriage, and Family in the Modern World*. Garden City, NY: Doubleday, 1985.

Kasper, Walter. *Sacrament of Unity: The Eucharist and the Church*. New York: Crossroad, 2004.

Lathrop, Gordon. *Holy People: A Liturgical Ecclesiology*. Minneapolis: Augsburg Fortress, 1999.

Linn, Dennis, Matthew Linn, and Barbara Leahy Shlemon. *To Heal as Jesus Healed*. Notre Dame, IN: Ave Maria Press, 1978.

McBrien, Richard P. *Catholicism*, chaps 21–22. Minneapolis: Winston Press, 1980.

McPartlan, Paul. *Sacrament of Salvation: An Introduction to Eucharistic Ecclesiology*. Edinburgh: T&T Clark, 1995.

Neal, Emily Gardiner. *Celebration of Healing*. Boston: Cowley Publications, 1992.

O'Toole, James M., ed. *Habits of Devotion: Catholic Religious Practices in Twentieth-Century America*. Ithaca, NY: Cornell University Press, 2004.

Polish, Daniel F., and Eugene J. Fisher, eds. *Liturgical Foundations of Social Policy in the Catholic and Jewish Traditions*. Notre Dame, IN: University of Notre Dame Press, 1983.

Rahner, Karl. *Foundations of the Christian Faith: An Introduction to the Idea of Christianity*, chap 8. New York: Seabury Press, 1978.

Riga, Peter J. *Sign and Symbol of the Invisible God: Essays on the Sacraments Today*. Notre Dame, IN: Fides Publishers, 1971.

Santa, Thomas M. *The Essential Catholic Handbook of the Sacraments: A Summary of Beliefs, Rites, and Prayers*. Liguori, MO: Liguori Publications, 2001.

Sarno, Ronald A. *Let Us Proclaim the Mystery of Faith*. Denville, NJ: Dimension Books, 1970.

Global Spirituality

Baum, Gregory, and Harold Wells, eds. *The Reconciliation of Peoples: Challenge to the Churches*. Maryknoll, NY: Orbis Books, 1997.

Berry, Thomas M. *Befriending the Earth: A Theology of Reconciliation between Humans and the Earth*. Mystic, CT: Twenty-Third Publications, 1991.

Chupungco, Anscar J. *Cultural Adaptation of the Liturgy*. New York: Paulist Press, 1982.

———. *Liturgies of the Future: The Process and Methods of Inculturation*. New York: Paulist Press, 1989.

Donovan, Vincent J. *Christianity Rediscovered: An Epistle from the Masai*. Notre Dame, IN: Fides/Claretian, 1978.

Fox, Matthew. *Creation Spirituality: Liberating Gifts for the Peoples of the Earth*. San Francisco: HarperSanFrancisco, 1991.

Keifer, Ralph A. *The Mass in Time of Doubt: The Meaning of the Mass for Catholics Today*. Washington, DC: Pastoral Press, 1983.

Lathrop, Gordon. *Holy Ground: A Liturgical Cosmology*. Minneapolis: Augsburg Fortress, 2003.

Muller, Robert. *New Genesis: Shaping a Global Spirituality*. New York: Doubleday, 1982.

O'Brien, David J., and Thomas A. Shannon. *Catholic Social Thought: The Documentary Heritage*. Maryknoll, NY: Orbis Books, 1992.

Peters, Ted. *Sin: Radical Evil in Soul and Society*. Grand Rapids, MI: William B. Eerdmans, 1994.

Schreiter, Robert J. *The Ministry of Reconciliation: Spirituality and Strategies*. Maryknoll, NY: Orbis Books, 1998.

Senn, Frank C. *New Creation: A Liturgical Worldview*. Minneapolis: Augsburg Fortress, 2000.

Snyder, T. Richard. *Once You Were No People: The Church and the Transformation of Society*. Bloomington, IN: Meyer Stone Books, 1988.

Volf, Miroslav. *Exclusion and Embrace: A Theological Exploration of Identity, Otherness, and Reconciliation*. Nashville, TN: Abingdon Press, 1996.

Conclusion

The sacraments are not an end in themselves; they are a means to an end. More precisely, they are means to many ends on four distinct levels of spiritual development.

On the individual level, they bring us to an awareness of who we are as Christians, called by God to self-transcendence and personal conversion. Baptism and confirmation, for example, invite us to stop living for ourselves and to start living for others, to die with Christ in the waters that dissolve our self-centeredness and to be reborn with a new spirit of self-giving. Penance draws us into a process of self-examination, reconversion, and recommitment to a career of continuous dedication to the ideals of the gospel. The Eucharist tells us to sacrifice our egoistic concerns and to become concerned with offering ourselves to God in union with Christ. And by consciously entering into what the sacraments symbolize, we allow them to transform our consciousness and our behavior so that we become the reality that they signify. We make it real. We incarnate it in our very being. And in doing so, we ourselves become sacraments signifying what God has done in us and what surrender to the spirit of Christ can do for others.

On the social level, the sacraments are means to the end of community building and social transformation. They make us aware of the interpersonal dimensions of our conversion and of our commitment to the task of self-transcendence. Christian initiation, for example, is nothing if it is not the beginning of a life shared with others. Christian marriage is not Christian at all if it is not a life of dedication to the well-being of one's spouse and children. Christian worship is not truly liturgy if it does not give us a sense of our union with and commitment to those with whom we pray. At the same time, by deliberately dedicating ourselves to what the sacraments symbolize, we open ourselves to a new dimension of interpersonal relationships, and we begin to participate in the reality that they signify. Christian community comes into being where it was not before, and it is intensified where it already existed. And when this happens, Christian families, friendships, parishes, schools, and other organized groups become sacraments themselves, signifying the transforming power of grace in human relationships and symbolizing the direction that the transformation of the human community should take.

On the ecclesial level, the sacraments make us aware of our heritage as Christians and our identity as Catholics. The sacrament of anointing, for example, reminds us that care for the sick and the dying is a perennial Christian concern and so we cannot be insensitive to those who are suffering nor blind to those who are dying if we call ourselves followers of Jesus. The sacrament of holy orders likewise tells us that the church in history is not the result of charismatic serendipity and so it needs organization in its ministry. The sacrament of Eucharist, in the same way, as the central and traditional act of Christian worship, identifies our own liturgy with the public prayer of Christians across twenty centuries and unites us with all ecclesial communities around the world that call themselves Catholic. By intentionally embracing such sacramental forms of worship as our own, we become members of the transhistorical and transcultural reality that they signify. We make it real in present history and in our present situation. And in doing so the church itself becomes an identifiable sign of Christ's presence in the world, a unified sacrament of the Christian message and divine grace. Finally, on the global level, the sacraments are a means to the transformation of the world and the salvation of the larger human community. At this level their effects (even their potential effects) are not as direct or immediate as those that they have (or can have) on the first three levels. Nevertheless, insofar as sacramental worship does effect a transformation of individual consciousness and personal behavior, insofar as it calls the church into being and energizes it as a medium of divine life in human history, to that extent sacramental worship plays a real role in the redemption of the world.

As Catholics today we must admit that the understanding of the sacraments that we inherited from medieval scholasticism and Tridentine dogmatism was rather limited. The effectiveness of the sacraments is not as neat nor as automatic as it once seemed to be. Their institution by Christ is not as directly traceable to Jesus of Nazareth as it once appeared to be. Even their numbering as seven is not as absolute and eternal as we once assumed it was. Nevertheless, that traditional understanding of the sacraments was about as broad and sophisticated as Christians could make it, given the limitations of human knowledge and social experience within which it developed.

In our own day, however, the social sciences have given us new instruments of analysis, our knowledge of history has become more detailed and nuanced, and new varieties of philosophy and theology have increased the number of perspectives from which we may view sacramental worship. Within such an expanded horizon we can see that the seven traditional sacraments are still valid and fruitful, but the meaning of their validity and fruitfulness has been transformed. Their validity today is rooted in their ability to express what is actually going on in the experience of individuals, local communities, the church as a whole, and humanity as such. And their fruitfulness is measured by the transforming effects that they have on persons, groups, the church at large, and the history of the human endeavor itself.

Afterword

In the introduction to this book, you were invited to interact with the information presented in it, with the promise that doing so would transform your thinking about sacraments forever.

If you have done the extra work of considering old and new ideas, of reflecting on your own experience, of making judgments about the claims being made, and of deciding what to do with your new knowledge, that transformation has hopefully happened—or at least it has begun. Especially if you took time to write to me about your objections and concerns, and if I was able to respond in a way that helped move your thinking process forward, you are in a different space now from where you were a while ago, both theologically and spiritually.

If you did not do that extra work but instead approached this as another book to be read, I hope that you have been intrigued by the possibilities it presents and challenged to rethink your understanding of the sacraments some time in the future. It is unlikely that you dismissed everything in it out of hand, for if you had, you would not have reached these last few pages.

It may take you a while to begin the lengthy process of rethinking sacraments from the inside out, and even if you have already begun to do that, you will find that the process keeps pulling you forward. Like traveling along an unfamiliar road, it leads to new discoveries and expanding horizons. In addition, Catholics carry a lot of linguistic and dogmatic baggage, and it takes a while to let go of habits and beliefs that we have lived with for as long as we can remember.

My own conversion, if you want to call it that, took place during the two years when I was writing *Doors to the Sacred*, confronting the twists and turns of liturgical development and observing how believers tried to make sense of their church's sacramental rites over the course of twenty centuries. But it was also preceded by four years in seminaries where I had the luxury of experiencing spiritual growth in a stable and supportive environment, by two years of intellectual self-appropriation with the help of Bernard Lonergan's writings, by three years of involvement in parish work and ecumenical dialogue, by eight years of teaching world religions at the high school and college levels, and by ten years of involvement with the Catholic charismatic renewal and similar religious movements. In addition, I had the advantage of growing up in the Tridentine church and being forced to rethink everything in the Vatican II church; I had the good fortune of receiving classical training in languages, philosophy, and theology; and I was blessed with a curious mind that kept me reading about psychology and sociology, anthropology and history, science and global issues long after I had graduated from school.

Your own background is unavoidably different from mine, where you are now is different from where I was when I started thinking seriously about sacraments, and the path you will take in reaching your own conclusions will be in many respects different from the one I took in reaching mine. I hope, though, that I have made some observations that make sense to you and that will help you on your own journey. If you are young enough, maybe you don't have as much baggage as us older folks, and so you will not have to work as hard at changing your understanding of sacraments. But if you are that young, you will have to work harder than we did at changing the church and the world.

Index

anointing
    and baptism, 46, 112, 114, 220
    and confirmation, 114, 200, 220–23, 241
    as ritual, 19, 90
anointing of the sick
    as ecclesiastical ritual, 47, 50, 115, 125, 131, 203–4, 241, 251
    as popular practice, 90, 115, 225
    meaning of, 47, 50, 89, 100–102, 191, 212, 223, 229, 235, 241, 251, 263
    new forms of, 47, 78, 91, 136, 150, 205
    one of the seven sacraments, 3, 26, 72
anthropology, 37, 42, 63, 65, 79
Aquinas, Thomas, 16, 124, 130, 142, 238–39
archetype, see symbol
Augustine, 9, 11, 16, 238

baptism
    and magical perception, 147, 159, 199
    as celebration, 99–102, 197–99, 212, 249
    as ritual, 35, 72, 83, 90–91, 111–14, 117, 124, 161–62, 183, 197–201, 218, 220–21, 228, 241
    effects of, 3, 12, 26, 42, 77–79, 89, 95–96, 131–32, 135–36, 146, 150,

151–53, 158–59, 184, 190–92, 233–235
    in Judaism, 197
    in the Holy Spirit, 220–21
    meaning of, 221, 223, 228–29, 241–42, 249
    one of the seven sacraments, 1, 196, 239, 262
Baum, Gregory, 39, 180–81, 242
Bell, Catherine, 65, 66, 82, 89

call, baptismal, 150, 198, 201, 215, 218, 250
Catechism of the Catholic Church, 3, 129, 168, 185, 189–91
character
    baptismal, 233
    priestly, 151, 233
    sacramental, 47, 132–33, 181
    charisma, 11–12, 56, 108–9, 110
Chauvet, Louis-Marie, 3–4, 155–60, 182
Christ, see also Jesus
    as sacrament, 110, 127, 140, 149
    as savior, 13, 153, 158, 192, 220
    as second person of the Trinity, 140
    becoming like, 41, 197, 212, 233
    church as body of, 41, 42, 135–36, 140–41, 148, 159–61, 166–67, 189, 195, 197–98, 201, 238, 241–43
    Eucharist as body and blood of, 73–74, 211–12